Treasures

Treasures of Truth

Frank Parker

The Pentland Press Limited
Edinburgh • Cambridge • Durham • USA

First published in 1997 by
The Pentland Press Ltd.
1 Hutton Close
South Church
Bishop Auckland
Durham

British Library Cataloguing in Publication Data.
A Catalogue record for this book is available
from the British Library.

ISBN 1 85821 515 3

Typeset by CBS, Felixstowe, Suffolk
Printed and bound by Antony Rowe Ltd., Chippenham

CONTENTS

PART I
FOOD FOR THOUGHT

PART II
FOR ALL SEASONS

PART III
DAILY LIVING

PART IV
THE WHOLE WIDE WORLD

PART V
PRAYER

PART VI
PRAISE AND WORSHIP

PART VII
EVANGELISM

PART VIII
JESUS IS COMING AGAIN

PART IX
THE POWER OF THE HOLY SPIRIT

PART X
THE SUPERNATURAL

PART XI
GOD'S BOOK

FROM THE PRESIDENT'S DESK

Frank Parker has been a personal friend for nearly forty years, during which I enjoyed a period of shared pastoral ministry with him in South West England. That gave me an opportunity to hear him preach and to appreciate his considerable communication skill – a skill that shines clearly through *Treasures of Truth.*

For fourteen years the author served the Apostolic Church as editor of its doctrinal magazine *Riches of Grace*, adding the special quality of his enlightening and edifying editorials, many of which are here compiled in this treasury. His calling and anointing as a teacher in the Body of Christ are evident in his writing, and I am confident that this book will serve to instruct and inspire the Christian faith of many.

The author is well-read and uses what he learns to illuminate his exposition of Biblical truth. His passion is to proclaim the uniqueness of the Lord Jesus Christ as Saviour and King – a fact that is made abundantly clear in these pages.

I wish this book every success, and I pray that the Holy Spirit will bless the written word of His servant, as for many years He has blessed his spoken word, for the Kingdom and glory of God.

Philip W. Cawthorne
President, Apostolic Church Council,
Latimer Lodge,
Penygroes,
South Wales SA14 7PW

FOREWORD

It gives me great pleasure to be able to introduce this book entitled *Treasures of Truth*. The title is a clear indication of the contents, which are full of interest and contain many thought-provoking ideas.

For fourteen years the author was the editor of the Christian magazine, *Riches of Grace*, formerly the official publication of the Apostolic Church. The journal had a wide influence and touched over twenty nations of the world with Biblical, evangelical, devotional and Pentecostal truth and light.

This book now contains the distilled essence of some of the best editorials which appeared over the fourteen years of the author's editorship. It is a book to be dipped into again and again. Each time the reader will find some new gem of truth, which will challenge, stimulate and delight.

Treasures of Truth is a book firmly founded on Biblical revelation. Its wisdom is the wisdom of the Word of God, but the book also contains information about the great thinkers and philosophers of the past, and includes quotations from many significant personalities in the history of Christianity.

Although a very readable book for everybody, *Treasures of Truth* has a built-in design feature which will be of special interest to Bible teachers and preachers seeking to find relevant material for special occasions, such as Christmas, New Year, Easter, Ascension Day, Whitsun and Harvest. Other sections of the book deal with a stimulating wide range of subjects, enabling each and every reader to discover some real 'Treasures of Truth'.

My association with the author has been a long and happy one, as together we have worked to extend the kingdom of God in the East of Scotland and in other parts of the country. It is, therefore, with a measure of fulfilment as well as joy, that I can wholeheartedly recommend this book.

BRYAN E. LEWIS
(Apostolic Church Superintendent,
Edinburgh Area)

ACKNOWLEDGEMENT

My first grateful acknowledgement is to the Lord, who enabled me to produce the material for this book in the context of busy pastoral duties, over a period of many years. Faced monthly with a blank sheet of paper and a deadline for the printer, it was only the Lord's constant inspiration that helped me to produce the requisite 168 editorials on time, as the fleeting months flew into years.

Because of the protracted period of time over which the articles were produced, it was inevitable that some of the more complex themes were addressed more than once. However, as one reviewer has observed, the approach each time has been from a slightly different angle, thus enabling the reader to assimilate gradually what might have been virtually indigestible if taken at one sitting.

I have tried conscientiously to acknowledge, within the context, each source of material from which I have quoted. If any have been inadvertently overlooked, I ask your pardon.

My thanks are also due to my colleague in the ministry, Pastor Bryan E. Lewis, whose drive and enthusiasm were a constant encouragement to me in the task of preparing this book. I am quite sure that without his dynamic stimulation my editorials would still be in the cupboard, and not in this book.

Furthermore, I sincerely thank all those people who have supported this publication from their financial resources. Together with God's help, you have enabled that which was impossible to become possible.

Finally, I express my thanks to the directors and staff of the Pentland Press Ltd, whose unfailing courtesy and efficiency have played such an important role in the ultimate presentation of this book to the general public.

FRANK PARKER

PART I

FOOD FOR THOUGHT

Items 1 – 22

1. WORDS

The world is full of words. They are spoken in streets and shops; written in countless books, magazines and newspapers; beamed throughout the earth on radio waves in hundreds of dialects and languages; stored in a million files; and programmed into computers and word processors by a host of operatives world-wide.

Man has a fascination for words. He analyses and records them in dictionaries. Men like Cruden, Young, and Strong have spent a life-time compiling Biblical Concordances. Roget has amazed the literary world with his Thesaurus.

The course of history is changed by signatures beneath words contained in treaties, pacts and agreements. Commerce and communication flow through the nations in rivers of words. Fax machines convey instantly in words the thoughts of men from one continent to another.

The ability to be articulate in words is one of the qualities which distinguishes man from the lower orders of creation. Perhaps this is one reason for man's endless preoccupation with words. Authors and playwrights make their point with the clever use of words. Poets delight us. Comedians entertain us. Professors enlighten us. Teachers instruct us. Words crystallize original thoughts, convey them to others, and store them for future generations.

Because of man's unique gift with words, we know what God said to Moses and to Abraham and to David. We know what Jesus taught in His parables, what He prayed to the Father, and what He said on the cross. We have become aware of our responsibility to preach the gospel to all mankind, because we can understand words.

Mao Tse Tung understood the power of words. His thoughts were encapsulated in slogans and inscribed on the backs of his army's tunics. Millions of Chinese soldiers marched cheerfully to their deaths, brainwashed by the powerful words emblazoned on the battle-dress of the men marching in front of them.

The cosmic conflict commenced with words. God spoke to man and said, '*You can eat from every tree in the garden except that one.*' Satan challenged the justice and fairness of God by saying to the woman: '*Can it really be that God has said, "You shall not eat from every tree of*

3

the garden?"

The issue boiled down to a decision over words. Would mankind be obedient to God's will expressed in terms of simple words? Or would Satan's deceptive way with words win the day? The tragic state of the world today reminds us of the sad result of that original Satanic strategy.

When it came to the testing of the last Adam, Jesus of Nazareth, it was a different story. The issue was the same. Loyalty or disloyalty to the commands and requirements of God expressed clearly in His revealed word.

After fasting for forty days and being now in a state of physical weakness and bodily exhaustion, Jesus defeated Satan by adhering faithfully to God's word. Those wonderful words of His allegiance to the Father's will, '*It is written*', overcame the subtle strategies of Satan, and Jesus remained victorious. Thus did the last Adam succeed in a hostile wilderness, though the first Adam had failed in a Paradise.

Not only is God's word vitally important, but the Bible teaches us that our own words are a matter for careful consideration too. Jesus said that we would have to give account for every idle work spoken. Words are precious. '*A word fitly spoken is like apples of gold in pictures of silver.*' Words can hurt or heal; depress or uplift; create fear and anxiety, or inspire with courage and determination.

The panic-conveying words of the ten spies who were afraid to possess the promised land prevailed over the faith and courage of Caleb and Joshua. As a result, two million Israelites wandered for forty years in a harsh wilderness instead of entering the land flowing with milk and honey. Words can damage and destroy. Or they can encourage and comfort.

In the ultimate analysis, if human philosophy does not accord with divine revelation in every respect, it will not stand the test of judgement. For God will have the last word. Jesus said: '*The word that I have spoken will judge you in the last day.*'

The genius of human intellect, however brilliant, must always be submitted to the truth already revealed in God's word. Safety lies only in allegiance to God. 'It is written,' will always win the day over. '*Can it really be that God has said?*'

4

2. CARING FOR THE EARTH

God had great plans for mankind. He made both male and female in His own image, a privilege granted to no other order of created beings. God blessed them and told them to be fruitful and increase in number. *'Fill the earth and subdue it,'* God said.

He gave them authority and dominion to rule over the lesser orders of creation. Great honour and real dignity were bestowed by God on man, the crown of His handiwork. But God's plan also made provision for man to co-operate with Him in the development of creation. *'The LORD God took the man and put him into the Garden of Eden to work it and take care of it.'*

Man was God's vice-regent upon earth; his privileges included rulership over many realms of creation. But his responsibilities included work – and that work included the duty of taking care of the earth.

How grieved God must feel over the mess that man has made of Planet Earth! Wars have wrought a wilderness out of a Paradise. Industrial pollution has made a wasteland of the green earth, and has turned rivers and seas into poisonous cesspools, creating a toxic threat to hundreds of species of living things.

As man destroys the rain forests, he is at the same time cutting off the branch supporting his own survival. Commercial expediency and financial greed have blinded the human race to the long-term devastating effects of such thoughtless action.

In an article about the tragic accident which occurred some years ago at the Chernobyl nuclear reactor, *The European* newspaper reported in April 1991 that the full consequences of Chernobyl will never be known. American scientists estimate there will be 40,000 deaths from cancer over the next 40 years. In 1988 there was an evacuation of 2,000,000 Soviets from the Ukraine and Byelorussia. The reactor core will remain hazardous for the next seven billion years!

In his pursuit of power, man has created and unleashed upon his own environment a frightful, Frankenstein-like monster which can no longer be controlled!

But there are even worse things spoiling the earth than nuclear contamination. The Bible says: *'Murder pollutes the land.'* Terrible as murder is, it is but one foul fruit of the poisonous root called sin. Sin is man's opposition to God. It is his attempt to ignore God and His laws, and to manage Planet Earth and all its resources without any reference to, or acknowledgement of, the Creator.

Man cannot properly care for the earth if he ignores God's plan and purpose.

The titanic tragedies of floods and famines focus our attention on the millions of victims who suffer such appalling loss of life and property. We can hardly imagine misery on such a scale. But sometimes these disasters are caused by the human factor. Some experts believe that the terrible flooding of Bangladesh was caused initially by the destruction of forests, normally retaining soil at the source of the river in the hills far away to the north.

Famines could often be alleviated if man's inhumanity to man were to cease, and if the abundance of prosperous nations could be shared with the poverty of needy lands, unhindered by political or military interference.

In an article in *Voice of Victory* magazine, John Avanzini wrote:

'Last fall my wife and I were in a small farm town in Iowa. It was harvest time there and the corn was everywhere. They had a bumper crop. Every storage space was full and corn was still standing in the fields because they didn't know what to do with it. At that same moment, in Africa, two and a half million babies were starving to death. But they wouldn't move the corn out of Clear Lake. They simply let it sit there idle because if they shipped it out free to the starving masses, it would signal to the market-place that there was a surplus, and the price of corn would fall three or four cents a bushel.'

Caring for the earth involves much more than caring merely for the environment. It must begin with caring for each other. And **caring** always means **sharing**. Only by following God's principles can we fulfil God's purpose for mankind and for Planet Earth.

3. GOD AND GOVERNMENT

God governs the universe by the free exercise of sovereign authority over every sphere of existence. His government is not an oppressive regime. It is not a penal system. His wise and loving providence regulates the lives of men and women, controls the course of history, and orders the orbits of the planets.

From the microscopic, invisible structure of the atom to the myriad stellar worlds of outer space, God upholds all things by the word of His power. His word is continuously creative. Constantly He renews the face of the earth, caring for every form of life.

God's word of Government is eternally issuing from the sapphire splendour of His dazzling throne. Angelic beings fly swifter than light to do His bidding. Suns and stars in galactic empires, millions of light years across, hear the word of His power and expand or explode according to His sovereign decree. Demonic spirits shudder at the thunder of that voice from the throne, and all the powers of darkness know that they are ultimately helpless to frustrate the ongoing purpose of the Eternal! Why? Because God is sovereign in government and almighty in power. He brings His own will to perfect fulfilment in every realm of the universe.

How does this concept of an omnipotent God of government fit in with the evidence in the world indicating hostility to God and rebellion against His will?

God has given mankind the precious privilege of exercising the power of choice. It is an awesome responsibility, but it is one of the factors which set men above the animals. Men are made in the image of God and have the capacity to make intelligent choices. Animals, on the other hand, live largely by instinct and are incapable of making ethical distinctions or moral decisions.

Where He does not find the loving co-operation of mankind, and in cases where people do not voluntarily submit to Him, God nevertheless weaves the dark threads of their sullen rebellion into the bright design of His own pattern, thereby causing the wrath of man to praise Him by contributing to the overall programme of His eternal mosaic and plan. Where the world will not recognise God's rule, He will over-rule.

Ultimately the universal declaration will be: 'The Lord God Omnipotent reigneth!' One day every knee must bow to King Jesus and every tongue confess that Jesus Christ is Lord to the glory of God the Father.

God is a great God and when I contemplate Him, I stand in awe, marvelling at His sublime wisdom, eternal majesty and sovereign grace! I am fascinated by the concept of the omniscience of the Almighty. Nothing in the past, present or future is outwith or beyond God's knowledge!

How incredible to realise the implications of God's omniscience! Every action in the history of mankind is known to Him. Each word spoken and every thought that has ever been conceived are clear to the Eternal God. He knows what you will think tomorrow, what you will say, how you will react. He knows before you do! He has always known from eternities past, the origin, development and destiny of every being in the universe. The past, the present and the future are focused in the eye of God with the clarity of an eternal NOW. That is omniscience.

God, in knowledge and foreknowledge, providentially guides and controls each tiny detail in the life of every human being, fitting even the perfect timing of events together like a jigsaw, and weaving the apparently insignificant into the supremely important fabric of His own eternal purpose.

On this planet live five thousand million people, each one an internal universe of a myriad thought patterns, a galaxy of emotional and spiritual potential, constantly shifting between time and eternity. Five billion threads on the mystic loom of life are being perfectly woven into the second seamless robe of the Master of the Universe.

Trust Him! He knows what He is making of your life.

4. BIBLICAL THERAPY

God is concerned about a suffering world. His heart is touched by the misery of mankind. He wants to heal their hurts and forgive their sins.

Over thirty-five centuries ago God spoke to Moses from the burning bush in the desert at Horeb: '*I have indeed seen the misery of my people in Egypt. I have heard them crying out because of their slave-drivers, and I am concerned about their suffering. So I have come down to rescue them . . .*'

The way in which God implemented His desire to alleviate the misery of the Israelites, was to send Moses to demonstrate His power before Pharaoh, and to declare His word: '*Let my people go!*'

God's great heart of love reaches out to the whole of humanity – not merely to Israel. That is why He sent His beloved Son, Jesus, to live amongst mankind and to die for our sins on the cross. During His earthly ministry Jesus brought healing to thousands. He made them *whole*, reaching the depth and source of every problem – not just treating the symptoms.

Following His resurrection and ascension in exaltation to the right hand of the Father, the Lord Jesus sent the Holy Spirit to fill and inspire His church to continue the work of spreading the good news. God's offer includes forgiveness of sins, healing, assurance, and eternal life. It is His will that His people exercise a therapeutic ministry toward broken humanity.

Sometimes people are healed and made perfectly whole in an instant by the miraculous power of God. But on other occasions the healing process is a gradual one, and Christians are involved in sacrificial and loving ministries of patient counselling toward people who still hurt from their emotional and psychological wounds.

Counselling is an important function in the church. There is a sense in which it has become very popular despite the exacting nature of the demanding work involved. Seminars have been conducted all over the country so that Christians can be properly equipped to deal with the complex problems confronting the church in these days of unprecedented difficulties. This preparation has been in the wise providence of God. The multitudes converted as a result of the Billy Graham Missions brought many problems with them into all the churches, and scores of needy people will require patient and loving counselling for some time. There is a Biblical therapy for every hurt – a Scriptural solution for each problem. But each individual person must be treated gently, with a Christlike sensitivity. We need the anointing of God's Spirit for this task.

Whilst recognising and accepting the skills of psychiatry and psychotherapy, we must be soundly Biblically-based in our counselling.

Dr Laurence J. Crabb has pointed out that the essential problems of mental disorder are all dealt with in the Bible. The psychotherapist is struggling to find the answer to resentment, insecurity, anxiety, fear, irresponsibility, guilt, loneliness, underdeveloped conscience, feelings of emptiness and meaninglessness, and other problems of an interpersonal nature. There is a solution in God's word.

The Bible points the way to the living Jesus – the ultimate answer to all our needs. Biblical principles of personal counselling must, therefore, be clearly understood and applied in each individual case.

Humanistic psychology views man as the centre of the universe, and does not recognise the need for God. But the application of Biblical therapy to a personal problem inevitably confronts the patient with certain propositional truths from God's word. For example, man was made in the image of God, but has become distorted because of sin. Nevertheless, Christ has dealt with that sin at Calvary, thereby redeeming mankind. This clearly implies that man is of inestimable value to God, and from this perspective, people can see that they are worthwhile beings. If they let God work in their situation, they find renewed hope and purpose in life. Christ is the answer to human despair.

Dr Maurice Wagner believes that people need a sense of belonging, of worthiness and of competence. These are important factors in the development of a healthy self-concept.

When someone is brought into a saving relationship with God the Father, that person is assured of belonging. Dr Wagner writes:

He is pleased to call us His son. This gives us a position with Him in His family. We know we are somebody to God. We have been redeemed from being a nobody. The idea of being a nobody never again will have any validity. When it threatens us we can firmly reject it in the reassurance of God's promises.

It follows quite logically that when a person becomes aware of his relationship with the Lord Jesus Christ, the Son of God, he is assured of his own worthwhileness. And as he relates to the Holy Spirit (who makes Christ real to him), he gains a sense of competence. The Spirit shows him from God's Word that, through Christ, he can do all things, and he discovers that God's Holy Spirit is the source of all personal guidance, comfort, and power.

These principles are effective maxims of Biblical therapy. When believed and applied, they work wonders.

5. OPEN TO GOD

It has been suggested that the human mind is, in one respect, like a parachute. It's not going to be much use unless it is open!

Oscar Wilde, on the other hand, expressed the view that an ever open mind is no better than an ever open mouth!

What can we make of these two concepts? There is a measure of truth in both statements. To make progress, we must open our minds and hearts to new ideas, fresh revelation and expressions of thought that are perhaps different from our own entrenched prejudices. But we must also guard our minds from Satanic influences, and close our hearts against the infiltration of sin and the world. Somehow we must reach a point of equilibrium when our minds are open to God, but alert to the subtle suggestions of the enemy.

The Bible has a lot to say about the human mind, and urges us towards the experience of the renewed mind. The Apostle could write: 'But we have the mind of Christ.' What a stupendous claim!

Paul could never have received divine revelation if he had closed his mind and heart to God and remained locked in his Pharisaical traditions of formal religion. On the other hand, it was Paul who urged the Ephesian Christians to wear the whole armour of God as protection against the wiles of the devil. An important item of that equipment is 'the helmet of salvation.' The helmet protects the head, the symbolic centre of mind and thought.

The Psalmist said: 'You have covered my head in the day of battle.' We are in a day of battle. Our minds are assailed from every quarter by the philosophy of humanism and the psychology of Satan. The god of this world entices us into the web of materialism by a thousand attacks a day upon our thought-life. The helmet of salvation will enable us to keep our minds open to God and closed to Satan.

The hymnist T.T. Lynch has crystallised the thought into verse:

> Tender Spirit, dwell with me,
> I myself would tender be;
> Shut my heart up like a flower
> At temptation's darksome hour;
> Open it when shines the sun,
> And his love by fragrance own.

In his charming book of meditations and poems entitled *No Strange Land*, former international Director of the Leprosy Mission, Eddie Askew, draws attention to the penetrating insights of the great Swiss psychologist Carl Gustav Jung, who was concerned at the tremendous increase in international tourism. Jung could accept travel for work's sake, but constant travel for travel's sake disturbed him, and he asked some very profound questions: 'What inward journey was the traveller running away from? Was he substituting his exploration of new lands for the need to explore the mountains and deep valleys of his own personality? Was he running from himself, and from God, to get lost in a relatively safe external world?

Of course, to be fair, we must remember certain things to keep this matter in perspective. In Jung's day, for example, the world was relatively much safer than it is today. Furthermore, the great psychologist was himself very widely travelled in connection with his work, so he was not deprived of that dimension of living. But most important of all is the fact that few people share Jung's enthusiasm for introspection of the psyche, and if it came to a choice, most of us would opt for a world-tour rather than an exciting session of psychoanalysis.

But the question remains. Are people running away from themselves and from God? Yes. Many are. They would rather do anything than obey the Biblical command to examine themselves in the light of God's word.

We have nothing to fear if we will open up to God. He is willing to forgive, cleanse and change us. But if we close our hearts and minds to Him, we are on a free-fall to disaster with an unopened parachute that can never help us.

6. THE FORMATION OF CHARACTER

Joseph, more than any other Old Testament character, typified the life and experience of the Lord Jesus.

For example, Joseph was the beloved son of his father; he was hated and rejected by his brethren, who conspired against him. He was stripped and sold for silver. He was tempted but did not sin; he was unjustly accused and cast into prison. Two other prisoners were bound with him (the butler and the baker); one was saved and the other was destroyed. Joseph possessed great wisdom and spiritual insight; he was eventually exalted to the throne and great power was given him. His word was to be obeyed, and he became the means of great blessing to all nations (by supplying them with food in a time of famine). At all times he was in complete submission to the will of God for his life.

What a beautiful prophetic picture of the experience of the Lord Jesus! It helps us to realise how important a character Joseph was in the sovereign purpose of God.

Psalm 105 is a song of praise to God for the fulfilment of His covenant promise to Israel. It was used as a hymn for congregational worship, inspiring the people to call to mind God's faithfulness and providential care. In surveying the history of God's people, the psalmist shows how the Lord used the tragedies of life to pave the way toward Israel's triumphs.

One such apparent tragedy was the personal history of Joseph described in verses 17 to 22:

'He sent a man before them, even Joseph who was sold for a servant: whose feet they hurt with fetters: he was laid in iron: until the time that his word came: the word of the Lord tried him. The King sent and loosed him; even the ruler of the people, and let him go free. He made him Lord of his house, and ruler of all his substance; to bind his princes at his pleasure; and teach his senators wisdom.'

This record tells us four things about Joseph and the formation of his character:

1) **He was humiliated**: *'Joseph, who was sold as a servant' (Ps. 105 vs. 17).*

Joseph was not dragged off into slavery by a foreign power or by an invading army. Terrible as that fate would have been, Joseph's lot was far worse. He was cruelly sold as a slave by his own brothers, who were envious of his father Jacob's favours toward him, and jealous of his profound spiritual insights revealed by his prophetic dreams.

His was a bitter cup, full of wormwood and gall; humiliated and hated by those who should have loved and protected him! Joseph was sold into slavery by his brethren.

2) **He was hurt**. *'Whose feet they hurt with fetters' (Ps. 105 vs. 18)*.

Who can begin to assess the agony of this sensitive soul as the cold treachery of his brethren dawned upon him?

How hurt he was to realise how hated he was! Each phase of this dark experience hurt Joseph. The **family plot** against him: the **fearful pit** into which he was cast; the **financial profit** made out of his personal grief; all these were terrible wounds in the heart of Joseph.

But not only was he hurt spiritually and psychologically – he was hurt and injured physically as well: *'Whose feet they hurt with fetters.'*

Twenty silver coins slid into Judah's bag, and the Midianite merchants lowered a rope into the pit where Joseph had been thrown. His hopes – raised momentarily by his rescue from the pit – were cruelly dashed as rough hands seized him and fastened the terrible chains of slavery upon his hands and feet. Joseph, weeping piteously, implored his brothers for mercy.

Joseph's brethren watched as the Midianites remounted their camels. The last in the line grabbed Joseph's chain and with a cruel slash of his whip dragged the bewildered young slave away from his homeland into the heathen land of Egypt.

The journey to the land of the Pharaohs was long and arduous. Joseph limped along through the fierce heat of the eastern sun, his mind in a daze, his heart hurting too much for words, his feet chafed and bleeding from the cruel chains.

In Egypt Joseph was sold again – this time to Potiphar, the captain of the Pharaoh's guard.

Potiphar soon recognised the outstanding qualities of the young Israelite, and made Joseph his chief steward.

Joseph's feet and ankles had just healed nicely, when he was falsely accused by Potiphar's wife and then clapped in irons in the prison-tower! *'He was laid in iron' (Ps. 105 vs. 18).* Fettered and manacled again, Joseph once more found himself the innocent victim of what appeared to be a cruel and capricious fate. But a wise and sovereign God was working His purpose out, through the events of Joseph's life.

Joseph lay in the straw on the floor of the dark tower. The iron chains had begun to re-open the old wounds. His heart breaking for sorrow, he remembered his dreams and his high hopes for the future. In that lonely experience: *'The word of the Lord tried him' (verse 19).* Emotionally exhausted, Joseph fell into a fitful sleep.

3) **He was helped**. *'The king sent and loosed him, even the ruler of the people, and let him go free' (Ps. 105 vs. 20).*

While Joseph was in prison, the Lord was with him in a special way and caused him to be trusted by the keeper of the prison, who shewed him favour (Genesis 39 vs. 21-23). In this way Joseph was helped.

Joseph had been in prison for some years when two new prisoners were brought in and locked up. Both were officials in the royal palace, and both had offended Pharaoh. One was the king's butler; the other man was his baker.

Joseph, now a 'trusty' in the gaol, was given the task of looking after them. A few months later both men had dreams which troubled each of them. Joseph could see by their faces that there was something wrong, so he asked them why they were so sad.

Both men related their dreams, explaining that their anxiety arose because they did not know the meaning of their dreams.

It is an illuminating comment on the strong character of Joseph that even in the prison he had kept in constant contact and communion with God. When a crisis arose – as it had now (in relation to the interpretation of these dreams) – Joseph was in vital touch with God, and he was able to exercise his gift and thus alleviate the anxiety of the palace officials over the meaning of their dreams.

In tragic and adverse circumstances, the Lord had enabled Joseph to retain his integrity and his insight into spiritual things.

'Within three days,' said Joseph to the king's butler, 'You will be restored to your former position: Please speak up for me then and ask the king to set me free.'

'As for you,' he told the baker, 'within three days Pharaoh will have you hanged!'

And so it came to pass, just as Joseph had predicted. But tragically, the butler, having been restored, then forgot all about his former fellow prisoner, Joseph, who languished on in the tower in lonely frustration. Once again: *'The word of the Lord tried him; (Psalm 105 vs. 19).*

It was two long and difficult years later when events began to move again in Joseph's favour. This time it was Pharaoh's turn to be troubled by strange dreams that he could not interpret.

After all the magicians and wise men of Egypt had failed in their efforts to find the interpretation of the King's dreams, it finally dawned on the butler that the man with the answer to the problem was in the prison!

So he told Pharaoh about Joseph and about his ability to interpret dreams accurately. The Psalmist describes the next scene: *'The king sent and loosed him' (Ps. 105 vs. 20).*

We can trace God's hand and see how Joseph was helped in his prison experience (The Lord will always help us through our times of darkness and difficulty).

Joseph was helped by the keeper of the prison, who showed him favour; he was helped by his own kindness in being willing to interpret the dreams of the palace officials; and he was helped by the king, who 'let him go free' (Ps. 105 vs. 50).

Through it all, the Lord of Sovereign wisdom was helping Joseph.

4) **He was honoured.** *'He made him lord of his house, and ruler of all his substance to bind his princes at his pleasure; and teach his senators wisdom' (Ps. 105 vs. 21-22).*

It was just going to be another of those monotonous, weary days of prison routine for Joseph. Suddenly there was a commotion in the keeper's quarters; then he hurried into Joseph's cell, closely followed by Pharaoh's representatives.

Joseph was instructed to shave and to change his garments. (The palace officials had brought appropriate clothes with them).

Just as his whole life had been dramatically changed on that terrible day when his brothers had sold him as a slave (how often in his lonely moments had he re-lived that agonizing trauma!), so now he was being swiftly swept from prison to palace, as the purpose of God moved inexorably forward for the provision and preservation of Israel.

So it was that Joseph found himself standing before Pharaoh. He had suffered in prison for fourteen years! But to him alone God had entrusted the answers to the problems of the Ruler of the eastern world!

Miraculously, the years of tragedy, slavery and agony had not embittered Joseph. His humble, God-glorifying responses to Pharaoh revealed Joseph's deep love and unwavering loyalty to the Sovereign Lord Jehovah.

e.g. 'It is not in me, **God** shall give Pharaoh an answer of peace' (Gen. 41 vs. 16).

'**God** hath shewed Pharaoh what He is about to do' (Gen. 41 vs. 25 and 28).

'The thing is established by **God** and **God** will shortly bring it to pass' (Gen. 41 vs. 32).

Joseph had been 'laid in iron'. Now the 'iron' was in his soul. He had become a man of steel who could speak to the Sovereign of Egypt.

So Joseph interpreted the king's dreams, which predicted seven years of plenty, followed by seven years of famine. By the power of God's Spirit, Joseph was able to give Pharaoh outstanding administrative advice. The wisdom of God – 'Forasmuch as **God hath shewed thee all this**, there is none so discreet and wise as thou art: thou shalt be over my house and according to thy word shall all my people be ruled.' (Gen. 41 vs. 39-40).

Thus was Joseph promoted to honour and became the ruler of an empire. His character had been forged in the fires of adversity. He had been humiliated and hurt beyond telling. But the Lord helped him in every phase of his life. Ultimately **God** honoured His faithful and fruitful servant, Joseph. 'For them that honour me I will honour' (I Sam. 2 vs. 30).

7. CHRISTIAN HEALTH

Beloved, I wish above all things that thou mayest prosper and be in health, even as thy soul prospereth. (III John 2).

'He healed them all' (Matt. 12, 15).

Despite the tremendous advance of medical science, millions of people still suffer from sickness, pain and disease. As one scourge of mankind is conquered, another raises its malignant head to threaten the health of the human species. Ironically, it seems as if the progress of civilization brings with it new diseases, and a multitude of psychological disorders not suffered by previous generations. The pressure of modern life takes its toll, and in some places even the old problems remain unsolved – the pains unalleviated.

Also there are sicknesses which are inward – deep scars of the spirit, running sores of the soul – hurts, wounds, grievances, resentments and fears – emotional disturbances bringing people into bondage, inhibiting their joy and their freedom of expression.

The compassion of Christ remains unchanged. He still longs to heal us all. But often, before healing comes, there are certain adjustments we must make. Confession, forgiveness, self-humbling, and restitution may all be necessary before we can receive His healing touch. This principle is particularly true in the case of spiritual and emotional healing, but it also applies to other forms of healing.

Let us consider some of the spiritual disorders amongst Christians requiring God's healing:

Loss of feeling. One of the distressing features of the disease of leprosy is the destruction of the ability to feel pain. Terrible injuries can be sustained by lepers without them experiencing the danger-signal of pain.

Spiritually speaking, such a condition is even more deadly! Yet many Christians suffer from it. They do not feel pain in their hearts at the sufferings of others. They are insensitive to the plight of broken humanity in a lost world, destined for wrath and judgment. Millions of souls fall daily into an eternal hell – but the spiritually insensitive Christians feel nothing – and because they **feel** nothing, they **do** nothing about it.

Oh for the spirit of Christ, who was **moved with compassion**, and therefore sought to heal hurt people! In the words of Herbert Lockyer: 'There are diseases, worse and deeper than bodily diseases – stings of conscience, deadness of heart, blindness to divine truth, paralysis of energy to serve God, hideous **inner leprosy**.'

'In His name, I shall cast out devils' says Alexander Smellie, 'the demons of sin, the selfishness of pride, of worldliness – from my own heart and from the hearts of others. Jesus in me ought to bruise Satan under His feet today.'

'In His name I should lay hands on the sick, and they should recover. Those quiet, cooling, rest-giving healing hands – how I covet them as mine! But, instead, my touch is feverish and I only inflame and intensify the malady I seek to cure.' **Have you ever felt like that?**

Another current complaint amongst Christians involves **loss of appetite** for the things of God – a kind of spiritual anorexia nervosa!

Anorexia nervosa is described by the dictionary as 'a psychological illness in which the patient refuses to eat over a long period. It results in emaciation and, if untreated, in death by starvation.' How important it is for all Christians to feed regularly and eagerly upon Christ – upon His word, His presence, and His fellowship.

If you starve yourself of spiritual substance, you will become weak, dispirited and apathetic. Your vital support will be withdrawn from the cause of Christ, and you'll become a 'drop-out.' As a result, the spiritual warfare in your sector of witness and worship will sustain a serious setback.

A quaint little verse puts it like this:

> For want of a nail, the shoe was lost,
> For want of a shoe, the horse was lost,
> For want of a horse, the rider was lost,
> For want of a rider, the battle was lost,
> For want of the battle, the kingdom was lost –
> And all for the want of a horse-shoe nail!

So hear the call of the Master to you today: **'Come and dine!'**

Thirdly, **loss of perception** is a disability that can seriously inhibit Christian progress. Many professing Christians suffer from '**spiritual dyslexia.**'

('**Dyslexia** is a learning disorder causing impairment of the ability to read'.) People with this problem look at words, but they cannot make any sense of them. Consequently reading and writing for the dyslexic become an impossibility. Are there Christians like that in the spiritual realm? Yes! There are folk who open the Bible, but to them it makes no sense at all. They cannot discern God's revelation in His word. They suffer from a lack of spiritual perception. The cure for this **spiritual deficiency** is constant dependence on the Holy Spirit for light and understanding, coupled with a disciplined determination to pursue systematic Bible study. There are many useful aids to study, currently available to the sincere student.

Spiritual sclerosis is yet another form of sickness prevalent among Christians. (Sclerosis is a **hardening** process. It can affect arteries, nerve-endings, or the spinal-column.) Once the hardening process has set in to a Christian's **spiritual** life, that person is in grave trouble. Attitudes toward God and man become hard and bitter. Prejudices become more deeply entrenched. Change and progress become almost impossible, whilst ritual and formality are welcomed.

It is difficult for sufferers from this spiritual sickness to become involved in vigorous on-going programmes of evangelism. Consequently many precious souls go to a lost eternity.

Dr James Kennedy has reminded us of some startling statistics: 'If you could win **1,000 persons for Christ every night of the year**, how long would it take you to win the whole world for Christ? Answer: **Over 1,000 years!** But if you could win just **one person** for Christ **each year**, and then train each person to win **one other person** for Christ **each year**, how long would it take to win the whole world for Christ? Answer: **Just 32 years!**'

'Today, if you will hear His voice, **harden not your hearts!**'

Much more could be said about various other sufferers from spiritual disorders. (About **spiritual haemophiliacs** for example – who never seem to stop bleeding from wounds they received twenty years ago!)

But let the words of the poet H. Twells sum it all up:

'O Saviour Christ, our woes dispel:
For some are sick and some are sad
And some have never loved Thee well,
And some have lost the love they had.'

21

'And some are pressed with worldly care
And some are tried with sinful doubt
And some such grievous passions tear
That only Thou canst cast them out.'
'Thy touch has still its ancient power;
No word from thee can fruitless fall;
Hear in this solemn evening hour,
And in Thy mercy heal us all.'

8. THE THEORY OF EVOLUTION

It is amazing how such an incredible notion as evolution has gripped the minds of millions. So deep-rooted is this theory of evolution that it has assumed an almost unassailable place in the philosophy of mankind. But thoughtful people are challenging the evolutionists.

Evolution is taught as an accepted constituent element of the educational system. Fair enough! Students should learn about it. They should, for example, know who Charles Darwin was and what he believed. But the unfairness of the system consists in the exclusion from the educational curriculum of any serious attempt to acquaint pupils with the credible alternative – creationism. Students should be expected to regard the scriptural record of creation as a valid alternative to the theory of evolution.

Evolutionistic doctrine attacks God. It renders Him redundant. If the world sprang into being by chance, and every living being 'evolved' in process of time, then God as Creator, Sustainer and Governor is disposed of. This is a satanic idea. Clever people may believe in the theory of evolution, but such a concept springs from a God-hating philosophy. The Apostle Paul wrote about 'doctrines of demons.' Evolution is one of them. It is satanic in origin, and the logical implications prove that the theory of evolution is ultimately atheistic at heart.

The theory of evolution attacks the person and work of the Lord Jesus Christ. It denies His involvement in creation and in the cohesion of the universe. It renders unessential His redemptive work and His ultimate Kingship over mankind and the earth. If man is evolving upwards instead of being a fallen sinner in need of salvation and reconciliation, then the work of Jesus at the cross of Calvary becomes superfluous. It is the aim of the devil to deny the person of Christ and to discredit His work. Evolution is the deceptive mask behind which Satan hides his real philosophy, viz, that mankind does not need the Saviour.

The theory of evolution attacks man. It robs him of his dignity and of his destiny. Man was made in the image of God. Evolution asserts that he evolved from the lower animals. Because of the materialistic nature of their philosophy, evolutionists are forced to deny that man has a glorious future to co-operate with God's arrangements for subduing, and ruling over, the earth.

Evolution offers no hope to mankind. It is a doctrine of despair.

The theory of evolution attacks the Bible. It contradicts the written word of God. The final implications are so subtle. If the Genesis record cannot be trusted, why should people be expected to believe any part of the Bible? Thus Satan has undermined the confidence of mankind in the Biblical revelation of truth. Millions have been caught in this web of diabolical deception.

Evolution violates the intelligence of students. They are expected to believe, without question, an absurd theory, asserting that this complex universe with its myriad forms of life, is the product of chance. Evolutionists can give no explanation for the origin of matter, nor can they explain why atoms, molecules and elements behave as they do.

Evolution is anti-God, anti-Christ, anti-Bible, anti-Man and anti-intelligence. The theory is sustained by the energy of satanic spirits influencing and dominating the minds of unregenerate, unbelieving and unrepentant people.

A God-rejecting world eagerly accepts evolution because He is not required in their system of doctrine.

Take off the blinkers. Give yourself the chance to see that God is right after all.

9. RELIGION AND POLITICS

'Religion and Politics don't mix.'

How often have you heard that mindless assertion? If enough people keep repeating it, everybody will eventually believe it to be true. But, as Anatole France said, 'If ten thousand people say a foolish thing, it is still a foolish thing.'

The dictionary definition of the word 'politics' is: 'The art or science of power and government'. 'Religion' is defined as 'The expression of man's belief in and reverence for a superhuman power or powers regarded as creating or governing the universe.'

Those two definitions have a lot in common. They are both concerned with power and government. Logically, on the basis of semantics alone, religion and politics are not incompatible. In the cycle of events both in the religious and the political spheres, people's beliefs ought to influence the way in which their society is governed.

Christ's command, 'Render therefore unto Caesar the things which are Caesar's and unto God the things that are God's', was never intended to be a policy of separating the sacred from the secular. It merely clarified the scope of human responsibility. In the ultimate analysis, *all* is God's. As David Pawson has suggested, nothing is really secular except sin. God is concerned with everything in His universe.

The Bible makes no artificial division between religion and politics. Christian convictions must find expression at every level of social government, right from the local scene to the amphitheatre of national and international politics.

The scriptures exhort Christians to pray for kings and for all that are in authority so that standards nationally will be improved. Much of the social disorder existing today in Britain arises from the failure of believers to pray in line with Biblical principles. Obviously Christians cannot be effective prayer-gladiators in the political arena if they do not take an intelligent interest in these matters.

Our nation is deteriorating daily. Unemployment alone is fomenting bitterness, anger, frustration and despair in millions of young people. This generation is ripe for revolution. The conditions calculated to precipitate it are being aggravated by Marxists determined to undermine

25

the social structure in Britain.

Marxist policy involves the infiltration of trade unions, local and central government and positions in education – in particular, the teaching profession and the media. Their aims include the disruption of production, the initiation of strikes, and the demoralisation of youth by encouraging permissiveness and the use of drugs.

Marxists have been virtually unhindered in pursuing these subversive tactics because the Christians have been brain-washed into believing that 'Religion and politics don't mix.'

Believers have not involved themselves in political matters. Very few have become trade union leaders, local councillors, or Members of Parliament. The result nationally has been tragic. The positions of governmental influence have been occupied in many cases by people whose aim is to destroy the fabric of our society. Their success has been undeniable. The rot has set in, and it may well be too late to eradicate it.

Marxist dedication will certainly never be shaken by a Christian ethic that detaches itself from the mainstream of life in our nation. Christians must stand up and be counted in each governmental stratum of society.

Christians ought to be politically concerned about the future of children in this country. Why are teachers forced to take strike action? Why is the health of babies, mothers and children still placed in jeopardy because of lack of finance for hospital resources and staff? Some doctors have to work unreasonably long hours under tremendous pressure because funds do not allow an increase in the number of medical staff.

Whether your money is used to maintain an arsenal of weapons with an unprecedented potential for horrific destruction, or whether your taxes are channelled into providing a better future for your children by giving teachers and doctors more reasonable working conditions, is really a matter for political decision. But ultimately these are ethical matters.

There are no easy options or smart answers.

When Jesus comes He'll sort things out. His kingdom will be a political kingdom. In the meantime, He expects us to do something about the situation today.

10. THE NOTICE BOARD

With breaking heart and distraught mind, the young man walked sadly through the streets of Plymouth. His leaden steps brought him eventually along Gordon Terrace, where he happened to glance up wearily at the structure of the Apostolic Church.

The church notice-board caught his eye, and he picked out the name and telephone number of the minister.

Soon, the young man was pouring out his heart to the Pastor on the telephone. The Pastor made immediate arrangements to meet him, and then brought him to the manse.

A tragic story unfolded. The young man, Albert, had been visiting Freedom Fields Hospital, where his wife, – in her early twenties, – was suffering from cancer. He needed someone to pray for her, and to counsel him.

Prayer-warriors were alerted, and the people in Devon and Cornwall prayed for Albert, for his wife Helen, and for their young son.

The weeks went by. Then one day the telephone rang in my home at Porthleven, Cornwall (where I was Pastor at that time).

It was my colleague, Pastor Philip Cawthorne, ringing from Plymouth:

'*Frank, they are discharging Helen from Hospital. Nothing more can be done for her. She is going to her home in Marazion in Cornwall. Will you call and see her?*'

I readily agreed.

The sun was shining in a cloudless sky as I drove along the narrow streets of the quaint old village of Marazion, near Penzance.

I looked over the sparkling blue sea toward St Michael's Mount, with it's fairy-tale castle rising to meet the azure dome of the sky. Beyond that, the long grey finger of the coast-line thrust itself into the ocean. I could faintly discern Penzance, Newlyn – and Mousehole. The Penlee Lifeboat house stood on that coast. Little did I think on that golden day, that death and destruction would eventually overtake the Solomon Browne Lifeboat and her heroic Cornish crew. Nor could I then imagine the sleepy village of Mousehole one day becoming the centre of world-attraction, and the focus of a colossal financial fund.

All that was far into the future as I turned off the main road and threaded

27

my way through the enchanted Cornish lanes toward the Marazion Pottery where Helen had her home.

I drove the car gingerly over the rickety wooden bridge which just managed to span the reed-covered stream running beside the Pottery.

The air was warm and still. The birds were singing and it seemed as if I had reached Paradise early, as I knocked on Helen's door.

When she appeared, I came back to earth with a shock. Death had set his mark upon her. It seemed so incongruous in such an idyllic setting, where all was a joy to life.

Her weak and slight frame was crowned by her bright face, from which her eyes shone like two dark pools. She smiled sweetly. Beside her stood her small son – an exact replica of herself. The situation tore at my heart.

We chatted for a while. She made no complaint, expressed no bitterness. Yet, as far as I knew, she had not up to then professed to be a Christian.

So I talked to her about the love of Jesus, and a few minutes later she prayed with me and acknowledged Him as her own personal Saviour.

How loving and merciful God is! What tender care he bestows upon His loved ones!

I said Goodbye to Helen, drove back over the little bridge, and went home.

I never saw her again. Not long afterward, the Lord took her home to be with Himself where there is no pain or death.

Two special things stand out in the incident I have related. One is the undeniable evidence of God's sovereign and saving grace. Helen was evidently one of God's elect children. To bring her to Himself, He moved through a chain of events that only He could have planned and foreseen.

The other thing is this. God used a church notice board as one of the vital links in that chain of circumstances which led up to Helen's conversion.

But what if nobody had bothered to paint and maintain that notice-board?

11. LIBERTY

'Man was born free', wrote the eighteenth century French political essayist, Jacques Rousseau, *'and everywhere he is in chains.'* What kind of a man was Rousseau? And what was his philosophy of freedom?

He was born in 1712 in Geneva, of Swiss, French and Italian descent. His father was a watchmaker and the boy had little formal education. At the age of 13 he was apprenticed to an engraver who was unkind to him. Three years later he crossed the border, arriving eventually in Turin, where he became a Roman Catholic and studied music and Latin. He then moved to Annecy, where he spent the next ten years before trying his fortune in Paris at the age of 30. There he lived in worldliness without much thought of God. He became a companion of Voltaire the infidel, and of Diderot and d'Alembert, who had been appointed to edit the famous *Encyclopédie*. Rousseau was asked to contribute articles on music and political economy.

He was popular with the great ladies of Paris and became associated with a girl named Thérèse Le Vasseur, who bore him five illegitimate children. These he irresponsibly and uncaringly deposited one by one on the steps of the hospital for foundlings.

Rousseau continued to expound his philosophy about the virtues of the 'natural man', and to write on republican ideologies. He also wrote about music, composed an opera, and immersed himself thoroughly in the social life of eighteenth-century Paris.

His conscience being briefly stabbed into wakefulness, Rousseau went back to Geneva in 1754 and became a Calvinist. But soon he returned to Paris, where he was invited to occupy a cottage in the forest of Montmorency and was quickly involved in a romantic situation with the Comtesse d'Houdetot.

Rousseau's writings increased and he produced a novel, *La Nouvelle Héloise*, in 1761, containing idyllic descriptions of the countryside. His *Le Contrat Social* was written in 1762, outlining a theoretical constitution so popular in his day. The philosophy of the social contract demanded that the individual would hand over himself and all his rights to the community. Personal freedom was sacrificed to the rule of the greater number. (Does this concept remind you of heavy shepherding being practised in some Charismatic circles today?)

Rousseau's book was well-written. (His prose has been described as 'unforgettably eloquent'.) But, as historians have pointed out, the *Social Contract* was full of false arguments that appealed to the infamous Robespierre and later on to the Nazis. Rousseau's much-quoted statement *'Man was born free and everywhere he is in chains'* appears in Chapter One of the *Social Contract!*

Having settled in Paris, he wrote various other books, beginning a volume entitled *Dialogues,* in which he made an attempt to explain his philosophy of a return to nature and to justify his past conduct. But although his writing was pleasing to read, his exposition of his beliefs and doctrine exposed a mental unbalance now plain for all to see.

In 1778 Rousseau went to live at Ermonville, where he died in July of that year. Was his classic maxim true? Is man *'born free'*? Yes, and no. Politically and socially some privileged folk *are* born free. But nobody is born free from sin, as the Apostle explains in his letter to the Romans. Man needs a Liberator. His name is Jesus.

Poor Rousseau! After almost sixty-six years of pleasing himself in what he thought was freedom, he found himself in chains together with the rest of mankind!

The ancient wisdom of David the Psalmist provides the real prescription for a life of true liberty: *'I will walk about in freedom, for I have sought out your precepts.' (Psalm 119 vs. 45).*

The word *precept* comes from a Hebrew root meaning a *mandate of God.* A mandate is an authoritative command or instruction. A life of liberty comes by recognising the authority of God – not by making up the rules as you go along. That is what Rousseau tried. But it didn't work.

12. THE SPIRIT OF OBEDIENCE

Obedience is not a simple matter. It can be rational, but at other times it can be irrational. It is often motivated by subtle and complex forces, making the psychology of obedience a fascinating and thought-provoking study.

'Failure to obey the law,' writes Professor Stanley Milgram *'. . . is the hallmark of criminality. Yet an excess of obedience may also present grave moral problems.'* This maxim has been demonstrated historically by Nazi Germany. Swayed by the hypnotic rhetoric of Adolf Hitler, a whole nation was deluded into believing itself to be the Master Race and moved obediently to fulfil the Fuhrer's despotic will. Political and military machinery was set in motion for the extermination of 'inferior' peoples. In such a misguided heady climate of megalomania, S.S. Officers like Eichman could easily justify the destruction of six million Jews by claiming that he was merely being 'obedient' to orders from a higher authority. Such fanaticism is surely an example of irrational obedience.

But rational obedience is a foundational factor in any civilized society. *'It makes good sense,'* continues Milgram, *'to follow the doctor's orders, to obey traffic signs, and to clear the building when the police inform us of a bomb threat.'* According to Milgram, *'Human society as we know it could not exist unless a capacity for obedience were present in its members.'*

The question that perplexed the mind of Professor Milgram was this: *'How is it possible that a decent kindly person may, in a short time, find himself killing others with ease?'* He was, of course, referring to the terrible transformation wrought in societies by war. Young people are called up into the armed services and are sent to kill the young people of another society. They are taught to obey. Their obedience is rewarded. Their disobedience is punished. There are no simple answers to the complex questions that spring to mind in such circumstances. Clearly, obedience is a crucial factor and a very subtle dynamic.

There can be a superficial obedience, an outward show, whilst all the time a sullen resentment or a seething rebellion festers within the heart. This is the kind of 'obedience' rendered by prisoners to their jailors. But is such an attitude capable of producing real obedience? It seems clear that true obedience is a matter of the spirit. In fact, the Apostle told the church at Ephesus that the spirit of Satan is at work in those who are disobedient. The arena of spiritual conflict is the human will. If your will is energised by Satan, you will live in disobedience to God. If, on the other hand, your will is controlled by the Holy Spirit, the outcome will be a life of glad submission to God's will.

But most important of all, your outward obedience will reflect the true spiritual submission of your heart and will. There was a delight in the heart of Jesus to do the Father's will, even when it involved the pain of the cross. Christ's obedience was not a charade. Neither was it a grudging submission to His Father. An inward, holy dynamic energised His whole life, which expressed itself in terms of true obedience.

The Russian scientist Ivan Pavlov could alter the behaviour of dogs by his work on conditional reflexes. The animal's responses to stimuli could be confidently predicted by the physiologist, following his work upon them. This led some behaviourial psychologists to experiment on human beings in order to obtain their complete 'obedience' to commands. Brainwashing was the terrible sequel to Pavlov's experiments with animals. Can such psychologically induced responses be included in the category of real obedience? I don't think so. If obedience does not spring spontaneously from a heart of love which longs to please the Master – then it is not the quality which God desires. It may look like obedience. But it is something else.

Obedience – or disobedience – to God have equally far-reaching but opposite effects. The Apostle made this quite clear when he wrote to the Romans: *'For just as through the disobedience of the one man (Adam) the many were made sinners, so also through the obedience of the one man (Christ) the many will be made righteous.'*

The crucial importance of a true spirit of obedience can never be over-emphasised. It can be produced in the human heart only by the gracious power of the Holy Spirit, and it is the hall-mark of Christlikeness.

Acknowledgements to The Oxford Companion to the Mind, *edited by Richard L. Gregory, published by Oxford University Press, 1987, by permission of Oxford University Press.*

13. THE QUESTION MASTER

In the Christian community the phrase, *'Christ is the Answer'* is in danger of becoming a cliché. Congregations sing with gusto: *'Christ is the Answer to my every need'*. The chorus goes with a swing and everybody enjoys the sense of confidence expressed musically.

I would not, of course, deny the truth of that assertion. Christ *is* the Answer . . . But only if you know the right question. Only if you understand your true problem. Take, for example, Paul's reassuring words written to the Philippian church: *'And my God will meet all your needs according to His glorious riches in Christ Jesus'*. If ever a Biblical verse contained the essence of the comprehensive truth denoted by the phrase 'Christ is the Answer,' it is that verse written to the Philippians.

The trouble is that most people do not realise what their real needs are. Allowing for the context of the Apostle's words, which dealt with the sacrificial financial giving of the Christians at Philippi, there is a persistent tendency to regard our 'needs' exclusively in terms of material values.

A new car is required; a better music-centre; a bigger house; more fashionable outfits – we regard these as our needs. So, according to the Scripture, we can confidently ask God to supply these things. Most Christians in the Western world have these, and many more, possessions, and God does supply such items in response to faith when it is in line with His purpose.

The point I am making is that our concept of our true needs ought not to be limited to the realm of materialism. What about our desperate need for holiness? For Christlikeness? For a deeper prayer-life? For a passion for souls? For more of the power of God in our own experience and in our churches?

We should elevate our vision to see the promise of God in a new light, and seek to understand our true needs from the divine perspective. Then we can confidently claim God's promise, because our expectations will be in line with His will and purpose.

Christ can never be the complete Answer to our needs so long as we keep presenting Him with inferior problems, or continue to ask Him the wrong questions.

From an examination of the gospels, it seems to me that Jesus asked more questions than He answered. He did this, of course, not because He didn't know the answers, but in order to probe the understanding of those who were listening to Him.

The Christ who is the Answer is also the great Question Master. As the sharp sword of His word cuts through the traditional prejudices enshrouding the mind, light begins to dawn. The dark clouds that inhibit a clear understanding of God and His purpose start to disperse. The sun of revelation shines, and the Spirit of the Lord graciously enlightens the eye of the understanding.

One day Jesus asked His disciples this question: *'Who do people say the Son of Man is?'* After some very disappointing answers from the others, the heart of Jesus was gladdened as a shaft of divine revelation penetrated the mind of Peter and the big fisherman cried out with supreme confidence: *'You are the Christ, the Son of the living God!'* That tremendous truth became articulate in the Apostle, only because of the unique wisdom of the Question Master.

It can be a fascinating and rewarding study to trace through the gospels the searching questions of Christ. At first sight some of them seem very strange. How would you feel, for example, if you were at sea in a small boat when suddenly a furious storm threatens to swamp the ship? You and your friends struggle to prevent the little craft from capsizing, but the fury of the hurricane intensifies. One of the crew, in desperation, wakes the Saviour, who, exhausted from His work, is sleeping through it all. As He rises to His feet, Jesus asks you this question: *'Why are you so afraid?'* In the circumstances, wouldn't you consider that an unusual question?

The gospels contain many more such thought-provoking questions of Christ. The Apostle John gives us some insight into the mind and motivation of the Master: 'When Jesus looked up and saw a great crowd coming towards Him, He said to Philip, "Where shall we buy bread for these people to eat?" He asked this only to test him, for He already had in mind what He was going to do.' The ultimate result of Christ's question was the feeding of a vast multitude, thereby illustrating the tremendous truth of His claim: *'I am the bread of life.'*

Certainly, Christ is the Answer. But He can become the answer to your needs, only as you are prepared to listen sensitively to His searching questions.

14. THE PARADOX OF APOSTLESHIP

'God is light and in Him is no darkness at all'.
'Moses drew near unto the thick darkness where God was'.

A God of glorious incandescent light, dazzling in brilliant splendour! Yet a God enshrouded in thick darkness. These two concepts illustrate the paradox that is at the centre of things in the Being and dealings of God.

At the heart of the universe is a cross.

Golgotha's cross is a series of profound paradoxes. The sublime mysteries, for example, of the sinless One being made sin; of the Blesser of all mankind becoming a curse; of the immortal Prince of life tasting death for every man; of a holy God suffering in agony so that guilty sinners might share eternal bliss in glory!

A paradox is a situation exhibiting inexplicable or contradictory aspects. God seems to work in paradoxes which are not subject to simple analysis. The blood-red reasoning of Calvary defies the understanding of the brightest intelligences of men and angels. The logic of the cross is a paradox. The mysteries of Golgotha are not unravelled by a Mensa-level intellect. But they can be grasped by the logic of faith.

The Scriptures highlight another paradox: *'He shall baptise you with the Holy Ghost and fire' (Luke 3.16).*

'He who believes in me as the Scriptures said – from his innermost being shall flow rivers of living water. But this He spoke of the Spirit.' (John 7 vs. 38-39).

Fire and water! Two apparently contradictory concepts – yet both equally applicable to the power of the Holy Spirit.

Paradox is evidently a divine principle. The idea appears yet again in the ministry of Apostleship: *'And God has appointed in the church, first Apostles' (Cor. 12.28).* But Paul also wrote: *'For I think God has exhibited us apostles last of all, as men condemned to death; because we have become a spectacle to the world, both to angels and to men' (1 Cor. 4.9).* As Moffat puts it: *'God meant us apostles to come in at the very end, like doomed gladiators in the arena.'*

Apostles, first in government, in authority and in responsibility -yet exhibited as those condemned to die, paraded in public.

This is a graphic allusion to cross-bearing – the condition of discipleship

35

and the vital qualification for apostleship.

An Apostleship proclaiming a non-sacrificial triumphalism unrelated to the crucifixion of self, will issue eventually in a sterile, dictatorial and spiritually powerless bureaucracy, devoid of revelation and lacking a true sense of vocation.

On the other hand, an Apostleship crucified, risen, and suffering with Christ will shake the very gates of hell, and make an impact on this generation.

Paul described the paradoxical avenues through which the ministry of apostleship was expressed:

'By honour and dishonour, by evil report and good report; as deceivers and yet true; as unknown and yet well-known; as dying and behold we live; as chastened and not killed; as sorrowful, yet always rejoicing; as poor yet making many rich; as having nothing and yet possessing all things' (II Cor. 6 vs. 8-10).

The paradox of the cross is at the heart of fruitful Apostleship.

15. 'WHY?'

The story is told of the defeated Napoleon, brooding in his exile over a map of the world. Placing his finger upon Great Britain, the frustrated despot exclaimed bitterly: 'But for that red spot I would have conquered the world!'

That incident captures the imagination. We can visualise another would-be World Dictator viewing the globe that he had longed to govern. In helpless rage Satan had to confess: 'But for that red spot I would have conquered the world!' That spot was Calvary, reddened with the blood of the cross.

At Calvary the wisdom of God frustrated the strategy of Satan. The power of God defeated the forces of sin and darkness. The love of God endured the horrors of the cross; and the sacrificial blood of Jesus made full atonement for a world's sins.

Satan could do no more. At the cross the demonic hordes of hell exhausted themselves in malicious ingenuity and cruelty. Jesus absorbed it all in His great heart of unconquerable love, and then died sinlessly and willingly in accordance with the Father's gracious plan of redemption.

There is an eternal magnetism in the cross of Calvary which compels us to draw near, and, with wondering eyes to gaze upon our crucified God! There is a majesty in the Man of Calvary, a dignity superseding the proud dynasties of emperors. The Lamb of God, bleeding, suffering, dying for our sins on that awful cross, demonstrates the majesty of a kingdom that is not of this world. There is a mystery in the Calvary-sufferings of God's Son. The cross is the deepest mystery of the universe – the wisdom and the power of God.

Profound mystery is in the stern silence of the Father, as all heaven reeled from the agonizing pleadings from that innocent Sufferer nailed to Golgotha's cross . . . 'My God . . . Why? . . .?' It has been said that God never answers the question 'Why?' Faith accepts the apparently cruel mystery of the Father's will, and trusts Him when it cannot trace Him.

In a cellar in Cologne, Germany, after World War II, these words were found written on the wall: 'I believe in the sun, even when it is not shining; I believe in love, even when I feel it not: I believe in God, even when He is silent.'

There is a mystery in unanswered prayer. But Jesus trusted his Father even though no answer came to his tormented question . . . *'Why?'* Jesus died with his question still unanswered – but with his trust still unbroken. The Father vindicated the faith of His Son by raising him from the dead and appointing him as King and Judge of all the Universe.

Calvary remains the wonder of the ages; crowned with majesty, clouded in mystery, drawing us with an irresistible magnetism to the gentle Sufferer on that blood-stained cross.

16. 'THE RIGHTEOUS KING'

'For the righteous LORD loves righteousness.
(Psalm 11 verse 7).

God is absolutely righteous in character and activity. In an unrighteous world this revelation of God is reassuring. But the Psalmist also poses a *moral problem* – a dilemma in moral philosophy: 'If God be all-powerful and absolutely righteous, why is so much unrighteousness in His world?' There are no smart answers to questions like that. But remember, God's sovereignty is not tyranny. People are not puppets programmed to behave correctly when God presses the right button. God could take no pleasure in such mechanistic behaviour.

There is a further implication: since the righteous Lord loves righteousness, He expects His justified people to correct the evils arising from a context of social unrighteousness. Christians should know where they stand on issues like apartheid, divorce, abortion, drugs, anti-semitism, sex, political involvement, contraception, alcoholism, immorality and capital punishment. And the world should know that Christians stand with God on these matters. His position is, of course, made clear in His written word – the Bible. The Christian world-view, therefore, must always be Biblically orientated. Nothing should be left to mere philosophical speculation, or to humanistic reasoning.

A *spiritual maxim*, or principle of conduct, is also contained in the Psalmist's statement. Each believer's personal life should be regulated by that principle of righteousness. The Bible frequently warns about religion without righteousness. No amount of religious activity can ever become a substitute for real righteousness, nor make a wrong thing right.

The righteous LORD loves righteousness – but it is absolute righteousness that He loves. It is His own righteousness. Consequently the righteousness in mankind that pleases God is the product of His own grace which first justifies believers (imputing to them the perfect righteousness of Christ), but which also enables them daily to express Christ in righteous behaviour through transformed lives.

King David's words also presuppose a *final kingdom*. It is the righteous LORD who loves righteousness. This sovereign LORD is the righteous

39

Ruler of the universe. It follows, therefore, that the righteous King is bound to have a righteous kingdom. In the ultimate analysis, 'Jesus shall reign', and the sceptre of His kingdom is the sceptre of righteousness. David's Psalm prophetically implies certain judgment.

From the eternal perspective, 'The LORD reigneth. He is King forever!' From the eschatological perspective, God is moving all things toward the inevitable ultimate goal of the millennial reign of His Son upon Planet Earth. But from the spiritual perspective, 'the kingdom of God is within you', and kingdom principles must be applied by all believers to every national, social and ethical issue confronting the church today.

17. FAMOUS WOMEN

Women have made their mark in history. Some have been famous and noble, while others have been infamously wicked.

The Bible contains the record of all kinds of women. There was Eve, the first human being to commit sin; and Sarah who, through faith, bore the son of promise in her nineties! There was Ruth, a stranger in a strange land, a woman whose name is synonymous with faithfulness; and there was Esther, whose beauty swept her from a lowly homestead to a queenly throne, and whose intelligence and courage saved a nation.

Who can forget Mary the mother of the Messiah? Or the un-named little woman whose tremendous faith drove her weak body through overwhelming opposition to touch the tassel of Christ's robe, drawing from him virtue that wrought a miracle!

The names of other women in Scripture conjure up such scenes of horror that we would rather forget them. God, however, has seen fit to place their abhorrent wickedness on everlasting record. Whose blood does not run cold at the mention of the evil Queen Athaliah? This woman's ambition for power rivalled that of Lucifer himself! The Bible says: *'She arose and destroyed all the seed of the kingdom' (II Kings 11 vs. 1)*. She murdered potential kings so that she herself could reign over the land. It was a woman whose quick resourcefulness hid little Joash in the house of the Lord for six years until the time came when he could be crowned king of Judah. That brave woman was Jehosheba – perhaps you've never even heard of her – but she was the means of preserving the royal line of kings and of maintaining the principle of godly government in the land. The foresight of courageous Princess Jehosheba is in sharp contrast to the destruction and violence of the wicked Queen.

Crowns cannot create character. Jezebel and Herodias were also queens; but their behaviour was by no means queenly. They were a disgrace to royalty because they abused their power in order to persecute the prophets of the Lord.

But of all the notorious wicked women in the Bible, the worst of all was the treacherous Delilah. Her pride and insensitivity, her greed for silver, and her consuming desire to ingratiate herself with the Philistine aristocracy, cost the people's leader his eyes and drove him into the cruel

41

bondage and drudgery of the enemy's prison grinding-house. Her deeds were worse than those of any other woman, because she appealed ostensibly to the best and highest emotions in a man – love and trust. Delilah's deception brought judgment on the Judge!

Enough of these gloomy meditations! Let us consider some women of a more beautiful nature. The history of the church has been illuminated by a host of sparkling jewels of womanhood, many of whom have contributed to the ministry of worship by hymn-writing. Fanny Crosby wrote 'Blessed Assurance', and Frances R. Havergal penned 'Take my life'. But it is God's Word which puts womanhood into true perspective: *'Who can find a virtuous woman? For her price is far above rubies' (Proverbs 31 vs. 10).*

18. JESUS – HEIR TO ALL GOD'S RICHES!

The resurrection of Jesus Christ brought to humanity many tremendous benefits, and had an effect on every realm of the universe.

In heaven, the crucified, sinless, risen God-Man blazed the trail to the throne of glory and sat down (as the Proto-Type of a new order of mankind), on the right hand of the Majesty on high.

On earth, people now experience a glorious deliverance from the fear of death and the power of the grave. New hope has dawned for the human race because Jesus is alive!

In the infernal regions, Satan is still reeling from the shattering blow dealt to the kingdom of darkness by the resurrection of Christ. The devil will never recover his authority. The keys of hell and of death are now securely held in the nail-pierced hand of the risen Lord!

To the redeemed, one of the most exciting features of the resurrection is that it has enabled Jesus to become the Executor of His own will and testament.

Being the Son of God, Jesus is the heir of all things. But God, with gracious generosity, has appointed the elect to be joint-heirs with Christ. To secure this eternal inheritance for believers, it was necessary for Jesus to shed His blood and die upon the cross. He then rose from the grave and ever lives to implement the distribution of the inheritance to the beneficiaries.

The risen Christ is not only the gracious Provider, but also the effective Mediator of the inheritance. He is both Testator and Executor. This unique office is His by virtue of the cross and the resurrection.

In his book, *The Lord of All*, H. Brash Bonsall relates an illuminating incident from the life of Richard Flockhart, a well-known Christian in Edinburgh.

Flockhart used to visit, in the Tolbooth Jail, a criminal condemned to death for forgery. 'Richard,' cried the condemned man, 'I have left you all I have in my will!' Flockhart, however, exerted all his efforts to save the man's life, with the result that the forger was reprieved.

Later, a friend of Richard's wife left her all she had in her will. After the woman's death the will fell into the hands of unscrupulous lawyers who, by manipulating a legal technicality, deprived Richard's wife of her entire fortune.

After that, the godly and somewhat philosophical Flockhart used to say: 'I never got my legacy because the testator did not die. My wife did not get hers because the testator did not come to life to ensure its terms were observed!'

Thank God, there are no such loopholes in His testamental arrangements!

In his letter to the church at Corinth the Apostle is eager to emphasise: *'Christ died for our sins . . . He was buried, and He rose again the third day' (I Cor. 15 3-4).*

Every believer can now sing with J. Mason:

'Christ is my Meat, Christ is my Drink,
My Medicine and my Health;
My Portion, mine Inheritance,
Yea, all my boundless Wealth'.

19. POWER!

'. . . YOU shall receive power after that the Holy Ghost has come upon you . . .' (Acts 1:8).

The vital need of the church today is the **power** of the Holy Ghost. We need the ministry of the Spirit to create that which is lacking and to revive that which is dead.

There are four particular areas of deficiency in which the Spirit of fullness desires to move and to give a new supply of **power** from the reservoir of His eternal resources:

1 **Vision** – Power to Look.
2 **Passion** – Power to Love.
3 **Mission** – Power to Labour.
4 **Fusion** – Power to Live together.

Let us consider them in turn.
1. Vision – Power to Look.
When men see Jesus, something happens! Vision transforms! The fearful and disheartened disciples had their depression changed to joy when they saw the risen Lord. 'Then were the disciples **glad** when they **saw** the Lord' (John 20:20).

The martyr Stephen **saw** Jesus in glory (Acts 7:55-56). He had Spirit-given **power** enabling him to **look** beyond the death-laden stones and the murderous mob. Stephen had spiritual **vision**, and it gave him **victory**.

When Saul of Tarsus saw Jesus he was immediately transformed from a persecuting bigot into an obedient servant of the Lord (Acts 9:6).

The prophet Isaiah and the patriarch Job were also dramatically changed when they saw the Lord (Is. 6:1 & 5 and Job 42:5-6). A **vision** of Him puts things in perspective and shows us our need for cleansing and holiness.

'Open my eyes Lord, I want to see Jesus,

45

To reach out and touch Him, and say that I **love** Him.'

Adoration and love flow from a true vision of Jesus. This brings us to the second thought:

2. Passion – Power to Love.

Vision creates passion. A vision of His Calvary love produces a response of love in our hearts. 'We love Him because He first loved us.' The passion He creates in us is not a surface-slush emotional feeling. It is not superficial sentimentality, but a deep sacrificial love for Jesus.

Such a love issues in loyalty to Jesus and to the Word of God. 'If you **love** me, keep my commandments.'

Jesus condemned lack of passion. To the church at Ephesus the risen Lord said: '. . . I have somewhat against thee, because thou hast left thy first **love**.' (Rev. 2:4).

The early church continued steadfastly in the Apostles' doctrine, in fellowship, in breaking of bread, and in prayers (Acts 2:42). Also they had an outreach to the world, revealing a **passion** for souls. They **loved** Jesus and they sought to win souls for Him.

If passion is the product of vision, then the outcome of passion must surely be **mission** – the outreach to others – working for Jesus. This is the third thought:

3. Mission – Power to Labour.

'The **love** of Christ constrains me!' cried Paul. David Livingstone, motivated by the same dynamic, declared: 'The love of Christ **compels** me!'

David Brainerd, Henry Martyn, Mary Slessor, C.T. Studd, William Booth, Robert Raikes, Jim Elliott, and countless hosts of others, moved in **mission** because of a **passion** burning in their souls.

Such a flame should fire the whole church – not just a few illustrious names – but all! The whole body of Christ must move in Holy Ghost **mission** to reach the world for Jesus!

Jesus said; 'As the Father sent me, **so I send you**.'

He was sent on His great redeeming mission on the basis of the **passion** in the heart of God.

'God so loved' – that is passion.

'That He gave His Son' – that is mission.

And so the Son of Man came to seek and to save the lost.

Finally, there is the thought of fusion.

4. Fusion – Power to live together.

God's master-plan for world-evangelisation is the one-ness of His people (John 17:21).

The **purpose** of this fusion is that the **world** will believe. It is the work of the Holy Spirit to create that unity, and it is the duty of the church to maintain it (Eph. 4:3). It is not something future – this unity exists now.

The **pattern** of fusion is the God-head (John 17:21-22). The harmony that is in the God-head must be demonstrated in the church which is the body of Christ. Then the **world** will believe.

The **power** to live together in this one-ness of perfect harmony is the vital need of the church today!

20. AVAILABILITY

ARE YOU SOMEONE WHOM GOD CAN USE?
'. . . Ananias! And he said, Behold, I am here, Lord.'
(Acts 9 vs. 10).

Ananias was the sort of person whom God could use. The Bible doesn't tell us much about his background. He is described as **'a certain disciple,'** and we know he lived at Damascus.

Before we go on to analyse Ananias a little more closely, let us note certain suggestions about his character which are implied in that phrase: **'a certain disciple at Damascus.'**

It was no light thing to be a disciple of Jesus in the early church. The standards of Christian living were very high. The church was renowned for its purity, integrity and authority. Sin was discerned and swiftly judged (as in the case of a different man by the same name, Ananias – and his wife Saphira – Acts 5: 1-11). Yet the believers were being persecuted, and young Stephen had already sealed his testimony with his blood, becoming the first martyr of the church. Christian living was marked by suffering and sacrifice.

Furthermore, the zealous Pharisee, Saul of Tarsus, was at the height of his powers, carrying out an intense programme of persecution – and Damascus was next on his hit-list! No doubt, Ananias and his fellow-disciples at Damascus were undergoing considerable strain as the tension built up toward the arch-persecutor's impending purge of their churches.

With that background in mind, let us see what further light the Scripture sheds on this man – Ananias. The Biblical context for our character-analysis is Acts 9 verses 10-18. This passage reveals seven facets to the character of Ananias, and helps us to see more clearly why he was the sort of man that God could use.

Firstly, he was spiritual: '. . . and to him said the Lord in a vision, Ananias.' (vs. 10).

Ananias lived in fellowship with the Lord. He was a spiritual man with a capacity for divine revelation. When the Lord spoke to him, he recognised the tones of His Master. The Lord could have said of Ananias: 'My sheep hear my voice and they follow me.'

Ananias lived in touch with the realm of the supernatural. Like most of the early disciples, he lived his life in the dimension of the Spirit. He could receive the things of God in a vision, because he was a **spiritual** man.

Secondly, he was available: 'Behold, I am here, Lord.' (vs. 10).

It has been wisely said that God wants not our **ability**, but our **availability**. That is very true. God has all the power we need. He can supply all the ability necessary for every task. But the Lord seeks channels who are **available** to Him.

God looks for people who are **available** to do what He **wants**, to say what He commands, and to go where He sends them. If we will make ourselves available to God, He will make us **able** to do His will.

Ananias was such a man: '**Behold, I am here, Lord**,' i.e. 'I am available for your work Lord.' 'I am in the centre of your will.' 'I await your command.' 'I delight in your will and work.' 'I am here, Lord – I am **available** to you.'

Thirdly, he was teachable: 'And **the Lord said** unto him' (vs. 11-12).

So many mystics think they know it all! How many so-called spiritual people remain completely unteachable!

But Ananias was a teachable man. He had to listen carefully to the Lord's detailed instructions: 'Arise . . . Go . . . Inquire . . .' etc., etc.

Ananias was a balanced man. Not only did he have a capacity for perceiving visions, he could also comprehend articulate propositional truth – and adhere loyally to those words of God.

Fourthly, he was natural: 'Lord, I have heard by many of this man, how much evil he hath done to thy saints . . .' (vs. 13-16).

When we describe Ananias as natural, we do not mean that he was carnal. The word natural is used to show how human he was!

Ananias was like Mary, not like Zacharias. When the angel told Mary she would bear a child, her natural spontaneous response was: 'How shall this be . . .?' The question was permissible, it did not contain any element of unbelief.

Zacharias, on the other hand, expressed the unbelief of his heart when he made a similar outward reply to the angelic messenger who had foretold the birth of John the Baptist: 'Whereby shall I know this?'

(It is an illuminating illustration of the penetrating powers of the sublime messenger to discern **the spirit** in which the words of reply were uttered in each case.)

The natural response of Ananias was not condemned by Jesus, who went on gently to reassure his servant about the purpose of God for Saul, to whom Ananias was being sent with a message!

Fifthly, he was faithful: 'But the Lord said unto him, Go thy way . . . and Ananias went his way.' (vs. 15-17).

Having understood the Lord's instructions, Ananias faithfully obeyed them. It could not have been easy for him to contemplate laying his hands upon the man who was largely responsible for the imprisonment, suffering, and death of his fellow-believers in Jerusalem. But the Lord had spoken. That was enough for Ananias – he obeyed the Master. Ananias was a faithful man.

Sixthly, he was merciful: 'Putting his hands on him, he said **Brother Saul**.' (vs. 17).

As King Saul had been at the mercy of young David, who twice spared the jealous monarch's evil life – so Saul of Tarsus, blind and helpless, was now in the hands of Ananias of Damascus.

Ananias could have thought: 'Now's the time to give this persecutor a taste of his own medicine!' But the Bible gives no hint of any spirit of revenge in the heart of Ananias.

The first word he spoke to Saul was a word of love, of mercy, of forgiveness, of acceptance, of faith in the promise of Jesus, and of confidence in His transforming grace! It was a family word: '**Brother!**'

Ananias was **merciful** to the man who had shown no mercy to others. Likewise did the twentieth-century widows of the martyred missionaries in Ecuador shew mercy to their husbands' murderers, and took the Gospel to the Auca Indians, and pointed them to the Saviour.

Finally, he was powerful: 'And **immediately** . . . he received sight.' (vs. 18).

Ananias, under the mighty anointing of God's Spirit, laid his hands upon Saul and told him that the Lord Jesus was now about to restore his vision and fill him with the Holy Ghost.

This happened **immediately**! His sight was instantly restored, he was filled with the Holy Spirit, and was then baptised in water.

What a change from the proud Pharisee who had set out just a few days before, to persecute the followers of this Lord Jesus!

The instrument of God's dealings with Saul was the obedient Ananias – a powerful man – because he moved in the dimension of the Spirit. Therefore signs and wonders and miracles attended his simple ministry to Saul.

Thus did the obedient co-operation of one obscure, yet godly disciple lead to the involvement of the great Apostle Paul in the plan and purpose of God!

How important it is to 'walk in the Spirit' and to be continually available to God!

The promise of God for these Pentecostal days is: 'Your young men shall see **visions**!'

Have you ever had a vision from God?

You never know to whom God will send you! You never know the full purpose of God for the souls to whom you witness; or for the children whom you teach in your Sunday School class!

When a soul is saved, you never know what God's ultimate plans are for that person. It is vital to be faithful in your tasks for the Lord, however insignificant or routine they may seem to be.

Many years ago, Mordecai Ham, an old evangelist, was conducting a tent campaign in America. Night after night he faithfully preached the gospel, and gave the invitation for sinners to come to Christ and be saved.

One night, a tall, fair-haired, teenage lad made his way down the sawdust aisle to receive Jesus Christ as his Saviour and Lord.

That young man was Billy Graham, destined by God to preach the gospel in 62 nations, and to speak to more people about Christ than any other person in the history of mankind!

Mordecai Ham had no inkling of that golden future when he watched that tall blond lad coming to Christ. The old evangelist was just faithfully fulfilling his ministry for the Lord. He was **available** that night for God to use him; and God gave him the privilege of leading to Christ the greatest evangelist the world has ever seen!

So, keep yourself **available** to God – because you never know . . .!

21. THE SUPREMACY OF CHRIST IN HIS
HEADSHIP

The supremacy of Christ is a glorious reality.

In a glowing passage in his letter to the Colossians the Apostle Paul outlines the various realms in which Christ exercises supremacy (Col. 1:15-20).

He is supreme in His ability to express perfectly the invisible God: *'He is the image of the invisible God . . . '* Christ is supreme in His superiority over every order of creation: *'. . . the first-born over all creation.'*

He exercises supremacy in His universal power of creativity: *'For by Him all things were created . . . '* The Apostle continues to exalt the prerogatives of Christ in the realms of heaven and earth, visibility and invisibility, time and eternity. Christ is supreme over all thrones, powers, rulers and authorities, whether they be temporal or spiritual.

He exercises supremacy not only in the sphere of creativity with regard to the universe, but also in the realms of destiny and purpose for the universe: *'All things were created by Him and for Him.'*

He is supreme in His priority – *'He is before all things.'*

He is supreme in His ability to sustain the whole universe in perfect cohesion: *'In Him all things hold together.'*

As the swift river of revelation sweeps over the mighty themes of the personality of Christ, His ability, deity, creativity, superiority, priority – and His sovereignty in controlling the destiny of mankind and of all angelic orders – the Apostle introduces a startling truth: *'And He is the head of the body, the church.'*

This elevates the church into the divine perspective. God sees the church set in the context of universal creation, destiny and glory. And God has been pleased to constitute His Son, Jesus Christ our Lord, as supreme Head of His church. Headship, therefore, is a matter of the highest importance.

Church historians have suggested that Christ's supremacy in the headship of His body, the church, was the first truth for the church to lose historically and doctrinally. (This, of course, does not mean that Christ ceased to be Head of His church at any time. It means rather that, under the cunning attack of Satan, the church began to lose its grip on certain spiritual and theological realities.)

It has also been pointed out that the doctrines which were undermined and which were lost to the church for centuries have been restored historically by God in the reverse order from that in which they disappeared.

For example, the last truth for the early church to lose was the doctrine of justification by faith alone, and this revelation was one of the first that God restored after the dark ages.

A former Secretary of the W.E.C., Len Moules, outlined the great programme of God's 'Operation Recovery' through history. The following sums up his views:

In the fourteenth century, through Wycliffe, Hus and Savonarola, God restored to the church the vital truth of the inspiration and importance of the Word of God. By means of the Lollards in the fifteenth century, He taught successful soul-winning through personal witnessing. The great turning point of history came under Luther in the sixteenth century when the Reformation swept Europe, and God graciously restored to His church the meaning and truth of justification by faith alone. The impact of this doctrine can never be estimated, but it laid the foundation for all the restoration-work that was to follow in the teaching and theological experience of the church. God used the Puritans and Quakers of the seventeenth century to open the eyes of Christians to the truth of the priesthood of all believers; whilst in the eighteenth century Wesley and Whitefield proclaimed a full and free salvation with its fruits of sanctification and holiness. The great evangelical awakening followed in the nineteenth century with its social reforms, and the establishing of missionary societies and evangelical missions.

The twentieth century has seen the Welsh revival, and more recently, the Charismatic renewal movement, during which God has poured out His Holy Spirit on thousands of churches. There has followed a restoration of the fullness of a pentecostal experience with a fresh understanding of the importance of the gifts of the Spirit and revelation upon the ministry gifts of the ascended Lord. Apostles and prophets and the other ascension ministries are now widely recognised, and the importance of their function is taught world-wide.

It has been said that at this point in history many of the renewed churches are losing their impetus and are without direction or destiny. If this is true, then the cohesive factor which is missing must be the governmental reality of the Headship of Christ.

This truth, like so many of the other precious doctrines, has been pioneered in the twentieth century by the Apostolic Church, and a renewed emphasis upon the importance of Christ's Headship within the contemporary context must surely be a top priority-function for our movement today.

Headship was the first truth to be attacked and to disappear. As early as AD.64 the Apostle revealed this fact:

'. . . his unspiritual mind puffs him up with idle notions. He has lost connection with the Head . . .' (Col. 2:18-19).

That is the problem today. Groups of believers have lost connection with the Head. Individuals as well as churches are floundering in a situation where, as in the time of the Judges, 'every man does that which is right in his own eyes.'

But God is faithful to His restoration programme historically. If the truth of the Headship of Christ was the first to be lost, it will be, and is being, restored in all its fullness in these last days.

If, as a movement, we still have a part to play in God's work of restoration, then we must be careful not to lose our connection to the Head. Whilst recognising the inevitability of change and the need for progress, we must nevertheless tread cautiously upon the pathway of pragmatic arguments propounded by the devotees of devolution, lest ultimately we miss the dispensational purpose for which God brought us into being.

Don't lose connection with the Head!

22. CROWNED WITH GLORY AND HONOUR

The King of heaven has always been crowned with glory and honour. On the eve of His crucifixion, Jesus spoke about His glory with the Father, before the world began. The preincarnate Christ had ever worn the crown of essential deity, of eternal sovereignty, of creatorial energy, of co-equality with the Father.

The majesty of the eternal Christ was the central attraction in heaven. With adoring wonder the seraphim encircled His throne, their faces veiled from the dazzling splendour of His countenance, ceaselessly crying: 'Holy, holy, holy is the Lord Almighty!'

In the fullness of time He laid aside His crown, stepped down from that flashing sapphire throne and entered the stream of human experience via the womb of the virgin. The pre-incarnate Christ became the incarnate Christ Who died on the cross for the sins of mankind.

The Roman soldiers crowned Him with thorns before they dragged him to Golgotha and nailed Him to the cross.

No monarch in the history of the human race ever wore such a diadem! Nobody but Jesus of Nazareth, the King of the Jews!

This crown of thorns is highly significant. Thorns were not part of God's creation. No thorns grew in the Garden of Eden. Thorns are the result of the fall of man, the emblem of the curse. When Adam sinned, God said: 'Cursed is the ground because of you . . . It will produce thorns and thistles . . .'

Jesus the Lamb of God, shedding His blood on the cruel cross, was crowned with the symbol of the curse. What are thorns? Botanists believe that every thorn is an undeveloped bud. A thorn is the emblem of arrested potential.

If Adam and Eve had not disobeyed God, they could have produced a sinless race. The natural creation would never have known the intrusion of weeds, thorns or thistles. The unparalleled Edenic beauty would have been reproduced each year with increasing splendour and delight.

Satan, the malicious enemy, set out to spoil all that. The devil thought he had ruined God's purpose for mankind irrevocably. The sinning ones were driven from Eden, and the earth was cursed by God.

But before He made the universe, God had foreordained a Lamb, a

Kinsman-Redeemer, who would not fail, but would extricate the human race from its plight and elevate it to unimaginable heights of glory and grace!

And so He came to Calvary, bearing His cross and wearing a crown of thorns – the emblem of humanity's inhibited potential – the symbol of the curse. There on Golgotha's blood-stained altar He gave His blameless life as a sacrifice for our sins. He redeemed the race. He broke the curse. He rose from the grave and He lives to apply to each believing heart the benefits He has secured.

Isaac Watts wrote:

'Believing we rejoice to see the curse remove,
We bless the Lamb with cheerful voice and sing His bleeding love.'

All who receive Him as Saviour are introduced into a new redeemed humanity – the sons of God. In Christ they find their true identity, and can develop their full potential without any inhibition.

Isaac Watts reminds us:

'In Him the tribes of Adam boast
More blessings than their father lost.'

On His return to heaven, Jesus was crowned in His manhood with the glory which He had enjoyed in His God-hood before the world began.

The cycle of glory completes itself. The kingly brow of God's Son is eternally encircled with glory and honour. 'Upon His head are many crowns!'

PART II

FOR ALL SEASONS

NEW YEAR

23. JUST A MINUTE!

What does the number 36,816,480 mean to you?

You could guess that it represents the population of a nation, or you might think it signifies the distance travelled by the latest scientific instrument through outer space.

But you would be wrong on both counts. The truth is much nearer home. 36,816,480 is, in fact, the number of minutes in a life-time of 70 years, (including 24,480 extra minutes in 17 leap years).

If you are 35 or over, you have already used up at least 18,408,240 of those precious minutes – and nobody can tell you how many minutes you have left!

The new year stretches before you like a plateau of untrodden snow. But instead of unsullied snow flakes, the future offers you the enticing vista of 525,600 unused minutes!

How will you use them? What footprints will you leave on the territory of Time?

Will you walk with God through the year? Or will you go your own way, disregarding the Saviour's call to follow Him?

'Time is money' asserts the efficiency expert. But actually Time is far more precious. Money can be banked. Time cannot. If you don't use Time when it is available, then that opportunity is forever lost.

In the words of Thomas Edison: 'Time is not a commodity that can be stored for future use. It must be invested hour by hour, or else it is gone forever.'

Use your time to serve the Lord. Follow Him through the year and learn to walk with God. When you die, there will be no 'extra time' or second chance to retrieve all the wasted moments and lost opportunities. 'Lost time is never found.'

'We speak of spending time,' declares John Blanchard, 'the Bible speaks of buying it!' 'You cannot kill time without injuring eternity,' warns Henry D. Thoreau. A wise old proverb sums it up: 'Kill time and you murder opportunity!'

Time is precious. It is not given us to waste, or to kill, or to spend on selfish pursuits. Every moment should be used wisely, with the ultimate glory of God in view.

Much can happen in a moment. How long did it take for Adam to taste the forbidden fruit? Just one unguarded moment – and sin with all its hideous aftermath was introduced into the human race. Luke explains that the devil tempted Jesus by shewing Him 'all the kingdoms of the world *in a moment of time.*' (Luke 4 vs.5). But Jesus did not fail. His moments were regulated by His Father's will.

Moments are uniquely precious. They have a miraculous potential for determining eternal issues. So let the Lord control your moments, then your eternal destiny will be secure.

24. EVERYTHING NEW

Towards the end of the book of Revelation the Apostle John records his vision of the enthroned Lord who spoke to him saying: *'I am making everything new.'* That must have been encouraging for John. He had seen some very strange things in his vision. Some were of great beauty and grandeur. What a thrill it must have been to see the risen Lamb of God approach the dazzling splendour of the Eternal and receive from the hand of Deity the scroll sealed with seven seals! How John must have longed to be among the heavenly throng as the redeemed, the angels, and the whole creation thundered their exalted praises to the worthy Lamb!

But the seer must often have trembled for the future of the planet as he beheld the devastating destruction of judgment falling relentlessly upon the inhabitants of the earth as the Lamb opened the seals of the book. Earthquakes, fire, plague and pain were outpoured upon land and sea in an inflexible programme of wrath. John saw many familiar sights vanish in the smoking fury of divine displeasure. He saw the earth scorched, the oceans poisoned, mountains fall and islands disappear beneath tidal waves of heaven's anger. He saw strong men cringing in caves, crying for the rocks to fall upon them to hide them from the wrath of the Lamb. John saw and heard the unsettling reversal of man's primeval instinct of self-preservation. Men sought for death, and could not find it. For death fled from them.

It could not have been easy for the Apostle of love, who had rested his head on the tender heart of Jesus, to witness and faithfully record such visions.

What a comfort therefore to his sensitive nature as these glorious words of hope issue from the flashing fire of the sapphire throne: *'I am making everything new.'*

Death, desolation and destruction are not the ultimate future for Planet Earth. Centuries before John heard those words of golden promise, God had told the prophet Isaiah: *'See I am doing a new thing.'* He is the God of new things. He is the God of renewal.

God has planned new heavens and a new earth. But before He introduces a new universe, God is going to renew Planet Earth, and for ten centuries there will be peace and prosperity among the nations in the kingdom of

Jesus. Earth will be greener than the greenest political party could imagine. Its ecological balance will be restored and renewed, exceeding the wildest dreams of every conservationist. God will produce renewal. And newness will create happiness.

There is, of course, a crucial contrast between God's programme for renewal and that of the conservationist. The Green Party supporters emphasise the environment, that which is, by definition, external. But God's programme starts with the human heart – the internal sphere of attitudes and relationships.

Each time a soul is born again, God gives an object lesson to the devil of His ability to make everything new. Whenever the Holy Spirit regenerates a person, changing a sinner into a child of God, the miracle is a prophetic indication individually of what God will ultimately do universally, by producing the new heavens and the new earth.

'Therefore if anyone is in Christ he is a new creation. The old has gone; the new has come.' It is this new life that produces the joy and happiness of the Christian. Newness and happiness. They are inseparable qualities. Joy is the logical sequel to the new creation. Happiness bubbles spontaneously from the fountain of newness.

These concepts are linked together in the phrase: *'A happy New Year.'* There is something inherent, deep in the human heart, that hopes for happiness to accompany the newness of another year.

Will there be happiness in the new year? If it comes to that, will there be anything 'new' about it?

Go through the year with the God of renewal. He will lead you into happiness, and every day can be a new adventure with Jesus.

25. NEW LIFE

This is the season when folk are making their New Year's resolutions – promising themselves to catch up and carry out all the things they had resolved to do the previous year.

How many have said to themselves: 'I'm going to turn over a new leaf'?

But the new leaf turns out to be very much the same as the old leaf. (Personally I don't see much difference between December 31st and January 1st. In most cases the only new thing is the calendar.) Am I being cynical? Perhaps I am, a little – but that's because turning over a new leaf (whatever that may mean) is not the answer. What people really need is not a new leaf but a new life! And that possibility seems so remote from reality in this materialistic world that folk rarely give it serious consideration.

But the Bible teaches not only the possibility, but the necessity of obtaining new life. If the words of Jesus: *'You must be born again'* have any meaning at all, they must offer a realistic alternative to the frustrating routine of 'turning over a new leaf', and that alternative is the receiving of a new life.

This new life is not something that you achieve. Rather it is something you receive. It's a free offer, open to all who have faith to accept it. *'If only one could have two lives,'* wrote D.H. Lawrence with a touch of wistful longing – *'The first in which to make one's mistakes . . . and the second in which to profit by them.'*

But those are not God's arrangements for living. Nobody gets two lives. As Dr Stephen Olford reminds us:

> *'Only one life, 'twill soon be past,*
> *Only what's done for Christ will last.'*

God has a better plan than giving us two natural lives. When we believe in Christ as Saviour and Lord, He implants within us by His Spirit a new kind of life altogether. This new life produces changes in the characteristics of the recipient. The metamorphosis is as dramatic as that which takes place when a caterpillar becomes a butterfly. The insect does not have two lives. Yet it becomes a new creature.

Jesus was always producing that type of startling transformation in people who expressed faith in Him. He gave them new life – and with that life came new hope, new prospects and new power to live victoriously. He changed the Samaritan woman from a social outcast into a successful soul-winner and evangelist. To the bed-fast paralytic He gave forgiveness of sins and the ability to walk again. To the blind He gave sight; to the deaf and dumb He gave the faculties of hearing and of speech; to the leper He gave cleansing; to the demon-possessed Mary Magdalene He brought deliverance, transforming her into His most ardent follower; and to Lazarus rotting in the grave, He communicated new life and perfect health.

To the tight-fisted tax-collector Zacchaeus, Jesus brought a spirit of generosity which so possessed the former skinflint that he amazed every Jew for miles around by restoring four times as much as he had stolen!

In each case Jesus gave a new life-power and a different life-principle from that which had been in control.

This new life is capable of ongoing and continuous change. The Bible teaches that Christians are to be constantly changed from glory to glory by the work of the Holy Spirit in their lives. A dead church with dry services conducted by formal and lifeless people is quite out of keeping with God's programme of new-life Christianity.

David Watson used to speak about a somewhat quaint announcement which appeared on a church noticeboard: *'Only the dead living in this parish may be buried in this churchyard.'* (At least it presupposes that people in that condition ought to be buried!)

How many 'dead' are living in your church? There's good news for you all: New life, eternal life, resurrection life is available in Jesus by the power of His Spirit. No assembly need remain dead with the threat of burial and extinction overshadowing it.

Jesus has come that you might have life, and have it more abundantly! David Watson must have been an astute observer of church notices. Here is another example of his: *'As churchyard maintenance costs are high, will parishioners please cut the grass around their own graves?'* (No doubt there would be a skeleton staff for that unusual work!)

New life will take you, like Lazarus, out of the grave. It will bring you into a fresh fellowship with Jesus.

New Life! It's free – get it today!

EASTER

26. THE PARADOX OF THE CROSS

'. . . they crucified Him . . .'   (John 19:14-18)

The Cross is a series of sublime mysteries and profound paradoxes. Collins' *New English Dictionary* describes a paradox as 'a statement seemingly absurd or self-contradictory, but really founded on truth; a statement contrary to popular opinion.' The cross was all of these things. The message of 'Christ crucified' was indeed a stumbling block to religious Jews and foolishness to the cultured Greeks.

But at Calvary God made His historic paradoxical statement to all realms of creation – and that statement, though misunderstood by mankind and misrepresented by Satan, was nevertheless founded on eternal truth, and it revealed divine wisdom, love and power.

Let us think about four of these mysterious paradoxes which God resolved at Calvary.

1. First, **the paradox of mystery and clarity.**

The cross is the greatest mystery in the Universe. Jesus uttered seven cries while nailed to the cross. The fourth, or **central** cry, was the cry of **mystery**. 'My God . . . **Why?**' There was no reply. Mystery is at the very heart of the cross.

There is the mystery of the Sinless One being **made** sin; the mystery of the Immortal tasting death; the mystery of a holy God suffering torture on a cross for sinful, rebellious man. These are sublime mysteries which all eternity will never fully explore.

Paradoxically, although Calvary is shrouded in mystery, yet it is, at the same time, a revelation of **clarity**.

The cross gives a clear revelation of the true nature of sin; of the character of fallen man; of the malice of Satan; and of the perfect love of God. Mystery and clarity meet at Calvary.

2. Next, consider **the paradox of simplicity and complexity.**

Golgotha – the place of a skull – speaks of a stripping away of all that is external and superficial – a complete removal of all sophistication.

Think of the simplicity of the materials used for crucifixion – two pieces of wood and three nails! With these primitive materials sinful men compassed the death of God's son.

Men have perfected ingenious and complicated methods of execution. Devastation and death can now be wrought on a colossal scale by means of laser beam death rays, biological warfare and nuclear power. Nation competes with nation in the mad race to accumulate vast stockpiles of incredible weapons for the destruction of mankind. It is the bitter fruit of dedicated years of scientific research!

Some years ago a Bulgarian dissident was murdered by an assassin who stabbed him in the leg with an umbrella, thus releasing into his bloodstream a metal microsphere containing a deadly poison beneath a film of wax. In time, the heat of the blood melted the wax, the poison entered the bloodstream, and the Bulgarian died. To what great lengths fallen men will go in order to accomplish their diabolical schemes!

But there was nothing scientific about Golgotha's cross! It was simple, stark, primitive, barbaric. Contemplate the simple cruelty of the method of death: Nailed to the wood, raised aloft, and left to die! What economy of ideas! The poet Gerhardt has captured the scene in verse:

> 'Extended on a cursed tree,
> Besmeared with dust, and sweat, and blood,
> See there, the King of Glory see!
> Sinks and expires the Son of God.'

Think now of the **complexity** of the cross. Despite the awful simplicity and cruelty of the cross, what God achieved at Calvary was nevertheless the fulfilment of a complex masterpiece of divine planning! The cross was, and still is, the power and the **wisdom** of God (I Cor. 1:23-24).

(a) It was the **demonstration** of prophecies fulfilled (I Cor. 15:3).

> 'The types and figures are **fulfilled**,
> Exacted is the legal pain,
> The precious promises are sealed;
> The spotless Lamb of God is slain.'

(b) It provided **redemption** and **salvation** for fallen humanity (Eph. 1:7).

(c) It wrought the **destruction** of Satan's power (Heb. 2:14-15).

(d) It laid the **foundation** for a new order of redeemed humanity (Rev. 5:9-10).

(e) It envisaged the **sanctification** and ultimate **presentation** to Himself of a glorious church (Eph. 5:25-27).

(f) It involved the **elevation** of the sons of God (Rev. 3:21).

What a complex and colourful tapestry God has woven from the simple threads of the cross!

3. Furthermore, there is **the paradox of ignominy and glory.**

At the time in history when Jesus suffered death by crucifixion there was nothing more full of **ignominy** than the cross!

Crucifixion was a shameful death – a public execution reserved for the lowest criminals. It was a terrible and ignominious way to expire – naked, helpless to brush away even the smallest insects that clustered tormentingly around the bleeding wounds, unable to shade from the fierce heat of the sun, or to hide from the cruel mockery of sinful, uncomprehending men! 'He humbled Himself,' declared Paul in amazement '. . . and became obedient unto death, even the death of the cross!' (Phil. 2:8).

The Jews falsely accused Him; Pilate unjustly condemned Him; demons tormented Him; His disciples forsook Him; cruel men crucified Him; religious men vied with ungodly criminals in their slander of Him; nobody understood Him. Even God the Father turned away from Him in His deepest need at the hour of darkness!

'Yea once Emmanuel's orphaned cry His universe hath shaken,
It went up single, echoless –
'My God, I am forsaken,'
It went up from the Saviour's lips amid His lost creation,
That of the lost, no son should use those words of desolation.'

In that dread hour 'the Lord laid on Him the iniquity of us all' (Is. 53:6). 'He was wounded for **our** transgressions, He was bruised for **our** iniquities' (Is. 53:5). It was our sin He bore. He was forsaken because of our shame. The ignominy of Calvary was **ours** – not His.

Now consider the **glory** of the cross. That the cross, appalling instrument of torture, shame and death, should have become the symbol adorning every church, is an eloquent tribute to the glory of the Christ

Who died at Calvary!

The cross was the unique glory of the Apostle Paul. 'God forbid that I should glory save in the cross of our Lord Jesus Christ' (Gal. 6:14).

Jesus **transformed** the shame of the cross by the glory of His own moral perfections.

Firstly, by the glory of His forgiving love. 'Father forgive them' (Luke 23:34). Secondly, by the glory of His transforming grace: 'Lord remember me' . . . 'Today shalt thou be with me in paradise' (Luke 23:42-43). And thirdly, by the glory of His patient suffering and endurance. Jesus endured to the full all that His Father required of Him. Then He gave up His spirit to God. 'When the centurion saw what was done, he **glorified God**' (Luke 23:47).

Thus, from the depths of **ignominy**, Jesus produced **glory** to God!

> 'Upon that cross of Jesus,
>   Mine eyes at times can see
> The very dying form of One,
>   Who suffered there for me;
> And from my smitten heart
>   with tears, Two wonders I
>   confess –
> The wonders of His glorious
>   love, and my own worthlessness.
>
> I take, O cross, thy shadow,
>   For my abiding place;
> I ask no other sunshine than
>   the sunshine of His face:
> Content to let the world go by,
>   to know no gain nor loss –
> My sinful self my only shame,
>   My glory – all the Cross!'

4. Finally, consider **the paradox of tragedy and victory.**

To the onlooker, Calvary was a colossal tragedy.

There was the tragedy of a young life ending on a cross. Jesus was just 33, in the prime of His perfect manhood, full of the joy of a sinless life lived in unbroken fellowship with God His Father. Nobody had more right to live than Jesus. Yet, 'He was cut off out of the land of the living' (Is. 53:8).

There was, also, the tragedy of a lost cause. The Leader on the cross, and the band of frightened disciples scattered and demoralised – what hope could there be now of His promises coming true?

Furthermore, there was the tragedy of the innocent good, being oppressed by the guilty and the evil. This tragedy has been re-enacted a thousand times through history. But Jesus was not overcome by evil. He overcame evil with good!

Calvary, to the unperceptive, seemed **an apparent tragedy**. But in reality it was, and is, an **accomplished victory**: 'It is finished' (John 19:30). This phrase is one word in Greek: 'tetelestai' – which means 'paid in full'. What a victory!

Taunted to abandon His Father's will, Jesus chose to remain in the centre of God's will even though it meant the **cross**. He evidently believed that it was better to come up from the grave than down from the cross. His was the victory of a **finished work**. Jesus completed the task allocated by the Father. He was victorious. Divine justice was satisfied. Holiness remained intact. Yet love could now reach out to believing sinners and justify them by the blood of Jesus.

The cross enabled God to remain just and at the same time to become the 'Justifier of him which believes in Jesus' (Rom. 3:26).

The **victory** of Calvary was a redemptive victory. 'He made **peace** through the blood of His cross' (Col. 1:20). In some ways, this could be regarded as the greatest paradox of all. That the **violent** shedding of His precious blood on the cross should have made **peace** and wrought **reconciliation** for all mankind, is indeed the wonder of Calvary!

God has made His historic and dynamic statement in the Christ of the cross. 'God has **spoken** unto us by His Son' (Heb. 1:12). To the unbelieving, Calvary remains an enigma, a paradoxical puzzle that history has never solved.

But to the believer, even though he might not fully understand the depths of mystery surrounding Calvary, the cross reasserts the values of eternal truth upon which all God's statements to mankind are founded.

At Easter-tide let every loving heart draw near again to the cross, and catch afresh the whisper of Calvary: 'Father **forgive** them.'

27. THE COSMIC LORDSHIP OF CHRIST

The Lamb of Calvary is the Lord of Glory. The Man Who died on the cross is the Monarch of the Cosmos. This is the true wonder of Easter: 'The Crucified is glorified, exalted at His Father's side, in Him I hide, I'm satisfied. The Crucified with power is glorified.'

'He is able even to SUBDUE all things unto himself' (Phil. 3:21).

Subdue is Hupotasso in Greek, meaning 'to set in array under'. It is a military term from **HUPO** – under, and **TASSO** – to set, arrange, ordain.

This word is used only twice in the New Testament. In this text, Phil. 3:21, and in I Cor. 15:28 '. . . all things shall be subdued unto him.'

In each case the word **SUBDUE** is linked to the phrases **'ALL THINGS'** and **'UNTO HIMSELF'**.

All things will be subdued by Him, for Him, and unto Him. He is able to set ALL THINGS in array under His own headship. This is an operation of sovereign government.

In His dealings with mankind we can trace the historical unfolding of His will. All things are moving inexorably toward their inevitable climax in God. He **creates, controls** and **consummates** all things in accordance with His own personal purpose.

Communist Russia 'subdued' her satellites and often devastated their lands with terror in the process. But God subdues His enemies by His inscrutable wisdom, fitting their very wickedness and hostility into the overall mosaic of His eternal plan. **The CROSS is the greatest example of this**. 'Him being delivered by the determinate counsel and foreknowledge of God, **YE** HAVE TAKEN, and by wicked hands have crucified and slain' (Acts 2:23).

The Psalmist said: '**Thou makest** even the wrath of man to praise Thee . . .'

God's matchless, irresistible, sovereign, omnipotent wisdom rules and over-rules *all things* in every realm, to *SET THEM IN ARRAY* under His *Lordship* in perfect harmony with that which He has ordained from the beginning.

Despite all the resistance of Satan and the forces of darkness, God's Kingdom shall come, and His will be done on EARTH, as it is in Heaven!

Some years ago the Lord spoke prophetically through Pastor

E.D. Hammond: 'He came to the sphere and realm of time; the COSMIC CHRIST, to redeem a lost humanity back unto the Father; to minister life, and by the application and flowing of the precious blood, to ultimately cause every realm and sphere that hath rebelled to be brought on the day of divine appointment, the day of restitution of all things, back unto the Father, presenting all the Kingdom, because of the mighty power unleashed at the place called CALVARY.'

The CRUCIFIED CHRIST IS THE COSMIC CHRIST!

Let us consider His cosmic lordship (Col. 1 vs. 16-17).

These verses reveal the work of the Cosmic Christ in creating and sustaining the universe. Because Christ is the Originator and Creator of the cosmos, everything He is in Himself is of **cosmic importance**. Because the universe **is still being sustained** and upheld by the word of His power, finding its cohesion in CHRIST, then everything He says and does is of **cosmic significance**.

His cosmic Lordship was challenged and attacked by Satan. The devil introduced the disorderly power and evil principle of **sin** into the universe, thus defying the CHRISTOS, and threatening the COSMOS with CHAOS. God's answer was the CROSS!

Calvary was not a local incident. It was an event of universal and cosmic significance.

Satan and sin set in **disarray** the realms created by CHRIST. God's work in CHRIST through the dispensations is to '**SUBDUE**'. i.e. '**to set in array under His Lordship**' all these disrupted realms. **THE CROSS IS THE LEGAL FORCE and the SPIRITUAL DYNAMIC WHICH ENABLES HIM TO DO SO** . . . 'Because of **the mighty power** unleashed at the place called Calvary,' all realms are being brought into subjection unto Himself. **ALL Realms**: eternal and temporal; spiritual and natural; visible and invisible; regal and legal; mystical and practical; social and moral; doctrinal and governmental; ecclesiastical and national.

Despite his defeat at Calvary, Satan still seeks to oppose the **Cosmic Christ** by belittling His person, and denying the Word of God. But Scripture underlines and emphasises the **COSMIC GLORY of CHRIST.**

The Cosmic Christ is the Creator, Controller, Redeemer, Sustainer and Governor of the Universe (John 1 vs. 1-3; Rev. 4 vs. 11; Rom. 8:22; Heb. 1:3; Phil. 3:21; John 5:22; Acts 17:31).

In exalting the Cosmic Christ, we do not seek to detract from the glory of the TRIUNE GOD. '... every tongue should confess that Jesus CHRIST is LORD, to the glory of **GOD the FATHER!**' (Phil. 2:11).

'**It pleased THE FATHER** that in **HIM** [Christ] should **all** fullness dwell' (Col. 1:19).

As **CREATOR** He reveals **the Majesty** of **His power** in **the Macrocosm** (i.e. The Universe of Outer Space). The sun is 93 million miles from the earth. It is a star, one of a galaxy in thousands of millions of stars scattered over an area of space some 100,000 light years across. Dr Filby writes:

'This galaxy is but one of **millions of such galaxies** scattered at distances of a million light years apart into the remotest depths of space!

'All is swift movement; the giant spheres travelling and whirling through space at incredible speeds. Light travels at 186,000 miles per second. Because of the distance of the sun from the earth, its light reaches us in about eight minutes. But the Dog Star Sirius is much further away, so its light reaches us in 8.5 years (so when we see the sun, we see it as it was eight minutes ago, and Sirius as it was 8.5 years ago).' These two stars are relatively near to Earth, in the context of the great universe. 'The Heavens declare the glory of God . . .' '**Great** is the Lord . . .'

Planet Earth is moving swiftly through space at this very moment! Dr D.W. Patten explains the Earth's four types of motion: (1) **Centrifugal** – Earth's rotation round its axis. It spins at 0.29 miles per second! (2) **Revolving Motion.** Earth orbits the sun at 18.5 to 25 miles per second. (It travels over 600 million miles per year during one revolution round the sun!) (3) **Galactic Motion.** Our Solar System is revolving round our galaxy (the Milky Way) at 12 miles per second. (4) **The galaxy itself revolves through the universe at 170 miles per second.**

Isaiah said: 'Behold the nations are as a drop of a bucket, and are counted as the small dust of the balance . . .' (Is. 40:15).

As Redeemer, the Cosmic Christ reveals the Mercy of His redemptive plan for Mankind. Redemption is more closely linked to Creation than most people realise. 'Through faith we understand that **the worlds** were framed by the **word of God**, so that things which are seen were not made of things which do appear.' (Hebrews 11 verse 3). **Note three special words:** (i) '**the Worlds**', in Greek **AIONS**, the 'Time-Worlds'. The word aion refers to a specific period, either future or past. The word suggests AGES, or the DISPENSATIONS of God.

(ii) 'Framed': in Greek **KATARTIZO**. 'To complete thoroughly. To fit together perfectly.' The time-worlds, the AGES, were **fitted** into God's predestined plan.

In the last phrase there is a reference to the VISIBLE UNIVERSE: 'things which are seen'. So in this text the **invisible** is linked with the **visible**; the **intangible** with the **tangible**; and the **non-material** with the **material**.

This shews that God had a **purpose** in view in creating the Universe and that this purpose is linked to His **dispensational** programme. So God made the COSMOS, and chose planet earth, in order to **develop** His mighty and merciful eternal **redemptive** programme for the destiny of Mankind. This concept is supported by Ephes. 3 vs. 8-11, where the Apostle introduces the **creative** work of Christ into an explanation of the **redemptive** eternal purpose of God for the church.

Scientists are puzzled by the question, '**HOW** was the Universe created?' God's word tells us something better. It tells us '**WHY**'! It was created as a **visible** platform on which the Lord could outwork historically amongst Mankind His eternal redemptive purpose, thus fulfilling the vision of God – the securing of a BRIDE (the CHURCH) for His SON and HEIR – JESUS!

(iii) **The Word**. But Faith understands **HOW**, as well as WHY '. . . by the **Word of God**.' (a) This Word is a **CREATIVE WORD**. It produced the Visible Creation: 'ex nihilo'. It implies that the TIME-WORLDS were fitted into a visible pattern with **MAN'S home – Earth – and Man's HISTORY – the development of God's purpose for Man. (b) It is also a Governing Word.** It produced the AIONS (time-worlds). God is the Architect of the Ages, the Great Designer and Developer of the Dispensations. Since TIME has no validity unless it is related to the progress or unfolding of a purpose, it is evidently implied that the WORD which '**framed**' ('fitted') the time-worlds is a **governing** word. (c) And since we know from other scriptures that God's purpose included Man, and that it made provision for his salvation, and that God involved Himself with a CROSS, then God's Word which framed the AIONS must be a REDEMPTIVE WORD. Therefore REDEMPTION is linked to CREATION.

In fact, **Redemption** was the prior thought: the LAMB 'was **foreordained before the foundation of the world**' (I Peter 2 vs.19).

73

As **Sustainer** and Controller He reveals the Mystery of His **wisdom** in **the Microcosm**: the tiny world of the atom. '**Upholding** all things by **the word of His power**' (Heb. 1:3).

In the same prophecy from which I quoted earlier, the Lord directed us to '**relate the vision Glorious to the space-age**'.

Scientists remind us that in this vast universe with its millions of galaxies, constructed by the Lord, He has used **only two basic kinds of building material: ELECTRONS** and the atomic **nuclei (protons and neutrons).** It is believed that the electrons revolve round their nuclei.

The atomic nuclei are positively charged, and the orbiting electrons are negatively charged. The electron of the hydrogen atom rotates 1,000 million million times around its nuclei in one second! Think of the power, the concentration, and the precision required to achieve that. **Christ upholds it by the word of His power!**

There are two fascinating factors about the atom, viz: **Tininess** and **Emptiness**. Erich Sauer has revealed some startling statistics about these factors.

'There are many billions of atoms in the tip of your finger.

One teaspoonful of water contains one million, billion, trillion atoms.

Your body contains 1,000 quadrillion atoms (i.e. 1 plus 27 noughts!)

On the head of a drawing pin there is room for so many atoms that if they were carried by an army, an atom to a man, marching four abreast, the march-past would take over 20,000 years!

The diameter of a hydrogen atom measures only one hundred millionth part of a millimetre.

Five million iron atoms placed side by side would cover less than 1/25th of an inch.' The atom is TINY!

But it is also almost EMPTY! Matter that appears so solid consists almost entirely of empty space. 'If the constituents of the atoms in 30 cubic feet of lead were packed together with no space between, they would take up less room than a pin-head! The atoms in the whole earth if treated in this way would compress to go into a fairly large building. The 1,000 quadrillion atoms of your body could be compressed into one single microscopic speck of dust!' (So the first lecture in Atomic Physics was given by God to Adam: '**Dust** thou art, and unto **dust** shalt thou return').

'If one whole atom had the same volume as St Paul's Cathedral, then its nucleus would be a tiny ball 1/5th of an inch in diameter. The rest would be empty space.'

Professor A. Titius described the atom as '**a system of connected events.**' This is a very enlightening description, for we seem to be face to face with the TIME-FACTOR again. For if the 'timing' of these 'events' were not perfect, the universe would disintegrate.

The reason it doesn't is because it is **upheld** by the Word of His Power. That same word framed the TIME-WORLDS. Can we extend the concept of the time-worlds into the heart of the atom? Each atom is a little 'time-world' in itself. Each is framed and fitted and upheld by the Word of His power.

The Universe is made of ATOMS. Atoms are mostly empty space. Therefore it is TIME and swift MOVEMENT which lend structure to the Universe. One scientist has suggested that this concept can be illustrated by thinking of a cycle-wheel. When it is still, there is space between the spokes, but it is **solid** when spinning.

So in the mighty stellar vastness of outer space, and in the incredibly minute universe of the atom, there is a symphony of majesty and wisdom. 'All things were **made** by Him' – the COSMIC CHRIST, and **sustained** by His Word.

Could this pattern of whirling galaxies in space and of spinning, orbiting electrons round atomic nuclei be based on the great prophetic prototype of the Glorious Throne of God as seen in VISION by EZEKIEL? (Ezek. 1).

The prophet saw those great gyroscopic whirling wheels, full of eyes, full of life, viewing and controlling the whole universe. They represent the glorious universal dominion of God's Throne.

This essential regal glory, this power of the Throne, is exercised governmentally over the spiralling galactic empires of outer space. Their own structure and movements reflect the pattern seen by Ezekiel in his vision. The same vital pattern is reproduced countless myriads of times in every tiny atom of Creation.

So God speaks out of the mystic majesty of His Throne, and we bow our heads and worship. Spiritual mysteries have become the governmental realities of the macrocosm, and the mathematical discoveries of the microcosm.

This is our Father's World! His Son, the Cosmic Christ, is the

EMPEROR and **Governor** of **the Universe**. He is LORD of all. And His LORDSHIP is a cosmic Lordship. We are heirs of God, and **joint-heirs** with our COSMIC CHRIST!

This is the glory of Easter! Jesus of Nazareth – Golgotha's provincial victim – **redeemed** mankind at the cross; **rose** from the grave; and now **rules** the whole cosmos from the Throne of God!

28. THE MAGNETIC POWER OF CALVARY

There is a mystic magnetism about Calvary, compelling us to draw near.

Jesus was crucified between two criminals. He was numbered with the transgressors. But the gaze of the crowd at Calvary on that first Good Friday focused upon the central cross.

Matthew wrote of the soldiers: 'And they crucified Him . . . and sitting down **they watched Him there**.' (Matt. 27 vs. 35-36).

Luke, describing the reactions of the crowd to the crucifixion, wrote: 'And the people stood **beholding**' (Luke 23 vs. 35).

Sitting or standing, soldiers or citizens – their eyes were toward the cross of Christ. And that is precisely what He had predicted: 'And I, if I be lifted up from the earth, **will draw all men** unto me' (John 12 vs. 32).

Almost two thousand years have gone since they nailed the Son of God to the cross. Yet today Calvary still exerts its magnetic influence over mankind. That mystic force, drawing us to His cross, is undiminished.

Calvary was the place of conflicting emotions and powers. On that historic day when Christ died for our sins, the powers of hell were outmatched by the wisdom of God. The cross brought into sharp focus the cosmic conflict between good and evil. The Lord Jesus Christ finally emerged in resurrection power as the undisputed Victor!

Let us consider some of the forces in the field of conflict at Calvary.

Think first, of the **Tyrannical Power of Sin.**

Sin had found its expression in the lives of the other two crucified victims. Both had been thieves. Both were now convicted criminals – justly condemned – and paying the full penalty for their crimes. **Death** by slow torture!

Strangely enough, they both had a hatred for the Lord Jesus. Mark recorded: 'And **they** that were crucified with Him reviled Him' (Mark 15 vs. 32). The true nature and power of the tyrant sin is here unmasked. 'They hated me without a cause.'

Sin had driven them to deeds of crime and shame. As they hung now upon their crosses, in their sins, that tyrannical power filled them with an unreasonable hatred for the very One Who loved them and agonized upon His own cross at their side. Sin blinded them to their own guilty condition, and they focused their venomous spite on the innocent Lamb of God.

Sin still does that today. Men are deceived by sin, degraded by sin, and eventually destroyed by sin.

The tyrannical power of sin drove those thieves to a cruel death. God's word is inflexibly true: 'The wages of sin is death' (Rom. 6 vs. 23). This principle is true in the spiritual sense – eternal death being ultimate separation from God.

The power of sin energised civic rulers and religious priests to mock Jesus in His awful death agony. Never forget that it was **religious** men who compassed the crucifixion of Christ. Any religion that deposes Christ from His rightful place becomes a vehicle of Satanic self-expression.

The power of sin caused the soldiers to torture and torment the Saviour. Sin deceived the people into rejecting the Messiah: 'Away with Him, Crucify Him.'

It was the tyrannical power of sin that had gripped the heart of the Governor, Pontius Pilate, and had driven him to the greatest act of public injustice in the history of the human race: to **scourge** and to condemn to death by crucifixion a Man Whom he knew to be absolutely innocent!

The power of sin still causes men to reject Christ, to refuse His rule, and to crucify Him afresh with their sinful ways.

Consider next, the **Triumphant Power of Love.**

Sin was the unchallenged Tyrant-King. But at Calvary, sin met the Master of every situation. 'Christ **died** for our **sins.**' He paid the penalty – death. Now all those who accept Christ as Lord and Saviour can be set free from the tyranny of sin. Sin was dethroned at Calvary. The deposed tyrant need lord it no longer over your life. 'Sin shall not have dominion over you.' For there is a power greater than sin. It is the love of God in Christ.

To appreciate more fully the tremendous power of love at Calvary, it is necessary to understand the cruelty of the cross.

Crucifixion was so degrading a death that it was reserved only for the worst criminals, guilty of the blackest crimes. No Roman citizen could be crucified – unless a soldier found guilty of desertion.

Death by crucifixion was not a Jewish method of execution. The Psalmist's prophetic description of death on a cross is, therefore, a striking proof of divine inspiration (Psalm 22).

The Romans probably learned the cruelty of the cross from the pagan Phoenicians or from heathen Carthage. Crucifixion was a method of execution so inhuman as to lead us to assume that it was demonically inspired.

Added to the physical pain, which was intense, there was the psychological suffering – the public shame of naked execution. 'I may tell all my bones: they look and stare upon me.' (Psalm 22 vs. 17).

Following sentence, the victim, having been fearfully scourged, was roped up and dragged like an animal to the slaughter. He was forced to carry his own heavy cross, the dreadful instrument of torture and death, to the execution site.

As the bleeding sufferer was pulled through the crowded streets, he would become the target of every malicious curse of a fickle population. Each victim ran the gauntlet of spite, becoming the immediate scape-goat for a hate-filled people's own self-loathing.

At the place of death the victim was sometimes offered a drugged mixture, to dull his senses to the shattering climax of an agony yet to come. (You will recall that the Saviour refused to drink this sedative. He chose to suffer every moment of pain clearly and consciously – Matt. 27 vs. 34).

The victim was then thrown to the ground, brutal soldiers hurling themselves upon him – and he was nailed, a helpless wretch, to his cross.

The nails were six-inch iron spikes, one driven through each hand, either in the nerve-centre of the palm, or through the tendons of the wrist – and one spike through both feet. As this violent and excruciatingly painful torture was being inflicted upon Him, the selfless love of Jesus was reaching out to His tormentors. The sublimest words ever to be heard on earth were uttered at the moment of greatest agony: 'Father **forgive** them; for they know not what they do' (Luke 23 vs. 34).

Raised aloft and dropped with a nerve-shattering thud into the hole, each writhing crucified victim became the spectacle of derision, scorn, or pity.

Death was agonizingly slow. Men have been known to linger, half alive, for three days on the cross – and their screams heard one and a half miles away.

Loss of blood, fever, thirst, blood-poisoning and exhaustion all took their toll. But crucifixion was death by eventual suffocation. On his cross, the victim's diaphragm was distended in such a way that in order to breathe he was required to force the weight of his whole body up on his pierced feet, and then to lower it again after each labouring breath, thus jolting his nailed hands.

That is why, when the Jews wanted all the bodies to be removed from the crosses before the Sabbath day, they asked Pilate to order that the victims' legs be broken. Once his legs were broken, a crucified man could no longer raise his body to draw breath, and he would, therefore, soon die from suffocation.

The soldiers smashed the leg bones of the two thieves – thus putting them out of their misery. But Jesus had already dismissed His spirit, and when they saw that He was dead already, one of the soldiers pierced the side of the Saviour with a spear (John 19 vs. 31-37).

Such, then, was the cruelty of the cross; and such was the incomparable power of God's Calvary-love.

Finally, contemplate the **Transforming Power of Grace.**

Before the Roman soldiers broke his legs and sent him into eternity, something had happened to one of the thieves. Looking at Jesus enduring such suffering in love and patience had wrought a change in the criminal's ebbing life. The penitent thief has been described as the model-convert. Certainly he illustrates the helplessness of a sinner, unable to lift a finger to change his ways or to save himself. But transforming grace wrought the miracle of change in this criminal in the closing hours of his life.

It has been said of the two thieves crucified with Jesus on that first Good Friday, that one was saved that none need despair, but one was lost that none might presume. It is a sobering thought.

The change in the penitent thief was dramatic. As the power of transforming grace worked in his sinful heart, he responded in remarkable ways.

He rebuked his companion in crime and dissociated himself from the former mockery and cursing of Christ. He recognised and confessed his own sin. He acknowledged Jesus as Lord. He sought mercy: 'Lord, remember me.' He expressed faith in a life to come, and in the ultimate authority and kingship of the Man who was nailed to the adjacent blood-stained cross: 'When **thou comest** into **thy kingdom.**' This convert could see more than all the scribes and Pharisees and religious rulers. He knew that the cross would not be the end of Jesus. One day this King would come into His Kingdom.

Jesus was not slow to respond to the faith which transforming grace had granted: '**Today** shalt thou be with me in paradise,' thus bestowing that 'blessed assurance' – the priceless possession of all true believers.

Man's sin, Christ's love, God's grace – these powers constitute the mystic magnetism of Calvary. drawing us ever nearer to our crucified Lord, to confess with Isaac Watts:

> 'When I survey the wondrous cross,
> On which the Prince of glory died,
> My richest gain I count but loss,
> And pour contempt on all my pride.
> Were the whole realm of nature mine,
> That were an offering far too small;
> Love so amazing, so divine,
> Demands my soul, my life, my all.'

29. FOUR DAYS IN ETERNITY

'He has been dead four days.' (John 11 v. 39).

Lazarus was the ultimate challenge to the claim of Jesus to be the Resurrection and the Life.

Death and decay had wrought havoc upon the body of Lazarus. It had lain in the tomb for four days before Jesus arrived on the scene.

With matchless confidence Jesus called him from his grave: **'Lazarus come forth!'** And he arose from that tomb.

John reveals an interesting insight into the cruelty and unbelief of the chief priests: 'But the chief priests consulted that they may put Lazarus also to death; because that by reason of him many of the Jews went away, and believed on Jesus.' (John 12 vs. 10-11). Satan wants to destroy men who cause others to believe on Jesus!

Lazarus had spent four days in Eternity. It is clear that he emerged from that experience with a unique capacity to cause **many** to believe on Jesus.

Oh to be like Lazarus – a man called back from Eternity – compelling others to acknowledge Jesus!

This quality resulted from what Jesus had done for Lazarus, rather than from what Lazarus could do for Jesus. It was a gift of His grace.

Just by **being** the new Lazarus, this man drew the crowds and caused them to believe on Jesus. He just had to **be himself** – the new man. What had happened to him?

1. **He experienced new life.** 'He that was dead came forth.' (John 11, 44). He had passed from corruption to resurrection. No transformation could have been more complete. Decaying for four days – yet raised in the fullness of a perfect, dynamic **life!** Changed instantaneously by the word of Jesus!

Jesus can still do that miracle. In situations of dearth, death and decay, He can bring **new life.** He can produce **new** men and **new** women.

2. **Lazarus found new liberty. 'Loose him and let him go.' (vs. 44).**
Lazarus emerged from the grave, but he was still bound hand and foot

82

with grave clothes, and his face was covered with a napkin.

Jesus directed his disciples to set the prisoner free! The **hands** of Lazarus were liberated, thus enabling him to embark upon new **service** for the Master in perfect freedom. His **feet** were set free, and he could walk freely in the Master's footsteps.

The cloth which bound his **eyes** was untied, bringing him fresh **vision**. His ears were uncovered and so he could **hear** the Master's voice and follow His commands. The bandage about his **mouth** was removed – and he could freely enter into praise, worship and witness.

The case of Lazarus thus illustrates a life that has discovered renewed **liberty**.

3. **He also received new love**. 'They made Jesus a supper and Lazarus sat at the table with Him.' (John 12 vs. 2).

From the isolation of the cold tomb to **fellowship** with Jesus at the supper table! What a contrast!

Many lonely souls spend their lives in cold sepulchres of silence and isolation. Jesus invites them to His table for fellowship and food. 'Come and dine!' Discover new love in the precious friendship of Jesus.

Lazarus came out of four days in Eternity to new life, new liberty, and new love. Whatever your experience, it cannot be stranger or more desperate than the case of Lazarus. What happened to him can happen to you – if you will respond to the voice of Jesus.

ASCENSION DAY

30. THE ASCENDED KING

Ascension Day is the least celebrated of all the Christian festivals and special events. Yet it is of supreme significance. Why has it been allowed to diminish in importance? I hunted through several diaries and calendars, but Ascension Day did not appear in any of them. Festivals, Bank Holidays, Mother's Day and Father's Day were all there. But there was no mention of a day to commemorate the bodily ascension of our Lord Jesus into heaven. Eventually, by calculating ten days back from Whit Sunday, I deduced the date of Ascension Day.

A reduction in the chronological importance of Ascension Day points to a devaluation of its spiritual and theological significance. This situation must be corrected. A brief survey of the Biblical relevance of the ascension reveals why this truth must not be further neglected.

There are ten salient features to consider:

First, Christ's ascension is related to the coming of the Holy Spirit in dispensational Pentecostal fullness to the church on earth. Jesus made His great offer: 'If a man is thirsty, let him come to me and drink. Whoever believes in me, as the Scripture has said, streams of living water will flow from within him. By this He meant the Spirit whom those who believed in Him were later to receive. Up to that time the Spirit had not been given, since Jesus had not yet been glorified.' (John 7: 37-39).

'Exalted to the right hand of God, He has received from the Father the promised Holy Spirit and poured out what you now see and hear.' (Acts 2, 33). These words of Peter refer to the coming of the Comforter on the day of Pentecost.

Second, the ascension of Jesus is related to His high-priestly work as Intercessor and Mediator: 'Therefore, since we have a great high priest who has gone through the heavens, Jesus the Son of God, let us hold firmly to the faith we profess.' (Heb. 4: 14).

Third, his ascension is related to His dominion over all spiritual and temporal forces: 'It saves you by the resurrection of Jesus Christ, who has gone into heaven and is at God's right hand – with angels, authorities and powers in submission to Him.' (1 Peter 3: 21, 22).

Fourth, Christ's ascension is related to His headship over everything for the church: '. . . God raised Him from the dead and seated Him at His right hand . . . And God placed all things under His feet and appointed Him to be head over everything for the church . . .' (Eph. 1: 20-22).

Fifth, His ascension is related to the distribution of Headship ministers to the church: 'When he ascended on high, he led captives in his train and gave gifts to men. It was he who gave some to be apostles, some to be prophets, some to be evangelists, and some to be pastors and teachers . . .' (Eph. 4: 8-11).

Sixth, His ascension is related to the perfect accomplishment of His redemptive work: 'After He had provided purification for sins, He sat down at the right hand of the Majesty in heaven.' (Heb. 1: 3).

Seventh, His ascension is related to His worthiness as the Lamb Who was qualified to receive the scroll from the enthroned One, break the seals, and implement the judgments of God upon the earth: '. . . See, the Lion of the tribe of Judah, the Root of David, has triumphed. He is able to open the scroll and its seven seals.' (Rev. 5: 5).

Eighth, Christ's ascension is related to His coming again in glory as King of kings: '. . . He was taken up before their very eyes, and a cloud hid Him from their sight. They were looking intently up into the sky as He was going, when suddenly two men dressed in white stood beside them. 'Men of Galilee,' they said, 'why do you stand here looking into the sky? This same Jesus, who has been taken from you into heaven, will come back in the same way you have seen Him go into heaven.' (Acts 1: 9-11).

Ninth, Christ's ascension is related to His office and function as the Universal Judge: 'Moreover, the Father judges no-one, but has entrusted all judgment to the Son, that all may honour the Son just as they honour the Father.' (John 5: 22-23).

Tenth, His ascension is vitally related to every believer: 'God raised us up with Christ and seated us with him in the heavenly realms in Christ Jesus.' (Eph. 2: 6).

Jesus is the first of a new order of redeemed and elevated humanity. He is the first-fruits of many brethren, and He is bringing many sons to glory, all like Himself, conformed to His image. '**If anyone is in Christ he is a new creation.**' (2 Cor. 5: 17).

Christ's ascension was dynamic. God took Enoch. The whirlwind

85

swept Elijah into glory. But Jesus overcame the law of gravity by His own inherent dynamic, and ascended into heaven by the exertion of His own volition.

His ascension was prophetic. The angels predicted that He would return one day just as He had gone up into heaven. He went up in a cloud, and . . . **'He shall come with clouds and every eye will see Him.'** (Rev. 1: 7).

His ascension was majestic. He is now crowned with glory and honour. When He returns, the diadem of eternal sovereignty will adorn His kingly brow!

Mark 'Ascension Day' in your diary. It's important!

31. 'RISEN, ASCENDED, GLORIFIED'

This is an age in which the fundamental doctrines regarding the person and work of Christ, are being challenged. Under attack are the facts of his virgin birth, his miracles, his deity, the value of his death, his resurrection and subsequent bodily appearances to many witnesses.

Unbelievers combine with hostile demonic powers seeking to undermine the glory and wonder of Jesus. Let me affirm that the Christ of Calvary is not only risen from the dead, but he is the ascended, glorified, exalted and enthroned majestic Lord!

Ascension ministries presuppose an ascended Master. Apart from the resurrection and ascension of Christ, there could never be any ascension ministries. They are an expression of his enthroned headship.

Before reaching a full understanding of the scope and function of ascension ministries, it is vital to grasp the basic concept of the glorious exaltation of the risen Lord. He has been elevated to unimaginable heights of glory, majesty, power and authority. In his letter to the Ephesian church, the Apostle Paul makes much of the ascension of Christ, and it is from the fourth chapter that we gain our knowledge about the ascension ministries.

But prior to all that, in the very early stages of his letter, the Apostle expresses his prayerful longing that his readers will receive Holy Ghost enlightenment to the eyes of their understanding, and thus be able to grasp the wonder of the amazing supremacy of the exalted Jesus!

Now this was not merely to involve them in a mystical experience of exultant joy and astonishment at the complete conquest of the Crucified. Although, of course, that is the inevitable emotional impact made by this revelation of Christ's Lordship. But the Apostle had a more practical purpose in view. He was praying for the church to understand that this exceedingly great dynamic energy, which had raised Christ from the darkness of the tomb to the dominion of the throne and had invested him with universal sovereignty, was the self-same power working in every Christian. That identical tremendous energy is available to every heart of faith, and can be applied in every human situation by everyone who believes.

This is possible because the grace of God has already involved the elect with the resurrection, exaltation and supremacy of Christ. Paul makes that point in the second chapter of Ephesians. He explains that what happened to Christ in his resurrection, ascension and glorification, happened also to the church. His phased programme of exaltation was not merely personal, it was representative. God has elevated His Son as the Federal Head of a new race and order of mankind – the redeemed, regenerated, transformed, Spirit-anointed people of God, living in faith, moving in ascension power, receiving and responding to the ascension ministries of the risen, ascended glorified Lord!

32. REACHING THE THRONE

Toward the turn of the fourth century, the saintly John Chrysostom, golden-mouthed orator and champion of the Christian faith, declared: 'Nothing will so avail to divide the church as love of power.' Subsequent events in church history have proved him right.

An overriding ambition that disregards the feelings of others and tramples underfoot all opposition is not in the spirit of Christ. It is more like Lucifer who, in his fearful bid for supreme power, threatened to exalt himself above the throne of the Eternal God! This terrible expression of self-will transformed an angel into a devil and became the fountain-head of evil from which sprang the poisonous waters of all sin, misery and despair still flooding the universe to this day.

The Lord Jesus manifested a nature that was in complete contrast to the rebellion of Lucifer. In a staggering demonstration of grace and love, Jesus stepped down from the throne that was eternally and lawfully His by virtue of His Godhood, laid aside His crown, divested Himself of the insignia of majesty, and vacated the glittering glory of heaven where He had ever been the centre of attraction to myriads of adoring beings. He came to the hostile darkness of a lost world and, by His incarnation, entered sinlessly into the total experience of a broken and suffering humanity. Instead of exercising the powerful prerogatives of deity, He lived a life of perfect obedience in utter dependence upon His heavenly Father. Whatever measure of power He had was granted to Him in His Manhood by the anointing of the Holy Spirit. As Peter revealed to the household of Cornelius: 'God anointed Jesus of Nazareth with the Holy Ghost and with power: who went about doing good, and healing all that were oppressed of the devil; for God was with Him.'

The perfect life of Jesus brought Him inevitably to the death of the cross. For such was the Father's will for Him. The cross was Christ's way back to the throne. In the eternities past He had occupied that throne in his Godhood, designing, creating, sustaining and reigning over the whole universe. But Golgotha projected Him in His Manhood right up to the pinnacle of supreme power. He is now 'the Lamb in the midst of the Throne'!

On the lonely island of Patmos, the Apostle John in his exile received a command from the risen Lord to convey to the luke-warm church of Laodicea how they could reach the throne:

'Behold I stand at the door and knock: if any man hear my voice and open the door, I will come into him and will sup with him, and he with me. To him that overcometh will I grant to sit with me in my throne, even as I also overcame, and am set down with my Father in His throne.'

Clearly, reaching the throne involves a responsive relationship with the Lord Jesus producing a life of victorious obedience to the will of God.

Lucifer never did reach the throne of power that he so much craved; his self-will prohibited him completely. It was the Man, Jesus Christ, who reached the seat of power and sat down on the right hand of the Majesty on high. The sceptre of universal dominion is swayed by the nail-pierced hand of the One who sweated blood in Gethsemane, breathing in agony those wondrously submissive words: 'Father, not what I will, but what you will.'

Because of His submission to the cross, the Father highly exalted Him. Jesus rose in triumph from the grave, and forty days later He ascended bodily into heaven – an event witnessed by many people, and documented in the New Testament.

From the throne, and in the power of His ascended Manhood, He urges the church to press forward in victory!

WHITSUN-PENTECOST

33. POWER TO PRESS ON!

The celebration of Whitsun, otherwise known as Pentecost, calls to mind the unique phenomena which accompanied the outpouring of the Holy Spirit on that first historic Day of Pentecost. The ecstatic utterances by the disciples in tongues foreign to their native language; the miraculous flames of fire which sat upon each head; the exuberant joy exhibited by them as they tumbled out of the upper room into the narrow streets of Jerusalem where they were immediately accused of being drunk at nine o'clock in the morning; the love, the enthusiasm and the new boldness they displayed – all these signs marked them out as true Pentecostals – filled to overflowing with the Holy Ghost and power.

Mention to someone today that you have a Pentecostal experience and you will inevitably obtain the response: *'Oh, you believe in speaking in tongues.'* The concept of manifest phenomena persists to this day. Thank God for it. It is no disgrace to have an experience similar to that received by the early church. The disgrace is in a denial of our need for the Pentecostal power.

Speaking in other tongues is, of course, only one aspect of the Pentecostal experience. But it is the one which seems to stick in people's minds. I wonder why that is?

Jesus said: *'Wait in the city of Jerusalem until you are endued with power from on high.'*

He had previously told His followers to preach the gospel throughout the whole world. But Jesus knew they could not do it without the power of Pentecost. Consequently 120 disciples gathered in the upper room at Jerusalem, following the ascension of Jesus. They prayed and waited for ten days because they believed the promise of Jesus: *'You will receive the power when the Holy Spirit comes upon you; and you will be my witnesses in Jerusalem, and in all Judaea and Samaria, and to the ends of the earth.'* Only the power of the Holy Ghost could enable them to fulfil the great commission.

Their prayerful patience was rewarded. The Holy Spirit came down to them on the Day of Pentecost direct from heaven with the sound of a rushing mighty wind. His gracious visitation was accompanied by the other signs which I have already described.

The same day, Peter preached a reasonably simple sermon to the people who had crucified Jesus, and three thousand were converted!

Subsequently the early church grew by leaps and bounds. Great numbers were added to them. Whole communities turned to the Lord and were saved. In many places miraculous signs and wonders, healings and deliverance from demons, accompanied the preaching of God's word with Pentecostal power and enthusiasm. The Gospel spread like a prairie fire. The prediction of Jesus had come to pass. Those who had waited for the Pentecostal experience did, in fact, become His dynamic witnesses throughout the earth, and the Kingdom of God increased.

It seems to me that the hallmark of Pentecostalism in the early church was successful evangelism issuing in church-planting and growth at a phenomenal rate. So I really wonder why Pentecostals are labelled now as 'tongue-speakers', instead of 'soul-winners' or 'church-planters'?

What I am saying is this: A Bible-based genuine Pentecostal church will be full of enthusiastic soul-winners making a social impact on their community.

One further point. The people who were involved in receiving the true Pentecostal experience from God were enabled by His Spirit to press on against all odds. Pentecostal power is the power that drives you on to persevere.

The record of events surrounding the Day of Pentecost is in Acts Chapter 2. The opening verses deal with the mighty energies and unique signs which accompanied the coming of the Holy Spirit. The middle of the chapter describes the anointed evangelism of Peter, resulting in the salvation of three thousand people. But toward the end of the record, these words appear: *'And they continued steadfastly in the Apostles' doctrine and fellowship, and the breaking of bread, and in prayers.'*

The power to press on is the power of Pentecost. Those who are truly filled with the Holy Ghost will be enabled to persevere.

34. THE SPIRIT, THE WORD, AND THE THRONE

In 1909, the author Grenville Kleiser compiled a series of sermons in ten volumes, entitled *The World's Greatest Sermons.*

One of these volumes – the first – is on my bookshelf. What gems from the giants it contains! It begins with a fourth-century sermon by Basil on the 'Creation of the World'. Then it moves progressively through the utterances of Chrysostom, Augustine, Wycliffe, Savonarola, Luther, Latimer, Melanchthon, and Knox. The book culminates in Calvin's sermon entitled: 'Enduring Persecution for Christ'.

No doubt the other nine volumes would proceed through church history, and include samples of preaching from Wesley and Whitefield, etc. (I have often wondered what those other nine books contain.) I know, from the early publishing date, that the compiler could not have included examples of the later teaching ministry by Dr Martyn Lloyd Jones, nor of the dynamic evangelistic preaching of Dr Billy Graham.

There is, however, a mighty message which merits a place in the series, *The World's Greatest Sermons.* It is the Apostle Peter's powerful proclamation on the day of Pentecost. So effective was this dynamic utterance that: 'the **same day** there were added unto them about **three thousand** souls' (Acts 2 vs. 41).

Peter's sermon was not exceptionally long. You can read it in a few minutes (see Acts 2 vs. 14-36). But Scripture was its **foundation**; Christ was its **focus**; the Spirit gave it its **force**; and a great harvest of souls was its **fruit**.

Consider just two sentences of Peter's sermon: '**This Jesus hath God raised up, whereof we all are witnesses. Therefore being by the right hand of God exalted, and having received of the Father the promise of the Holy Ghost, he hath shed forth this which ye now see and hear**' (Acts 2 vs. 32-33).

1. Peter evidently believed in the **Triune Godhead**, for he speaks of **Jesus** (the Son) being exalted by the very right hand of God. He explained that **the Father** fulfilled his promise, and that Jesus, from His exalted position in glory, sent **the Holy Ghost** to express the phenomenon.

2. Peter intended that nobody should ever forget that the Holy Spirit came from **the Throne of God** (Rev. 1 vs. 4). He is as much '**Lord**' as

Jesus is. The Apostle Paul emphasised this truth: 'Now the **Lord** is that Spirit' (II Cor. 3 v. 17). When you resist the Holy Spirit you sin against **Lordship** – against Deity. When you grieve the Spirit of God, you wound the heart of God.

The source of a true Pentecostal experience is the Throne of God. The Holy Spirit is continually at work to implement the regal rights of Lordship. He ever seeks to bring God's people to a place of total submission to the authority and headship of Christ. He came from the throne. He gently enforces the dominion of that throne. And He unceasingly works to prepare an obedient, submissive people for the glorious privilege of sharing the throne with our Lord Jesus Christ (Rom. 8 vs. 17; Rev. 3 vs. 21).

Total submission to headship is the true sequel to being filled with the Spirit.

3. The **Triumph of Jesus** was the joyful theme of Peter's message. '**This** Jesus hath God raised up' (Acts 2 vs. 32). '**This** Jesus' was Jesus of Nazareth, the miracle-worker, the God-approved and God-anointed Man whom the Jews had rejected, crucified, and slain (Acts 2 vs. 22-23). '**This**' Jesus was the subject of the Psalmist's prophecy (Acts 2 vs. 25-31). '**This**' Jesus had been sealed in the tomb. '**This** Jesus hath God raised up!' (How Peter exults in the glorious truth!)

The RESURRECTION. God raised Him up out of the tomb and back into the stream of history – 'Whereof we are all witnesses.' The resurrected Jesus had been seen. There were witnesses. Peter was one of them!

THE ASCENSION and EXALTATION. God raised Him up to the Throne, and crowned His sinless, victorious Manhood with majesty! 'Sit thou on my right hand, until I make thy foes thy footstool' (Acts 2:34-35). 'Being by the right hand of God, **EXALTED**'! (vs. 33).

From His lofty throne in glory, the Saviour administers the programme of the ages. There He patiently awaits the subduing of all His foes. But in order to make that desire effective, He has sent the Holy Ghost. And in order to implement the will of the Father, viz: the quelling of satanic forces and the evangelisation of the nations, He has brought into historic perspective that wondrous masterpiece – the Church which is His body!

From the context it is quite clear that the Lord intends to express His dominion and the authority of His Throne through the mighty instrument He has created – **the Church.**

Can you share the confidence of Isaac Watts? –

> 'Then let my soul arise
> And tread the tempter down,
> My Captain leads me forth
> To conquest and a crown.
> The feeblest saint shall win the day,
> Though death and hell obstruct the way.'

Why is such a glorious victory possible? Because the Holy Ghost has come to make good the thronal rights of Christ in every believer, and over every opposing force. Let faith arise to grasp this truth.

If the Resurrection was God's 'AMEN' to Calvary, then Pentecost was the 'HALLELUJAH' to the exaltation of His Beloved Son, Jesus!

35. A VALID PENTECOSTAL EXPERIENCE

'This Jesus hath God raised up, whereof we are all witnesses. Therefore being by the right hand of God exalted, and having received of the Father the promise of the Holy Ghost, he hath shed forth this, which ye now see and hear.' (Acts 2 vs. 32-33).

What was it that was shed forth on that historic day of Pentecost? It was the promise of the Father, the pentecostal phenomena – and it was obviously something that could be *seen* and *heard*.

The whole passage of scripture recorded in Acts 2 vs. 14-36 contains valuable information about the true evidence of a valid, Biblical, pentecostal experience.

God's Spirit is renewing the church today. The Charismatic revival is a reality. But there is always the danger of counterfeit manifestations. And there are also some sub-standard experiences masquerading as the fullness of the pentecostal blessing.

The Word of God is the only Court of Appeal by which our experiences can be assessed. God's Word, the Bible, is final and authoritative. Its authority is absolute.

If experiences do not measure up to the standard required by scripture, or if they do not conform to the principles and patterns revealed by the divine prototype, then those experiences are suspect. They are not valid pentecostal experiences.

Let us analyse this portion of Scripture in Acts 2 vs. 14-36, and assess our experiences in the light of God's Word. (We should keep in mind that the New Testament experience included *all* the facets of truth in our analysis, and was not evidenced by just one of them in isolation from the rest.)

(1) Firstly, *A valid pentecostal experience is revealed by an Allegiance to Scripture.* Peter declared: 'This is *that* which was spoken by the prophet Joel.' (Acts 2: 16). In other words, this experience is rooted in the predictive Word of God.

Today, some are saying: 'We do not need doctrine. Now that the Spirit has come, He will guide us.' They imply that they can dispense with the regulating influence and revelation of Scripture now that the Spirit has come.

But Peter emphasised that the pentecostal experience was the fulfilment of Prophecy. '*This* is *that*.' 'That' is the promise of the Word of God. '*This*' is a scriptural experience.

Jesus had opened Peter's understanding to understand the Old Testament Scriptures (Luke 24 vs. 45); and therefore Peter could relate his pentecostal *experience* to divine *revelation* – to the Word of God: '*This is that.*'

The Holy Spirit is the Spirit of Truth. He has come to lead us into all truth, and therefore *out* of all error.

God's word is truth, (John 17:17), and that word speaks of Christ, who is Himself truth (John 14:6). The Spirit takes of the things of Christ and shews them to the believer (John 16:15).

Clearly, any valid experience of the Spirit of Truth in our lives must bring us in line with the truth of God's written word, and must also produce within us a submission to the claims of the Christ of Scripture – for He is the ultimate truth – the Living Word.

Those who continue in error and darkness, in rebellion against the Lordship of Christ, should question the validity of their Charismatic experience. The same principle applies, of course, to all orthodox believers, and in particular to the classical pentecostalists.

Remember, the primary evidence of a valid pentecostal experience is an *allegiance to scripture*, which teaches *unswerving loyalty to Christ*.

(2) The second point is this: *A valid pentecostal experience is recognised by an Affirmation of the principles of Evangelism*. (Acts 2 vs. 21). Peter in his message on the Day of Pentecost proclaimed: '*Whosoever shall call on the name of the Lord shall be saved.*' That is a quotation from Joel 2 vs. 32; so Peter, still firmly rooted in Scripture, affirmed the great evangelistic principles of the Gospel. The obvious implication is that in the day of grace, the 'Whosoever' will have the gospel preached to them.

Paul quoted the same verse in Romans 10 vs. 13, and went on to expand the thought in verses 14 and 15: '*How then shall they call on him in whom they have not believed? and how shall they believe in him of whom they have not heard? and how shall they hear without a preacher? And how shall they preach except they be sent? As it is written, how beautiful are the feet of them that preach the gospel of peace, and bring glad tidings of good things.*'

It is clear that a valid pentecostal experience in any company of believers, must be accompanied by a sending forth of those who will preach the gospel of peace, and carry the glad tidings of *good things*.

Out of this basic rock of evangelism springs the fountain of hope, flowing out with irresistible logic and incomparable love to a dying world: *'Whosoever shall call on the name of the Lord shall be saved.'*

What is the content of that gospel of peace?

The details of the *'good things'* of the gospel are revealed in Acts 2 vs. 22-24.

Observe the three phases of the Sovereign action of God. (i) First, *the Sovereign action of God by the Historic Jesus (vs. 22). 'Jesus of Nazareth'* – that is a Person in space and time – the historic Jesus.

'A Man approved of God among you.' *'A Man'* – not a phantom; and remembered, known, and recognised as a God-approved Man ' ... among *you*, by miracles, wonders and signs *which God did by Him in the midst of you*, as ye yourselves also know.'

That is a clear description of the action of the Sovereign God working in and by the Historic Jesus.

Peter underlined the fact that the Instrument of God's choice had lived, worked, and died *amongst them*.

One of the *good things* of the gospel is surely this exciting news about the Historic Jesus, through whom the Sovereign action of God has been revealed.

(ii) The second phase is *the sovereign action of God at the Mystic Cross.* (vs. 23). The cross is (a) *An expression of the Wisdom of God:* ' ... Him, being delivered by the determinate counsel and foreknowledge of God . . .' But the cross is also (b) *An expression of the wickedness of man:* 'Ye have taken and by wicked hands have crucified and slain.'

The mystic cross combines Time with Eternity, and reveals how the sovereignty of God overrules, and uses for his own purpose, even the wickedness of men.

This revelation is also amongst the *'good things'* of the gospel of peace.

(iii) Thirdly, note *the Sovereign action of God in the Dynamic Resurrection.* (vs. 24). *'Whom God hath raised up'!* Here is another of those *'good things'*. These are *glad tidings of glorious truth*: 'Jesus is alive.'

God raised him up because it was *not possible* for death to hold him.

Why this impossibility? Because of the *sinlessness* of Jesus!

Death and Satan had no claim upon him. By dying the death of the cross, Jesus slew death itself, destroyed the power of the devil, and delivered those who were in bondage to the fear of death. (Heb. 2 vs. 14).

In His spotless life Jesus was approved of God by miracles, wonders, and signs. In His sacrificial death Jesus was approved of God by the mighty resurrection: 'God raised Christ by His glory'!

The risen, exalted Lord appeared to John on Patmos, exploiting His mighty conquest over death and the fear of death. (Rev. 1 vs. 17-18). Exultantly the Victor proclaimed: *'I have the keys of death and of Hell.'*

Christ is risen! Peter pressed the point home: (Acts 2 vs. 24, 32, 33) – *'God raised Him up'!*

(a) God raised Him up out of the *tomb* and back into Time. *This is historical reality*: 'Whereof we all are *Witnesses*.' (vs. 32).

(b) God raised Him up – on into Eternity and up to the *throne* of glory. *This is eternal majesty*: 'Therefore being by the right hand of God exalted . . .' (vs. 33).

This is glorious good news! It is precious amongst the *'good things'* of the gospel. It is a basic principle in evangelism. Only a risen Saviour can save! Only an exalted Lord can fill us with His Holy Spirit!

(3) Thirdly, note that *a valid pentecostal experience always acknowledges an Ascended and Glorified Lord-Christ (vs. 33).*

Peter explained that the phenomenon of Pentecost was the direct result of the exaltation of the Lord Jesus Christ. In other words, the exaltation of Christ marked the *initiation* of Pentecost.

A valid pentecostal experience involves measures of revelation and enlightenment by which certain crucial facts about Jesus are acknowledged and recognised. Let us consider them in turn.

(i) *His Eternal Lordship is recognised.* 'Being . . . exalted . . . he hath shed forth this . . .'

When the Holy Ghost came, He came with a purpose, viz. to prepare the body of Christ, the Church, as 'an habitation of God through the Spirit.' He came as the appointed Executor of the Godhead, to keep the promise of Christ: *'I will build my church, and the gates of hell shall not prevail against it.'* He came to endow and enrich the church, the Bride of the Lamb, with gifts and graces, to prepare her for the eternal destiny as the Queen of Heaven!

It is because of Pentecost that we expect the Rapture, when the Bridegroom will come for His prepared Bride. (I. Thess. 4: 16-17). *'The Lord himself shall descend from heaven.'*

On another occasion the scripture reminds us: 'We wait for *the Lord* from heaven.' Clearly, His Lordship is not only involved in the *initiation* of Pentecost, but is also vitally connected with the *consummation* of the valid pentecostal experience.

The Lordship of Christ is the *Alpha* and *Omega* of a true, Biblical, Charismatic, pentecostal experience.

(ii). *His Functional Headship is recognised.* (Ephes. 4 vs. 10-13 and Ephes 1 vs. 22).

This ascended exalted Lord has been constituted and given by the Father as Head over all things to the Church. He expresses that Headship through organic gifts and ministries in His body, the Church. His Headship can only be said to be fully acknowledged when those expressions of His government are also recognised, acknowledged, accepted and obeyed.

In other words, the risen Head gives tangible evidence of His governmental control, by setting the men of His choice in the ministry and administration of His church.

The Giver is honoured when His ministry-gifts of men are also honoured and recognised.

Pentecostal power always points to Apostolic government.

(iii) *His Universal Kingship is recognised.* (Acts 2 vs. 34-35). 'Sit thou on my right hand until I make thy foes thy footstool.' Here is the *expectation* of the *King!*

A valid pentecostal experience should certainly induce in us a practical loyalty to the claims of the King. But in terms of revelation, it should also give a true understanding of Biblical eschatology – the unfolding of God's purpose in the last days. We can leave the baffling mysteries of life to Him – confident that all His foes, and ours, will be subdued in God's time.

(iv) *His National Messiahship is recognised* (vs. 36). 'Let all the house of Israel know assuredly, that God hath made that same Jesus, whom ye have crucified, both Lord and *Christ.'*

The Christ is the anointed One – the *Messiah*. What a staggering revelation to the Jews! The Man Jesus, whom they had regarded as an imposter, subsequently rejecting and crucifying Him, was, in fact, their true Messiah!

Arising out of this thought of the recognition of His National Messiahship is the idea that a valid pentecostal experience should therefore lead us to a correct understanding of (a) the current signs of the times; (b) the interpretation and fulfilment of Biblical prophecy (in particular the prophet Daniel's interpretation of Nebuchadnezzar's dream); (c) the future function of Israel and the Gentile Nations; (d) the reality of the Battle of Armageddon; and (e) the pledge of Christ's return in glory and the establishment of His literal Millennial reign on this planet as the true Messiah of Israel, and the King of all the Earth!

Evidently a true, Biblical, personal Pentecost involves much more than speaking in tongues, or experiencing ecstasy, though we greatly treasure those scriptural signs. A valid baptism in the Holy Spirit will always issue in allegiance to God's word; loyalty to the Saviour; outreach in evangelism to lost souls; and loving submission to the Lordship of Jesus.

HARVEST

36. HARVEST TIME

What kind of harvest will there be for the Lord when He returns? Jesus himself asked the question: 'When the Son of Man comes, will he find faith on the earth'?

Will Jesus find faith in your heart? Will he reap a mighty harvest of faith from professing Christians world-wide? There can never be any kind of harvest if there has been no ploughing, no sowing of seed and no nurturing of the tender shoots. That is a fact which is self-evident in the realm of nature.

So, what kind of seed must be planted in order to expect a harvest of faith? How does faith come? 'Faith comes from hearing the message and, the message is heard through the word of Christ.'

The word of the Lord generates faith in the hearts of those who receive it. If Christians will fill their hearts and minds with the word of God, they will become full of faith.

It is men and women of dynamic faith who do exploits for God. This quality of life is so greatly needed in these dark and difficult days. The first martyr in the early church was a deacon by the name of Stephen. He was full of faith and of the Holy Ghost and he did mighty signs and wonders amongst the people. An examination of Stephen's defence before the Sanhedrin reveals an intelligent and thorough grasp of the scriptures. He had evidently fed upon the word of God and it was this factor which contributed to his successful, miraculous ministry, enabling him ultimately to be like Jesus in forgiving his enemies.

Faith comes by hearing the word of God. There is no other way to get it, to cultivate it or to preserve it. Faith enables people to launch out into new experiences with God. It empowers them to explore and pioneer fresh territory with the gospel. It equips them to exercise ministries of the miraculous.

When, from the comparative safety of his fishing boat, Peter observed the phenomenal sight of Jesus walking on the surface of the heaving sea, he cried out for a word from the Lord. Peter, like us all, was a strange mixture of faith and doubt. 'Lord!' he cried. That word expressed his faith. 'If it is you.' The word 'If' displayed his doubt. 'Bid me come to you across the water.' In other words, 'Speak to me Lord and, settle my doubts.' And the Master spoke just one word: 'Come.' That word was enough to generate extra faith, dispel all Peter's doubts and empower him to climb out of the boat and take that miraculous unprecedented journey across the waves toward Jesus.

'Faith comes from hearing the message and the message is heard through the word of Christ.' The seed was the word of the Lord. The harvest was an active dynamic faith.

Some Bible expositors take the view that the question of Jesus: 'Will the Son of Man find faith upon the earth?' should be rendered 'Will he find the faith upon the earth?' In other words when Jesus comes will He find the church believing and practising and holding fast to the 'Faith once delivered?' The Apostle Paul could say at the close of his life, 'I have kept the faith.' It is important to keep the faith; to shun heresy; to cling to that clarity of doctrine outlined in the scriptures.

The seed of God's word sown in the hearts of God's people will produce not only a dynamic faith, but also an adherence to the body of doctrine called 'the faith'.

Jesus is coming soon. His angels are preparing to reap His harvest. What kind of harvest will He find in your field?

It all depends on the kind of seed you have sown and on how well you have nurtured those early shoots.

37. SEEDTIME AND HARVEST

When the dry land appeared again following the judgment of the great flood, God made this promise to Noah: *'While the earth remains, seedtime and harvest, and summer and winter, and day and night shall not cease.'*

'Seedtime and harvest'. God coined the phrase. There is an element of logical inevitability about it. As winter follows summer, and as night comes after day, so harvest follows seedtime. No seedtime – no harvest. God has made the position very clear.

C. Peter Wagner has reported: *'Every week at least 1,400 new Christian churches are planted around the world.'* What a tremendous harvest the Lord will reap one day!

The Bible has a lot to say about sowing seed and reaping the harvest. Take, for instance, the words of the wise man in Ecclesiastes 11 verse 1: *'Cast thy bread upon the waters: for thou shalt find it after many days.'* In the book of the prophet Isaiah there is a reference to the joy of those who do the work of seed-sowing: *'Blessed are ye that sow beside* [or upon] *all waters, that send forth thither the feet of the ox and the ass.'* (Is. 32: 20).

'Cast thy bread upon the waters . . .' Whatever for? What use is wet bread? Why spoil a perfectly good loaf by throwing it into the water? Happily, Bible scholars have explained the real meaning of that verse. The allusion is to the River Nile and to the ancient custom of the local people: *'Cast thy seed* [i.e. bread-corn] *upon the waters when the river overflows its banks. The seed will sink into the mud and will spring up when the waters subside, and you will find it after many days in a rich harvest.'*

Isaiah underlines the thought: 'Blessed are you' (the expression in Hebrew is *'Very happy are you')* *that sow upon all the well-watered places.'* He goes on to speak about the feet of the ox and the ass. This refers to the practice of sending oxen into the water to tread the ground for sowing, before the seed is cast upon it.

Together the wise man and the prophet give us a clear picture of what it was like at seedtime on the banks of the rivers in ancient times. From this scene there emerge three important principles which are still relevant to our situation today.

First, **preparation**. *'Send forth the oxen to tread the ground for sowing'.*

This work was essential to the success of the final harvest. It was humble work. Patient work. Obscure work. Labour carried on out of sight – beneath the surface of the water. It was work which produced no immediate results. There was nothing to be seen after days trampling on the river bed. The waters looked the same on the surface. It was work done for others – for the sowers.

It was hard labour, and it was done in the mud!

All this hard work illustrates prayer – the only effective preparation for a spiritual harvest. Praying is work. Humble, patient, obscure, hidden, unselfish, unostentatious, hard work. But without it, the whole harvest is a hazardous hope, a mere pious dream.

All age-groups can pray. Everybody gets older as the years slip by. Don't give up. Pray! Maturity increases in beauty the more you pray for others. Preparation in prayer is the most vital part of any Christian work. *'If you are failing to prepare, you are preparing to fail.'*

The second principle is **dissemination**. This word means to scatter seed. *'Cast thy seed upon the waters.'*

Someone has said: *'Prayer was never intended to be a labour-saving device'* The intense work of prayer does not relieve us of our responsibility to witness and work in the hostile field of the world. The seed must be spread. The word of life must be presented to the unsaved.

*'Cast **thy** seed . . .'* This presupposes that you have already gathered seed in order to sow it. You must have your own personal deposit of the seed of God's word. It is a personal experience. You must be in touch daily with God so you will have the right word for each specific situation.

'Very happy are you who sow upon all waters.' You must give God's word to all kinds of people. Amy Carmichael has said: *'You can give without loving; but you cannot love without giving.'*

Here is God's prescription for happiness: Very happy are you who sow the seed of the gospel in the hearts of all kinds of people in many different places – in homes for the elderly, in hospitals, in prisons, in schools and colleges, in the streets and the shops, in the factories and on the farms. Spread God's life-giving word to your family and neighbours, to your friends and to the stranger you happen to meet. *'He who sows sparingly will reap sparingly.'*

Preaching and witnessing are not the only ways to spread the gospel. Visiting, loving and caring are also vital. A lost world needs your love.

G. H. Montgomery wrote: *'We need to be loved, and we need to give love . . . '* Many folk in the church are also hurting inside and they need the healing that only love can bring. *'Love never fails'* wrote the apostle. So spread the seed in love.

Finally, there is **expectation**. *'Cast thy seed upon the waters for thou shalt find it . . . '* Four factors are involved in expecting a harvest.

First, there is **faith**. Any harvest is a miracle. The farmer must believe in the unfailing processes of God's creative arrangements in nature, or he would not sow any seed. If you have prepared the ground with prayer, and sown the seed in love, then you must have faith to expect that God will produce a harvest of souls.

Then there must be **loyalty**. Your personal support of your local Christian group is vital. You are as important to God as anybody else. Ian Macpherson emphasised the importance of individual loyalty when, in *Blessings under the Cross*, he quoted:

'It was one vote that gave Oliver Cromwell control of England in 1656.

It was one vote that decided that English and not German was to be the official language of the USA.

It was one vote that transformed France from a monarchy into a republic in 1875. And it was one vote that placed Adolf Hitler in the leadership of the Nazi party in Germany in 1921.'

Your personal loyalty to Christ and your support of His cause locally could tip the balance of power in the unseen cosmic conflict, and change the tide of history.

In addition to faith and loyalty, there must be **harmony** – a spirit of loving unity amongst Christians. If you are really expecting a harvest of souls, you should be cultivating an atmosphere of loving care and unity in which to receive and develop them.

John Dresher wrote: *'The world does not understand our doctrinal differences, and does not care at all who is right and who is wrong. The world is only interested in whether or not we love one another.'*

Lastly, there has to be **patience**. *'Cast thy seed . . . thou shalt find it, after many days.'* How many days? Who knows? But this idea must not be distorted out of perspective. The farmer is only patient in terms of the natural laws of sowing seed and reaping harvests. Once he has sown the seed, he does not rush out the next day to reap his crop. He waits for the right season. He knows it will come. But he does not wait for three, five, ten or twenty years. If he does not get a harvest in due time, he knows there is something terribly wrong. And he takes steps to remedy the situation. So it is in the spiritual realm. Prepare the ground with prayer. Sow the seed liberally in love. Expect the harvest in God's good time. *'You will find it after many days in a rich harvest.'* The *'seedtime and harvest shall not cease.'* It is an immutable principle which applies in three cases. There will be an **Evangelical** harvest of souls; an **Ecclesiastical** harvest of the elect; and a final **Eschatological** harvest for judgement fulfilling the purpose of God.

38. THE BRIDGE BUILDER

In ancient Rome, a member of the Pontifical College, the highest college of priests, was known as a *pontifex*. The head of the college was called the *Pontifex Maximus*. The word *pontiff* is derived from the Latin *pontifex* and has its roots in an Etruscan word which came to mean: 'Bridge-maker'.

This is a very interesting concept. The real work of a true priest is to 'build bridges'. The supreme example is, of course, Jesus our great High Priest, Who, by His sacrificial offering at Calvary's altar, built a bridge enabling sinful mankind to come to a holy God.

Jesus was always building bridges. He saw how fragmented humanity had become and He longed to bring them together. So many things had been allowed to divide people and to keep them apart. Race, colour, class, creed and religion – all these things had become the occasion of dispute and had caused disintegration personally, socially and nationally.

There was not a more bitter prejudice than that held between the Jews and the Samaritans in the time of Christ. By His parable of the Good Samaritan, Jesus taught the meaning of compassionate neighbourliness. We are neighbours not merely to those folk who live near us, but we are to be neighbourly to all kinds of people who are in need, whatever their religion or class. It is a staggering philosophy. But if it were put into practice, it could solve the Protestant-Catholic problem in Northern Ireland and settle the Arab-Jew dispute in the Middle East.

Men have not been able to find a political strategy for an adequate solution to these problems. That is because the basic problem in humanity is spiritual rather than political. Christ is the answer. No-one else can do it. Nothing less than the implementation of His philosophy will suffice. The millennial reign of Christ upon earth will, in fact, demonstrate visibly and historically the truth of this proposition.

Jesus also built a bridge between rival factions preaching in His name. 'We saw a man casting out demons in your name Lord,' exclaimed His disciples indignantly, 'and we told him to stop because he doesn't belong to our little company.'

'Don't stop him,' replied the Master. 'Those who are not against us are for us.' What a great heart of love and understanding Jesus always had! With these words He built another bridge.

One of the most precious doctrines of the New Testament is the truth of the priesthood of all believers. Christians have been washed and liberated from sin by the power of the blood of Jesus. And they have been made a kingdom of priests unto God.

In this capacity, Christians are the greatest bridge-builders in the world today. By prayer and intercession they bring mankind to God. By witness and proclamation they bring God to lost mankind. What a bridge! It spans the gulf between time and eternity. It provides a means for the blind to cross over into light. It is the highway for the harvest of souls coming to Jesus. It conveys love from the Father's heart to broken humanity crying in despair. It brings the joy of heaven into the misery of earth. Millions groping in darkness, clutching at straws, longing for love, yearning for someone to care, can, with trusting tread, cross over into the gentle arms of the Saviour, their sad hearts thrilling to His words: *'I am the way'!*

One of my favourite songs is: 'Across the Bridge' sung by Jim Reeves. Let these inspiring words encourage you to follow Jesus the great Bridge-Builder:

> 'Across the bridge there's no more sorrow,
> Across the bridge there's no more pain;
> The sun will rise above the river
> And you'll never be unhappy again.'

CHRISTMAS

39. ROOM FOR JESUS

This concept of 'Room for Jesus' is a hackneyed theme. Authors and poets have written about it. Vocalists have sung about it – there is a well-known hymn entitled 'Have you any room for Jesus?' And every Christmas without fail, the story is retold about the baby who was born in the stable because there was no room for him anywhere else.

But the constant repetition of this theme does not make the subject unimportant or trivial. Never lose the wonder of the Christmas story just because you are over-familiar with it. Every time you sing a carol, think about the miracle represented in verse:

> 'Veiled in flesh the God-head see,
> Hail the incarnate Deity!
> Pleased as Man with men to dwell,
> Jesus, our Immanuel.'

The hymnist Charles Wesley had an exceptional gift of being able to crystallise theology into a few words of poetry.

The mystery and the miracle remain after almost two thousand years. There was no room for this 'incarnate Deity'. Immanuel was *persona non grata* in His own world. God had come down from heaven to be with men. But nobody seemed to know, or care, or understand.

Attitudes have not changed much over the centuries. How many people do you know who have really made room for Jesus?

If the head of state, or the reigning monarch, came to stay with you in your home, which rooms would you make available? You would be sure to provide top-quality accommodation. In fact, all your property would be open to your royal guest.

Yet when the King of Kings desires unlimited access to every department of your personality, you do the unthinkable. You lock Him out of those rooms over which you yourself wish to keep supreme control.

On the locked door of the room containing your cherished traditions and entrenched prejudices, you have a notice: '*Do not disturb*'. The Lord

Jesus wants to come in with new revelation and a fresh vision for the way forward. Open the door and make room for Him in your life.

All fullness dwells in Jesus. So He needs plenty of room. When you open up to the Lord, there is an inrush of new life, a surge of divine power. Unprecedented things begin to happen. Miracles take place when Jesus is given His rightful place in personal and assembly life.

The Apostle John was instructed by the risen Lord to send a letter to the church at Laodicea. Those Christians had fallen into a pathetic condition. Jesus said they were wretched, miserable, poor, blind, naked and luke-warm. But the real tragedy consisted in their self-delusion. They considered themselves to be self-sufficient and in need of nothing. They were assessing themselves in the light of materialistic values instead of from the perspective of the Spirit.

What had taken place to cause the degeneration of the Laodicean church? The answer is astonishingly simple. They had no room for Jesus in their ecclesiastical programme. He had been pushed outside the circle of their administration.

As he began to write the book of Revelation, the seer John received a vision of the exalted Jesus in the midst of the seven churches. That was His rightful place, the place of governmental centrality. From that position He exercised the prerogatives of administration, directing the course of correspondence flowing from the seer's pen.

But the Laodicean church had evidently rejected the governmental centrality of Christ. They had pushed Him outside the door of their experience. Patiently He pleaded: 'Behold, I stand at the door and knock.' Where was He? He was on the outside of the door, urging those Christians to repent and to make room for Him.

This Christmas, why don't you give Jesus a present?

'What could He possibly need?'

The keys to every room in your life.

40. CHRISTMAS GIFTS

During the emotive Christmas season people make it quite clear that they want joy, hope, peace and love, not misery, despair, war and hatred.

These four precious qualities were all conveyed in the angelic message from heaven to earth on that first Christmas night almost two thousand years ago.

'Fear not: for behold I bring you good tidings of great joy, which shall be to all people. Glory to God in the highest and on earth peace, good-will toward men.'

Since that time, people have tried everything to bring them the joy, the hope, the peace and the love they so deeply need. But these qualities as a permanent reality are found in essence, and are available in human experience, only through Jesus the Saviour, – God's love-gift to mankind. All other sources of these qualities will ultimately prove to be illusory and transient.

We must, however, always bear in mind that although Jesus is the real source of true joy, hope, peace and love, God's way of reaching suffering humanity is through the human touch and loving concern of His own people.

Jesus taught that to serve broken humanity is to serve Him; and to ignore the desperate needs of others is to neglect Him. People are crying out for someone to show them love, and it is the responsibility of the children of God to demonstrate His love in practical terms to the needy.

The poet has expressed the human longing in these verses:

'Everybody has some secret sorrow,
Everybody longs for someone to care,
Everybody hopes a bright tomorrow
Will bring the love they're longing to share.
Everybody dreams of a better day to dawn,
And everybody lives for the hope that's still unborn.
Every heart is burning with that eternal yearning,
Everybody wants to be loved.'

'Everybody wants a world that's peaceful,
Everybody longs to live without fear.
Everybody prays for someone special,
And knows that there is Someone Who'll hear.
Everybody seeks for a friend who'll understand,
And everybody hopes for the things that they have planned:
Everybody's waiting to end with all the hating,
Everybody wants to be loved.'

This Christmas, why not make a special effort to show the practical concern of Jesus to someone in need of your love?

In his book, *Miracle on the River Kwai,* Ernest Gordon quotes these lines:

'No one could tell me where my soul might be,
I sought for God, but God eluded me;
I sought my brother out and found all three –
My soul, my God, and all humanity.'

41. THE GOD-MAN

At His birth wise men brought Him gold. At His death he sacrificed something infinitely more precious than gold. The Apostle Peter reminds us: '. . . ye were not redeemed with corruptible things, as silver and gold . . . but with **the precious blood of Christ** . . .' (I Peter 1 : 18-19).

The propitiation of God's wrath against man's sin demanded the shedding of sinless blood. Adam's fallen race could not supply it.

The Son of God was the only hope. 'The Son of God loved me and gave Himself for me,' exulted Paul.

To save sinful man, to secure the elect, and to satisfy the outraged justice of Majestic Holiness, the Son of God was required to take the unprecedented step of entering the human scene through the womb of the virgin.

Two lines from H. R. Bramley's Christmas hymn describe with penetrating poetic insight this tremendous step of God's Son from heaven to earth:-

'He is that He was, and for ever shall be,

But becomes that He was not, for you and for me.'

The self-offering of the Son of God on the cross necessitated the incarnation. Bethlehem and Calvary are inseparably linked. In the sublime act of redemption, the incarnation and the crucifixion are two phases of one unique work.

On the high altar of Calvary's cross, Jesus the Son of God atoned for the sins of all mankind by the ultimate outpouring of His sinless, pure and precious blood.

Silver and gold would not do. The price was too high. Man's redemption required the death and sacrificial blood of the Lamb of God.

Why does Peter stress the contrast between the precious blood of Christ and the costly currency of men – silver and gold?

Perhaps for three reasons:-

First, silver and gold have their origin in the earth, but the atoning blood was shed by the God-Man Who came from Heaven above. Though born in a stable on earth, He nevertheless came from God in Heaven. Jesus said: 'Ye are from beneath; I am **from above**: ye are of this world; I am not of this world' (John 8 : 23).

Second, it is the work of men to mine the silver and gold, to process it, and to produce it in its final form as ingots, coins, ornaments or jewellery. But redemption by blood is wholly the work of God. The Apostle Paul declared: 'But when the fullness of the time was come, God sent forth His Son, made of a woman, made under the law, to redeem them that were under the law, that we might receive the adoption of sons' (Gal. 4 : 4-5). The Apostle here makes it clear that the Sovereign God initiated the incarnation at an appointed time in history, and that He overruled events on earth until His supreme purpose of redemption by blood was achieved at the cross by the death of His Son.

Third, the value of silver and gold fluctuates in relation to demand. For example, in the prosperous reign of King Solomon (in whose richly ornamental building schemes silver and gold were used extensively and liberally) there was such an abundance of silver in the land that it was estimated to be of almost no value at all! (See II Chronicles 9 vs. 20 and 27.)

The precious blood of Christ is, however, absolutely unique. Its stable yet priceless value arises from its rarity, its uniqueness. This is because the Lamb of God is Himself unique. He is the only being in the universe Who is both perfect God and total Man. This is a mystery that baffles the brightest intelligence of angels or men! In the words of E.L. Mascall: 'He is the God Who became Man: and the Man Who is God'.

This wondrous God-Man travelled from Bethlehem to Calvary, and from there up to glory, remaining the whole time absolutely sinless. His blood outpoured on the altar of Calvary was rare because of its sinlessness. His sacrifice was a 'once-for-alltime' offering. It can never be repeated. It **needs** never to be repeated. The rarity of His person, and the uniqueness of His sacrificial death on the cross, constitute the valid basis for Peter's description: '. . . the **precious** blood of Christ'.

His incarnation opened the heavens, inspired the angelic choir, and brought 'glory to God in the highest'. His sinless life and His obedient death brought such immense satisfaction to the Father's heart that, as Peter reminds us, 'God raised Him up from the dead **and gave Him glory**' (I Peter 1 : 21).

At this Christmas time, may we again behold His glory – that unique glory of the Babe of Bethlehem, the Christ of Calvary and the exalted God-Man!

42. 'A TREASURE THAT WAS ALMOST LOST'

'It is more blessed to give than to receive'. How many people in our avaricious society really believe that? So conditioned are we all by the materialistic context in which we live, that it is difficult to think of many (even in the church) who are genuinely convinced of the practical value of such a philosophy.

Yet this simple statement, expressing the profound principle of self-sacrifice, was made by the Lord Jesus Himself. This maxim is part of His teaching. It is a lesson that we all need to re-learn.

Paradoxically enough, you will not find these words of Jesus anywhere in the four gospels. The statement was, in fact, repeated by the Apostle Paul at an elders' meeting in Ephesus over a quarter of a century after the ascension of Jesus! Paul said: *'I have shewed you all things, how that so labouring you ought to support the weak, and to remember the words of the Lord Jesus, how he said: It is more blessed to give than to receive.'* (Acts 20 vs. 35).

What a sparkling gem of truth would have been forever lost, had the Apostle not quoted to the Ephesian elders those wise words of Jesus! In their Bible Commentary, Jamieson, Fausset and Brown have expertly expressed the situation: *'This golden saying was snatched from oblivion and here added to the Church's abiding treasures.'* Its true wealth, however, will not be realised unless the principle is put into practice.

The concept applies not only to the giving of money and material things. The idea is broader than that. It refers to your basic attitudes; to your whole life-style. It is, for example, more blessed to give your time and talents to the Lord and to His work, than it is to receive the approval and the applause of the worldlings because you have pursued their ambitious pathway to materialistic goals.

Spurgeon said to a young man: *'If God has called you to preach the gospel, I would not have you to dwindle down into a king.'* Such a life-perspective is rare today. Perhaps you need to re-assess your outlook, re-think your position, and, in the light of the philosophy of Jesus, re-set your goals in life?

God loves to give. He proved it by the incarnation. The Babe of Bethlehem was God's measure of giving. By the gift of His Son to mankind,

God emptied heaven of its brightest Treasure! Christ gave Himself at the cross in order to deal with our sin. God gives us His Spirit now to enable us to give ourselves to Him in worship, and to our fellow-man in loving service. Giving is the way to true joy.

43. THE PRINCE OF PEACE

Jesus is the Prince of Peace. He made peace by the blood of His cross, and He gives peace freely to every troubled soul willing to receive from His gracious, loving heart.

But peace of this quality is not cheap. It is costly. The high price of peace, however, is not paid by the people who need it – but by the Saviour who provides it. *'He made peace by the blood of His cross.'* A cruel and violent death by crucifixion was the price that Jesus paid for our peace with God.

'Wonderful, Counsellor, The Mighty God, the Everlasting Father, the Prince of Peace.' These thrilling titles of Messiah are proclaimed each Christmas with unfailing zeal. Great choirs sing of Him. Preachers declare the wonder of His Name. And the Scriptural record is regularly repeated throughout the world, reminding mankind of the living quality of the prophet Isaiah's inspiring announcement.

Christmas is the prelude to Calvary. Before Jesus could secure peace for mankind, He had to die a violent death on the cross. Before He could shed His precious atoning blood for our sins, He had to enter the stream of history and, excluding sin, share the human experience with broken and suffering people. The miracle of the Incarnation made all that possible. The Babe in the womb of the virgin-girl was the first step in the amazing process culminating in the wounds of death at Golgotha.

Isn't it wonderful how God brings peace out of chaos and violence? Sometimes a revolution is necessary before the new order can ensue. Looking back over the past years, some astounding changes have occurred in Eastern Europe.

The re-unification of East and West Germany is, perhaps, one of the most significant events of the latter half of this century. I was astonished at the swiftness with which this political miracle was achieved, following the removal of the 'wall'.

Not only in Germany, but in Czechoslovakia also, there have been revolutionary changes causing a tremendous improvement in religious freedom in the nation. The Bible Society relates the following testimony of a Christian lady from Prague. She describes what life was like for her family as Christians under the old regime:-

118

'I was born into a Christian family and so it was natural for me to go to church. For us, membership of (our) church meant being able to share in the heritage and traditions of our forefathers. This was especially important for us in the last forty years, because it helped us to understand and maintain our national identity. But during this time less and less people came to church because they were scared of losing their jobs, the possibility of studying, and so on.

'My father was a teacher and suffered persecution for forty years. This was because he didn't hide the fact he was a believer. When he refused to deny his faith he was punished by losing his teaching job for six years between 1954 and 1960. So he worked as a manual labourer, but was paid a very low salary. My mother too was paid poorly. During this time things were difficult for our family with four children. Oppression such as this was normal for all believers.

'The last forty years have destroyed spiritual life in our society. But that's not all – personal relationships, knowledge about our history and Christianity have also been destroyed. Many people are now coming to church and asking for Bibles and other Christian books.'

Compare this to events now, as described by Dr Jiri Luki, Executive Secretary of the Czechoslovakian Bible Society:

'Almost every day you can see something about religion on television. You can watch and listen to Christian programmes, even a Sunday School class on TV, and you can hear good things about churches and faith in God, which is all very new in our country. It is like a dream.

'The new challenge for the churches is to show by our life what it means to be a Christian. Many young people feel a certain emptiness through the atheist theology which was taught for more than 40 years in our country. They are seeking something and this is our great chance to help them discover Christianity.' [Acknowledgement to the Bible Society].

In every human heart there is a longing for peace. Not only for political liberty – but also for spiritual life; for freedom from the oppressive spirits of fear and guilt and anxiety.

A violent revolution took place at Calvary. Through the death of His Son, God produced life and liberty. This spiritual quality of peace is freely offered to the whole world by the Prince of Peace.

44. ON THE BRINK OF A MIRACLE

Wouldn't it be lovely if, this Christmas, God were to answer your prayers with a special miracle?

Don't give up hope. Here is a faith-inspiring true story retold by Billy Graham:

'A mother in an African nation came to Christ, and grew strong in her commitment and devotion to the Lord. As so often happens, however, this alienated her from her husband, and over the years he grew to despise and hate her new devotion to Christ.

His anger and bitterness reached a climax when he decided to kill his wife, their two children and himself, unable to live in such self-inflicted misery. But he needed a motive. He decided that he would accuse her of stealing his precious keys to the bank, the house, and the car. Early one afternoon he left his bank and headed for the tavern. His route took him across a footbridge extended over the headwaters of the Nile River. He paused above the river and dropped the keys in. He spent all afternoon drinking and carousing.

Later that afternoon, his wife went to the fish market to buy the evening meal. She purchased a large Nile perch. *As she was gutting it, to her astonishment, inside the fish were her husband's keys!* How had they got there? What were the circumstances? She did not know. But she cleaned them up and hung them on the hook.

Sufficiently drunk, the young banker came home that night and pounded upon the front door, shouting:- 'Woman, where are my keys?' Already in bed, she got up, picked them off the hook in the bedroom, and handed them to her husband.

When he saw the keys, by his own testimony, he immediately became sober and was instantly converted. He fell on his knees sobbing, asked for forgiveness, and confessed Jesus Christ as his Lord and Saviour!'

Isn't that an exciting story? God is so full of surprises! Whoever would have expected a routine visit to the fishmarket to result in a miracle? But it did! Because God is interested in the everyday events of life – however insignificant you may think they are.

Three things impress me in that story. First, God answers prayer in His own sovereign way, achieving what nobody else could ever do. The ingenuity of God is wonderful!

Second, He exercises Lordship over every sphere of creation. The Lord who told Peter to find his tax-money in the mouth of the fish still controls the animal realm – and He proved it by His providential authority over a humble Nile Perch! But His Lordship extends far wider and deeper than that. God holds the destiny of every human life in His Omnipotent hands. By the power of His grace in that husband's heart, God brought about a sudden and miraculous conversion.!

And third, although murder and destruction were the driving forces in the sinful life of that man – nevertheless the great heart of God was filled with love toward him, and the Lord brought him salvation.

That reminds me of the angelic message given on that first Christmas night when Jesus was born. God's loving attitude toward people is expressed in the words of the angels:-

'Glory to God in the highest, and on earth peace to men on whom His favour rests'.

God cares about you. So don't give up – you could be 'on the brink of a miracle'!

45. THE FRIENDSHIP OF IMMANUEL

Loneliness is one of the worst afflictions in our materialistic society. Some people have been known to wither away and die in solitary misery, without a friend in the world. Friendship is a priceless treasure. Without it, life is empty and poverty-stricken.

God never intended folk to be lonely. He knew that the idyllic conditions of Eden could never constitute for Adam the perfect paradise, without the compatible companionship of Eve.

Heaven is a place of harmony. It is populated with beings who live together in indescribable bliss under the smile and favour of a loving God. It was God's intention that the human race upon earth should be equally happy. He promised Israel *'days of heaven upon earth'* if they fulfilled certain conditions. Hatred, discord, war and social or personal unfriendliness are all foreign to God's will for mankind.

Man has allowed sin to wrench him away from fellowship with God. This estrangement has produced fear and suspicion, resulting in social disorder, personal rebellion and international threats. The shadow of nuclear war darkens the horizon of our generation. Violence, like a monster, stalks the nations of the world.

But God in His wonderful love found a way in which He could redemptively befriend mankind. He sent his Son, Jesus, to be the Friend of sinners and to demonstrate that unique friendship by dying on the cross for the sins of the human race. 'God was in Christ *reconciling* the world unto Himself.' Thus the way was opened up for God and mankind to be friends again. At the cross Jesus destroyed the enmity that sin had generated in the hearts of all mankind.

During His earthly ministry Jesus was described as the 'Friend of sinners'. This was a title somewhat scathingly applied to Him by His critics, who failed to understand His outreach to the lost and the broken. It was, however, nonetheless gloriously true of Him. Jesus was, and is, the Friend of sinners. His friendship does not express itself by His socialising with them in their sins, but by saving them out of their sins. His parents were instructed:-

' . . . you are to give Him the name Jesus because He will save His people from their sins.'

Seven centuries earlier the prophet Isaiah had predicted:- '. . . and they will call Him Immanuel – which means *"God with us".'* This clearly illustrates God's firm desire to befriend the human race, and the angelic message to the shepherds that first Christmas night underlines His benevolent attitude to the people of planet Earth. *'Glory to God in the highest, and on earth peace to men on whom His favour rests.'*

Immanuel has brought to us the grace of God. He is God's best gift to us, and embodies in Himself the favour of the eternal God toward a fallen race.

Because of Jesus, 'God is with us' in a unique manner. He has become the Saviour of every believing heart, introducing us into a new level of friendship with our great heavenly Friend.

The friendship of Jesus is consistent and dependable. He will not let you down. He has the capacity to love you despite all your failures. He can convey to you the reality of a true friendship, lasting not only for your lifetime, but through the untold ages to come. Give some thought to the stirring words of Joachim Neander:

> 'Praise to the Lord, who doth
> prosper thy work and defend thee;
> Surely His goodness and mercy
> here daily attend thee;
> Ponder anew
> What the Almighty can do,
> If with His love He befriend thee.'

At Christmas, remember the promise of Jesus: 'And surely I will be *with you always*, to the very end of the age.'

46. THE UNIQUE SPIRIT OF CHRISTMAS

There is something very special about Christmas. There is an indefinable quality, an elusive atmosphere, a mysterious excitement – feelings rooted in childhood, combining to make Christmastime absolutely unique. I suggest, for your consideration, there are four special ingredients in the Christmas spirit.

First, Christmas time is **Memory** time. You remember other folk with cards or gifts. Others remember you (hopefully!) in the same way. The only reason there **is** a Christmas is because God **remembered** lost mankind, and sent His Son from glory to Bethlehem's stable – the first stepping-stone to the cross. God **remembered** His promises, the types and the shadows, the predictions of the prophets: 'Behold, a virgin shall conceive and bear a son, and shall call his name Immanuel.' (Is. 7 : 14).

'But when the fullness of the time was come, **God sent forth His Son**, made of a woman, made under the law, to redeem them that were under the law, that we might receive the adoption of sons' (Gal. 4 : 4-5). In the multitude of memories that flood back into your mind at Christmas, consider the fact that God **remembered** you and gave His Son for you.

Second, Christmas is not only a time of **Memory** but it contains also an element of **Mystery**. In fact, the Bible calls the unique Christmas event a **Great Mystery**. 'And without controversy **great is the mystery** of godliness. **God was manifest in the flesh**' (I Tim. 3 : 16). Is there a greater mystery in the Universe? As Wesley so wonderfully expressed it:

'**Our God contracted to a span, Incomprehensibly made man!**'

Karl Barth, Swiss theologian of towering stature intellectually, suggested that the only way in which God could **unveil** Himself was by **veiling** Himself! What a mysterious paradox! Yet almost two centuries before Karl Barth expressed that view, Charles Wesley, that incomparable poetic theologian, had immortalised that mystic truth in verse:

'**Veiled** in flesh the Godhead **see**
Hail the incarnate Deity!'

Third, Christmas is pre-eminently a time of **Melody**. As soon as Guy Fawkes has been consigned to his annual flames, the contingents of Christmas carollers are marshalling their ranks to give forcible, if not tuneful, reminders that Christmas is a time for singing!

How dull this world would be without Christmas! What a sad place this planet would be if Jesus had not come! But He **did** come! '**When none was found to deliver me, Jesus came! Praise His name!**'

He came at that first Christmas time, and the whole world has been singing about it ever since. Yes, Christmas is a time of joyful **Melody**.

The poet has struggled to express this uniqueness in the poem, '**God gave us Christmas**'. Though the verse is somewhat irregular, the sentiments are clear:

'Christmas is a time of joy and love
When stars more brightly shine above,
When people laugh and children sing,
And music lives in everything.

Christmas is the colour of hope.
A gay rainbow of surprised delight,
Dancing through the past year's grey disappointments.
Sparkling and singing – smiling through to light.

Christmas lingers in the fragrance of flowers.
And glitters in each coloured light.
Each footprint in the snow spells CHRISTMAS,
And the music of carols fills the moonlit night.

Christmas is the time of giving, helping, sharing.
A time of loving, understanding – and of caring.
Christmas is the time when dreams come true,
When wars could end, mankind learn love anew.

God gave us Christmas
When He gave us Jesus
The lovely treasures that He brought,
Need never, never, leave us!'

What are some of the treasures that Jesus brought to this world? Love, joy, peace, salvation and good-will towards men. These gifts are generous expressions of the Father's loving kindness toward humanity.

Fourth, Christmas is a time to think of God's **Mercy**. How merciful God has been to this rebellious and hostile race! 'God so loved the world that He gave his only begotten Son' (John 3 : 16). The Christmas event is unquestionably the manifestation of **Mercy**: 'Through the **tender mercy** of our God, whereby the dayspring from on high hath visited us' (Luke 1: 78).

Mercy! That is the fourth ingredient in the Christmas spirit. Jesus said: **'Blessed are the merciful: for they shall obtain mercy'** (Matt. 5. 7). During the festive season, think of those who need the mercy of God: the refugees; the Christians who are persecuted; the hungry; those in prison for their faith; those who have no Bible to read; the orphans; the homeless; the chronic sick; the weak; the bereaved; those in hospitals, or old folks' homes; the forgotten; the condemned; the neglected; the unsaved, and the broken in heart. Think of them. Then reach out to them in the spirit of the Christ of Christmas, and show them **mercy** – for God has shown mercy to you.

PART III

DAILY LIVING

Items 47 – 53

47. 'SURPRISE, SURPRISE'!

Some years ago, a violent storm at sea caused a tragic ship-wreck. Only one man survived the devastation, and he was thrown by the fury of the waves on to a desert island.

When he had sufficiently recovered from his terrifying ordeal in the sea, his sad plight gradually dawned upon him. He was utterly alone! A castaway on a strange uninhabited island, thousands of miles from civilisation!

He rescued a few things from the wreck, dragged them to a sheltered spot, and began to build himself a little hut.

His task complete, the man placed his few belongings inside. Everything he possessed in the world was now in that frail shelter!

He prayed to the Lord for help and deliverance, as daily he anxiously scanned the horizon for signs of a passing ship.

After some months, his faith was tested to its limits. One day, on returning from a hunt for food, he was horrified to find his hut in flames.

All he possessed had gone up in smoke! The man stood rooted to the spot, overwhelmed by the cruelty of his fate. It seemed to him that the worst had happened. He had lost all! Why had GOD let it happen to him? Bitter tears scalded his cheeks.

But what seemed to be the worst, was in reality the best. To the man's limited vision it was the worst thing, but to God's inscrutable wisdom it was the best!

The next day a ship arrived to rescue him. **'We saw your smoke-signal,'** explained the captain.

Perhaps at some time during the year, you have felt just like this cast-away did, when he discovered his little world in flames.

A tragic bereavement; a sudden shock; a devastating illness; a family problem; a sad misunderstanding; a sharp change of circumstances – something happened, and you felt as if your life had gone up in smoke. You felt that everything had turned against you.

Jacob felt like that when his sons returned from Egypt to tell him that Simeon had been left there in prison, and that Benjamin must go back to Egypt with them before the Governor would grant them any more favours.

'And Jacob their father said unto them, Me ye have bereaved of my children; Joseph is not, and Simeon is not, and ye will take Benjamin away; **all these things are against me**'. (Gen. 42 vs.36).

How wrong he was! Yet how difficult it must have been for Jacob to realise, at that moment of despair, that the Lord was about to do something wonderful that would affect not only Jacob – but the whole purpose of God for generations to come!

It is when we stand before the blazing pyre of our hopes and ambitions – when we see our little world going up in smoke – it is just at that precise moment that faith must lay hold of the promise of God: 'We know that all things work together for good to them that love God to them who are the called according to His purpose' (Rom. 8 : 28).

God is sovereign, and God is love. In that sovereign love is our abiding security. The awareness of that sovereign love in our own experience brings deep peace, true joy, and constant victory.

That is why we can face the future with confidence and hope. God is on the Throne, and He will overrule every circumstance for our ultimate benefit and for His eternal glory.

48. THE COST OF NOT BEING A DISCIPLE

In A.D.320 forty Roman soldiers stationed in Sebaste, Armenia, confessed Christ as Lord and were condemned to a cruel death.

In biting winds and sub-zero temperatures they were taken to the shores of a frozen lake where blazing fires and hot baths were prepared.

Their Commanding Officer demanded that they renounce their faith in Christ. Upon their refusal to deny their Saviour, the forty brave men were stripped of their clothes and forced out to the centre of the icy lake to suffer martyrdom by freezing to death!

There is a legend that a vision was seen of forty angels, each holding a glittering crown over the heads of the dying soldiers. The astonished troops looking on from the lakeside could see the angels, but the Christians on the ice were evidently unaware of the angelic presence. One by one the courageous men began to succumb to an icy death, and to receive a martyr's crown.

But one of the condemned group, seeing the tempting glow of the fires, and thinking of the hot baths on the lakeside, could suffer the cold no longer. Tormented beyond endurance he recanted and returned to the soldiers standing near the fires.

As he did so, another man amongst the troops on the shore, seeing the fortieth angel still holding the crown, stripped off his uniform and ran out to the centre of the frozen lake crying: 'Angel I come! Angel I come!' and so he died with the Christians.

Jesus gave a warning to His church at Philadelphia: 'Behold I come quickly: hold that fast which thou hast, that no man take thy crown'. Rev. 3 vs 11.

To be a disciple of Jesus is not easy. It demands stern determination and enduring courage, together with a great deal of spiritual and moral stamina. Sometimes, as in the case of the forty Roman soldiers, discipleship can lead to a martyr's death.

In any event, following Jesus always means suffering and self-denial. His standards of discipleship are just as demanding today as they were when He issued His initial challenge almost two thousand years ago:-

'If any man will come after me let him deny himself, and take up his cross and follow me. For whosoever will save his life shall lose it: and

whosoever will lose his life for my sake shall find it. For what is a man profited, if he shall gain the whole world, and lose his own soul? Or what shall a man give in exchange for his soul?' Matthew 16 vs. 24-26.

Notice that it is in the context of the call to discipleship, that Jesus warns about the peril of materialism with its consequent insidious possibility of causing the loss of human souls! These solemn words were addressed to His closest friends and followers. They were not spoken to the ungodly. Yet Christians so often smugly apply this warning to the unbeliever.

The loss of your crown, even the loss of your own soul – can such a terrifying prospect really be possible? Jesus says that it is possible. The implications of this possibility are awesome.

Let us give heed to the wisdom of John Blanchard who, in his book, *'Gathered Gold'*, reminds us: 'It costs to follow Jesus Christ, but it costs more not to'.

49. 'DON'T YOU CARE?'

What a question to put to the compassionate Christ! 'Don't you care?'

This was not a sarcastic enquiry from His enemies, veiling their carping criticism and bitter hatred in a subtle innuendo. The question arose from His best friends, from those whom He had chosen to be His closest companions.

Mark graphically sketches the context:

'That day when evening came, He said to His disciples, 'Let us go over to the other side.' Leaving the crowd behind, they took Him along, just as He was, in the boat. There were also other boats with Him. A furious squall came up, and the waves broke over the boat, so that it was nearly swamped. Jesus was in the stern, sleeping on a cushion. The disciples woke Him and said to Him, 'Teacher, don't you care if we drown?' He got up, rebuked the wind and said to the waves, 'Quiet! Be still!' Then the wind died down and it was completely calm. He said to His disciples. 'Why are you so afraid? Do you still have no faith?' They were terrified and asked each other. 'Who is this? Even the wind and the waves obey Him!' (Mark 4 vs.35-41 NIV).

We might be forgiven for thinking that such terrible circumstances would mitigate their offence. But Jesus would not share our view.

In his account, Matthew adds a detail omitted by Mark and Luke, pointing out that before Jesus got up to calm the storm, He rebuked His disciples for their fear and lack of faith. (Matt. 8 vs. 26).

Jesus always had His priorities right! While the hurricane was howling, while the raging waves were sweeping over the little boat, Jesus took time to express His disappointment at His men's faithless attitude, which had obviously generated their panic in a crisis. Then, with awesome authority, He arose as the majestic Master of the situation, to deal conclusively with the thing that troubled them.

In the silence, they must have felt deeply ashamed of their foolish words: 'Don't you care?'

How irresponsible to charge Jesus with indifference! They had already seen His caring love for broken humanity. The whole spectrum of human suffering had confronted Jesus, who always cared about each individual. He still does! Never irresponsibly accuse the Lord of failing to care about you. Their attitude was also irrational. Exhausted by His arduous labours, Jesus had fallen asleep in the boat. As He slept, the fury of the storm broke upon them, but Jesus was so tired He did not wake up. The disciples woke Him. His sleep had been undisturbed by the storm. So how could this sleeping Man, apparently unaware of the circumstances of their terror, be blamed for indifference? The question was irrational.

Lack of faith allows fear to dominate the personality. Fear produces panic which generates irresponsible and irrational attitudes.

In the storms of your life, remember, Jesus does care!

50. OLYMPIC GOLD

'I have fought a good fight, I have finished my course, I have kept the faith: henceforth there is laid up for me a crown . . .'

(II Tim. 4 : 6, 7)

In the struggle to please the Lord, Paul always went for the 'gold'. Doing the will of God cost Paul pain and suffering, but he did not flinch from the pathway of eternal purpose.

Writing to the church at Corinth, he describes some of the things he had been called upon to endure in order to do the Lord's work and fulfil his calling and ministry:

'. . . in labours more abundant, in stripes above measure, in prisons more frequent, in deaths oft. Of the Jews five times received I forty stripes save one. Thrice was I beaten with rods, once was I stoned, thrice I suffered shipwreck, a night and a day have I been in the deep; in journeyings often, in perils of waters, in perils of robbers, in perils by mine own countrymen, in perils by the heathen, in perils in the city, in perils in the wilderness, in perils in the sea, in perils among false brethren; in weariness and painfulness, in watchings often, in hunger and thirst, in fastings often, in cold and nakedness. Beside those things that are without, that which cometh upon me daily, **the care of all the churches**' (II Cor. 11 : 23-28).

At the sunset of his experience, with all those sufferings behind him, Paul lies chained in a Roman dungeon awaiting a martyr's death at the hands of the infamous Nero. Who can deny the truth of his words to Timothy? '. . . I have fought a good fight, I have finished my course, I have kept the faith; henceforth there is laid up for me a crown of righteousness . . .'

In these words the Apostle sums up his tremendous life, illustrating his experience with pictures of a Greek wrestler, a Greek runner, and a Roman soldier. His whole concept was no doubt inspired by the Olympic games. 'I have fought **the** good fight.' This is a more accurate rendering. It speaks of the focus of energies on **the** fight. The Greek word is '**agon**', meaning: '**contest in the arena**'. The idea is of a contest which is on public view. Paul knew that the Christian life is not a picnic, but a conflict. It is a conflict observed by the world, and by principalities and powers. Paul could declare that he had agonised strenuously in this cosmic conflict. He

135

had not allowed himself to be diverted from the central pathway of God's will. His great powers of intellect, together with his spiritual energies and his physical efforts, had all been channelled into one mighty stream of sacrificial service for God and mankind.

'**I have finished my course.**' The word '**course**' is '**dromos**' in Greek, and it means '**the athlete's race-course**'. The Christian life is not only a fight. It is a race.

Life often seems like an **obstacle-race**, doesn't it? Praise the Lord for all the obstacles! By His grace they can become stepping-stones to progress in His will.

Some Christians seem to be in the **sack-race!** Inhibited by formality, fears, and traditions, they don't make much progress. They are in bondage. When Lazarus came out of his tomb, he was alive but **bound.** Jesus commanded his disciples: 'Loose him and let him go!' This ministry of deliverance is the responsibility of His disciples. Let us rise in faith to set His people free.

Others seem to be in the **egg and spoon race!** Their whole attention is given to petty, materialistic details, and they take their eyes off the goal. They lose the race – and the egg!

Still others, instead of pulling together, are locked in conflict and disagreement, hindering each other's progress in a semi-spiritual **three-legged** race. (If you want a good example of Christian co-operation, what about the **wheel-barrow race**? Those who reach the finishing line do so only because of the dedicated efforts of others. Therein lies a parable!)

Now, I know that all these races I have mentioned were not part of the great Olympic games, and I have strayed somewhat from the Apostle Paul's dignified concept. Nevertheless, the spiritual truth remains.

The greatest Greek race was the Marathon, deriving its name from the battle of Marathon between the Greeks and the Persians. The Greeks won against heavy odds, and a Greek soldier ran to Athens for a day and a night to announce the victory to the city magistrates. Running into the city, he gasped: '**Rejoice, we have conquered!**' They were his last words. His task cost him his life and he dropped dead. **He** had finished the race; completed his course, delivered his message; done his work.

Who could dispute that Paul's race was the greatest spiritual Marathon in the history of the church? And, like the Greek runner, Paul gave his life to deliver his message to men.

'**I have kept the faith.**' The Greek word for **kept** is **tereo**, meaning: 'to keep by guarding'. The Apostle knew about being kept by a guard. He was chained to a Roman soldier.

The **faith** was the deposit of truth and revelation entrusted to Paul. The Apostle had guarded it diligently against heresy, philosophy, and mockery. He was now about to shed his blood, rather than deny the **faith**.

'**Henceforth there is laid up for me a crown . . .**'. Paul **knew** he would get the 'gold'! Not the yellow metal medal of man's applause, but those priceless golden words from the lips of Jesus: '**Well done thou good and faithful servant. Enter thou into the joy of thy Lord!**'

What will the Lord Jesus say to you when you look into those eyes of fire at the judgment seat of Christ?

51. FREEDOM AND SERVICE

Set free to serve! The very idea is a paradox. Surely if a man is set free, he no longer has to serve? On the other hand, if he is in service to a master, how can he be really free? These conflicting concepts are resolved in Scripture. The paradoxical problem is solved in the exemplary life and obedience of Jesus.

The unregenerate mind has a fundamental misunderstanding of the concept of freedom. The average person believes that an unlimited ability to please himself constitutes freedom. But this unrestricted licence for self-indulgence is just another kind of bondage, resulting ultimately in compulsive or obsessional behaviour. Taken to its logical conclusion, such ungoverned lifestyle on a wide scale would issue finally in social chaos.

There is nothing wrong in wanting to be free. God does not want anybody to live a miserable inhibited existence of fear and anxiety. He wants us to be free. But our true freedom, viewed from God's perspective, is the right to live voluntarily within the orbit of His will and purpose. The boundaries He has set are not in order to limit the happiness of mankind, but to define the way of optimum spiritual and social welfare for all people.

There is, of course, a snag. People are born with a bias toward wrong. So it cuts across human nature to have to live within God's laws. In His great love, God provided a way in which people could acquire a new nature which would enable them to serve Him willingly with perfect freedom. The transformation is effected by the new birth wrought by the Holy Spirit when someone believes the gospel, repents, and accepts Christ as Saviour and Lord. The subsequent daily work of the Spirit in that newly regenerate person will gradually produce a life that becomes more and more like the life of Jesus.

Regenerated persons have two natures: the new life which is the gift of God when they are saved, and their own nature which they must learn to crucify and subdue. In the history of humanity only two men have existed without an old sin-biased nature. Adam, before the fall, and the Lord Jesus Christ Who was holy, harmless and undefiled and separate from sinners.

Jesus is the example for all believers, as the Apostle Peter has reminded us, and we must learn to tread in His footsteps. He is the model Servant, perfect in His obedience to the Father – even when it meant a cruel and horrifying death on a cross. Yet Jesus was perfectly free from any bias toward sin, and from any kind of sinful impulse or tendency.

Jesus, being the perfect Son of God, had every right to be free to make His own decisions in life. But He used His freedom to obey the Father's will.

The Bible says: *'Even Christ pleased not Himself.'* Nevertheless, He was free to please Himself (and had He done so He would not have chosen to do anything sinful). But He had an even higher concept of freedom than that.

Jesus voluntarily submitted Himself continually to the Father. He lived an exemplary life of absolute dependence on the will of the Father through the power of the Holy Spirit. The miracle of the perfect life of Jesus consisted not merely in His sovereign Godhood manifested in the flesh, but also in the daily demonstration of His Spirit-anointed sinless Manhood.

The Spirit enabled Jesus to serve the Father in absolute dependence. 'Whatever I see the Father doing,' said Jesus, 'that's what I do.'

'And whatever I hear the Father saying, those are the words I speak.'

This miraculous service of dependence was sustained and expressed in terms of prayer. Jesus, the God-man, lived a life of constant conscious fellowship with the Father through prayer.

This is the wonder of it all! In the history of the human race, the Man who was most free was the most dependent on God. Jesus achieved the most through a life of sacrificial service to God and mankind.

Christians are called to express their God-given freedom in the same way as Jesus did.

52. IN THE ARENA

The early Christians were no strangers to the arena. The clear area in the centre of the ancient Roman amphitheatre was known as the arena. There, chariot races were held, gladiatorial contests to the death took place, and spectacles of strength and skill were promoted to entertain the circus hordes who came to watch. In that dreadful arena, Christians were thrown to the lions, torn to pieces by tigers, burned alive, crucified, or forced to endure suffering and death in countless other ways of harsh cruelty. In the arena the blood of the martyrs became the seed of the church.

The Roman Empire, together with its proud rulers and its countless cruelties, has been swallowed up by the centuries. But the church of Jesus Christ remains.

The blood-red empire of Communism has more recently dominated the nations in a seventy-years' reign of terror. That totalitarian satanic system also persecuted the Christians, demolished church-buildings, banned the Bible, taught its children the philosophy of atheism, and sneered at the people who believed in God. But where is Communism today? It has been proved to be an economic failure, a historic disaster, and a philosophic illusion. God has blown upon the house of cards called Communism and it has collapsed. Its bemedalled paper-tigers have been swept away by the whirlwind of a Spirit-inspired revolution energised by the dynamic of prayer and faith in the hearts of countless Christians who refused to give up.

Like the Roman Empire, Communism is drifting away into history. Soon it will become a mere memory of a bad dream – a miserable mirage of a system that defied God and His people. The nightmare of Communism is over. But the Church of Jesus Christ remains – and it is thriving and growing and spreading all over the world. Almost two thousand years have gone since Jesus made His amazing promise: *'I will build my church and the gates of hell shall not prevail against it.'* But those words are as valid today as they were when they first fell from our Saviour's lips. History has proved that Jesus Christ is right and that His critics are wrong.

The concept of the arena-experience persists to this day. There is the sports arena for athletics; and the arena for boxing matches. There is the circus arena – or ring – where clowns, not gladiators, entertain the people.

The word is used also as a figure of speech. We speak about the political arena. In fact, the word 'arena' has come to mean any sphere of conflict, interest, or activity.

Some may be unaware of this fact, but all Christians are still in God's arena – the sphere of His cosmic conflict with the forces of darkness. Christians are a source of great interest to angelic intelligences. By the church, God is making known to principalities and powers His own great manifold wisdom. His Spirit is constantly active in the lives of believers as they wage war with Satan.

The outcome of victory is already secured. The battle was fought and won at Calvary. But Christians have to implement that victory by faith. And they are continually being resisted by the powers of darkness.

As the spirit, soul and body of the patriarch Job became the scene of the contest between the devil and God, so the church is now the arena in which God displays His grace to Christians, His wisdom to angels, and His victorious triumph over Satan.

Thousands observed the quiet courage of Christians in the Roman arena. Faced by certain death and suffering, the Christians often silenced the screaming crowds by demonstrating a tranquil trust in the risen Lord Jesus.

Have you ever thought about the effect upon Saul of Tarsus that the radiant face of Stephen had, as the church's first martyr of many millions to follow fell under those death-dealing stones?

Leila Gordievsky, forced by Communist authorities to remain separated from her husband Oleg for six long years, was watched constantly for all that time by the K.G.B.

Agents of the Secret Police had her under observation every minute of the day and night for those six years. That must have been a terrible ordeal for her.

Even though you may not realise it, Christians are in God's arena and are under intense angelic observation. Stand firm. You will receive the victor's crown when the contest is over.

53. MORE THAN CONQUERORS

How can we be more than conquerors? If we barely escape defeat, and scrape home with some sort of victory, we are ecstatic. But to be more than a conqueror – that seems so far beyond the normal expectation in Christian experience as to be almost incredible.

Nevertheless, that is precisely what the Bible teaches each Christian should be – absolutely and completely victorious in every circumstance. We are expected to be more than conquerors. And we can be enabled to live at that level.

When we think of the overcoming life, we usually equate it with victory over great forces – over Satan and the powers of darkness, over the hurdles of heresy confronting us in the Christian arena, and over the great and complex problems of life. The Holy Spirit does, of course, enable Christians to overcome all these things. But so often it is the little foxes that spoil the vine. We can denounce heresy but we cannot overcome jealousy. We can rebuke demons but we cannot rejoice at the exaltation of our brother. We can pass the public house without a desire to drink but we cannot resist the temptation to criticise our fellow Christians and to draw attention to their faults and weaknesses.

It is significant that the Apostle lists witchcraft together with hatred, discord, jealousy, fits of rage and selfish ambition in his catalogue of the works of the flesh – the acts of the sinful nature.

Haven't you met Christians who would raise their hands in holy horror at the thought of witchcraft, yet who think nothing of pursuing their own selfish ambitions? The Apostle condemns both because each springs from the same source – an uncrucified sinful nature.

There are other things over which we should be enjoying constant victory. We need to learn how to overcome discouragement, how to handle criticism (when we are on the receiving end!), how to rise above depression, how to rely on God's supply to meet all our needs, how to pray for those who treat us spitefully, how to love those who irritate us, how to deal with our fears, our insecurities, our inferiority complex, how to resist exaggeration.

The secret of becoming more than conquerors lies in two things: God's love and God's gift. We must rest in His love, and with simple trust we must receive His gift.

The Apostle deals with the sovereignty of divine love, assuring us that God makes all things to work together for good to the elect. He goes on to expound the wonder of God's personal predestined purpose for each believer, and this concept forms the foundation for the structure of his subsequent statement: 'We are more than conquerors through Him that loved us.'

Pastor Teddy Howells has said: *'We all believe in divine election when it affects us.'* How true! When we are called and honoured, then we rejoice in election. But if our brother is appointed to the place which we thought would be ours – how do we react then? It has been said that 'It is easier to weep with those who weep than to rejoice with those who do rejoice.' Let us remember the principle, 'When one is honoured, all in the body are honoured' – even when that favoured one is not you!

At such time, when your peace is threatened by the whispered insinuations of the enemy, learn to rest in the sovereignty of God's love. He has a personal plan for your life! Nobody else can ever be you, or do exactly what you can do in God. Nobody else has your family, your sphere of witness, your circle of friends, your personality or your testimony. You are unique in God, because you are chosen by God. It took a Calvary to save you, just as it did to save the Apostle Paul.

Rest in God's love. And trust in His gift. 'Thanks be unto God who *gives* us the victory through our Lord Jesus Christ'. Victory is his gift to believers. Of course it must be received by faith, and implemented in the power of the Spirit – but it is still God's *gift*.

This revelation emerged from the Apostle's discourse about death and resurrection. As there is victory for life, so there is overcoming power in the hour of death.

Some years ago I watched my own mother in her last hours upon earth. The eyes that had lovingly smiled upon me from my infancy closed in death. The white hair crowned the cold marble brow, and the frail hands that once had fed me, protected me, caressed me, were still. But there was no sense of defeat or despair. In life she had overcome weakness, illness, and blindness, by resting in God's love. At the hour of death victory was hers. It is God's gift to us all.

PART IV

THE WHOLE WIDE WORLD

Items 54 – 58

54. GOD'S MASTER-PLAN FOR WORLD EVANGELISM

The world's leading evangelists designated a 'Decade of Evangelism'. Programmes for church-growth, schemes for soul-winning, and plans for evangelistic outreach have never been more prolific in the history of the church. All these things are good. It is right to be burdened for lost souls, in the light of the imminent return of the Lord Jesus Christ.

Jesus is concerned about souls. His tremendous prayer in John 17 embraces all those who would believe on Him during the church-age, and reaches out in His boundless love to the whole world. He prays for the oneness of His people so that **the world** would be convinced of the reality of God's love, and thus would **believe** and **know** that God had sent Jesus to be the Saviour (vs. 20-23).

This prayer of Jesus reveals God's Master-Plan for World Evangelism, viz: **The perfect love, harmony and unity of all believers!** Where the glory and peace and joy of such oneness is displayed, there souls are saved and people are convinced of the reality of Christianity.

Churches lose their credibility in the eyes of the world when they promote schemes of evangelism from a home-base where this beauty of sacrificial love and harmony is not evident.

Jesus said: 'A new commandment I give unto you, that ye love one another; as I have loved you, that ye also love one another. By **this** shall **all men know** that ye are my disciples, if ye have love one to another' (John 13 vs.34-35). There is a clear relationship here between **our loving** and **others knowing**. True love in the church conveys understanding to the outsider.

We are to love one another **as He has loved us!** How did Jesus love? He loved freely, fully, faithfully and finally. 'Having loved His own, He loved them unto the end.'

Jesus loved sacrificially, selflessly, and supremely. He lived and died for others. 'Hereby **perceive** we the love of God, **because** He laid down His life for us: **and we ought to lay down our lives for the brethren**' (I John 3 vs.16). What a standard of love God expects from His people!

147

Jesus also spoke of the coming of the Holy Spirit to the believer, and the resultant effect upon the world. '. . . if I go not away, the Comforter will not come unto you; but if I depart I will send Him **unto you. And when He is come, He will reprove the world** of sin, and of righteousness, and of judgment' (John 16 vs.7-8).

There is evidently a relationship between the concept of a Holy Ghost-filled people, and the fact of conviction of sin in the world. The context demands that this conviction in the world results from the holy, loving, and powerful living of believers filled with the Holy Spirit. A holy church should make an impact upon an unholy society. It is this vital element of conviction of sin that is so often regrettably missing from many gospel crusades today.

The answer is for God's people to be filled with the Holy Ghost; with all the logical implications of prayerful, sacrificial, joyful, loving, victorious and holy living.

This is surely what Jesus expects of His people – and for which He prays in John 17 vs.17-23, indicating clearly the evident correlation between a church demonstrating the oneness of perfect love, and a hostile world coming to faith in Jesus Christ and to a knowledge of God's redemptive purpose in the earth.

Oneness is the key to God's Master-Plan for World-Evangelism. This vital oneness must be expressed in the unity of the Spirit **and** in the unity of the faith (Eph.4 vs.3-6). The prototype of this oneness is the harmony that exists in the Triune Godhead (John 17 vs.21-23). The same quality of perfect love and life that exists in the Godhead must be demonstrated in and through the church. '**Then**', said Jesus, 'the world will **believe** and **know.**'

How will this miracle of oneness be achieved? Jesus reveals the answer in John 17 verse 22: 'And the glory which thou gavest me I have given them; that they may be one, **even as we are one.**'

The Glory of God is the answer!

What is the glory that the Father gave to the Son? It is not the glory of essential deity, for that ever has been and ever will be Christ's by virtue of His being God the Son eternally.

The glory of which Jesus speaks in John 17 verse 22 is the glory of His exalted sinless manhood, which has been raised up from death and elevated to the right hand of the Majesty on high! The Man, Christ Jesus, now sits upon the Throne of God!

From that glorious pinnacle of power, Jesus the God-Man received the promise of the Father and sent the Holy Spirit in all His fullness of **glory** to indwell the church.

The Holy Ghost is the **Spirit of Glory** and it is His wondrous task to conform the millions of the redeemed into the image of God's Son, and thus to bring many sons to **glory**!

'What? Know ye not that your body is the temple of the Holy Ghost which is in you, which ye have of God, and ye are not your own? For ye are bought with a price: therefore **GLORIFY GOD** in your body, and in your spirit which are God's' (I Cor. 6 vs.19-20).

The people of God are a people of **glory**.

Jesus is going to possess '**a glorious church**, without spot or blemish'. It is this mighty army, charged with the dynamic energies of the **glory** of the exalted, victorious Jesus, that will implement God's Master-Plan for World Evangelism, causing the nations of this planet Earth to **believe** and to **know** that Jesus Christ is both Saviour and Lord to the glory of God the Father!

55. EXPANSION

'He shall have dominion also from sea to sea, and from the river unto the ends of the earth. And blessed be His glorious name for ever: and let the whole earth be filled with His glory'   (Psalm 72 vs. 8 and 19)

'Of the increase of His government and peace there shall be no end, upon the throne of David, and upon His kingdom, to order it, and to establish it with judgment and with justice for henceforth even for ever' (Isaiah 9:7)

God is a God of expansion. It is inherent in His nature. The principle expresses itself in creation – a single seed is sown, but an abundance of fruit is harvested. When a child picks up an acorn he holds a forest in his fist.

The Holy Spirit is continually seeking to impress upon God's people the extreme urgency of the need to expand – spiritually, in terms of Christian growth, and numerically, by way of evangelistic outreach.

The hour is late. The Lord is coming soon. Countless souls are rushing daily into a Christless eternity. Millions of others need the revelation of truth to enlighten them and unite them into the true army of the Lord.

Toward the close of the nineteenth century, Mushidi, the pagan king of Garenganze (later known as Katanga), spoke to Frederick Arnot, the missionary, with sobering truth: **'Monare, you, your book, and your God have come too late for me!'** (Where had the church been those 1,900 years?)

It is much later now, and the need is more desperate. The coming of the Lord is that much nearer. We must, however, proceed in line with God's word and in accordance with divine principles.

Five paradoxical principles of expansion can be traced in the Bible:-
1. Expansion through Persecution
'There was a great persecution against the church . . . and they were all scattered abroad . . . Therefore they that were scattered abroad went everywhere preaching the word' (Acts 8 vs. 1 & 4).

God never permits anything that He cannot use. In this case of the early church, the Lord decided to allow persecution to scatter the members. In wisdom and sovereignty God overruled, and that which Satan intended

150

should destroy the church was in fact used to multiply the church!

Persecution is on the increase. Under the totalitarian rule of godless Communism the church of this century has suffered persecution and martyrdom in many nations. There have been more martyrs for Christ in this sophisticated century than in all the previous centuries of church history put together. Satan persecutes Christians in many other ways apart from the oppression of Communism.

There is not only political persecution, there is ecclesiastical persecution, and social persecution.

History is repeating itself. But, '**so mightily grew the word of God, and prevailed!**' An outstanding example is the church of Dr Yonggi Cho in Seoul, Korea, which now has a membership of over 600,000. In a land once torn apart by war and ravaged by Communism, God has shown how He can implement the principle of expansion through persecution when His people are prepared to be faithful to Him in prayer and fasting. It is then that the gates of hell shall not prevail!

2. Expansion through Separation

The ecumenical movement calls for unity of the churches. Some advocate union with Rome. But God is still saying: '**Come out from among them and be ye separate.**'

Some nominal churches seek to attract the young with discos and dances. But the toys of the world will never attract this generation to the true church of Christ. There is enough dynamic magnetism in the person of the Lord Jesus Christ to attract young people to Himself. But the church must rightly represent Him.

Covetousness of the things of the world can stem the tide of progress amongst God's people. Remember the people of Israel and the sin of Aachan. God's programme for Israel was: '**Expansion**' – '**possess the land**'! But the sin of covetousness in one man hindered the whole nation from fulfilling the divine programme of expansion. That sin had to be uncovered, confessed, judged and cleansed before Israel could know victory again. Judgement must begin in the house of God.

3. Expansion through Restriction.

With this thought we come into deep waters. We touch the mysterious sovereignty of God overruling in circumstances calculated to frustrate His servants and to hinder His purpose. In such an experience we may be misunderstood, misjudged, misrepresented and maligned, but in matchless wisdom and sovereign power God turns the tables to such an extent that more is accomplished than would otherwise have been possible!

What holy frustration the Master felt! '**I have a baptism to fulfil, and how am I straitened till it be accomplished!**' What patience and self control and faith in the ultimate success of His mission!

The people tried to make Him a king by force. Bypassing them, He went on to Calvary; to the searing scourge, to the coronation of thorns, and to that prison of pain, the cross, where He was nailed hand and foot.

What powerful expansion issued from His restrictions! Millions have found a glorious release through His imprisonment. They have received life from His death.

Paul wanted to go to Spain, but he found himself in prison instead. But as a result, we have the Apostle's letters to the churches.

Much of the Bible was written in prison-circumstances, or by exiles and captives: e.g. Ezekiel, Daniel, Jeremiah, Paul, and the Apostle John on Patmos. David composed some of his Psalms while a fugitive fleeing from Saul. Thousands of years later another David – David Brainerd – was expelled unjustly from college. Frustrated because he could not obtain the qualification he deserved, but not embittered, he went as a missionary to the North American Red Indians, where he brought many precious souls to Christ, and laid his frail life down before he was thirty! Yale University, from which he was expelled, is famous today because Brainerd went there!

John Bunyan gave the world his *Pilgrim's Progress* from a Bedford jail, in which he was imprisoned for preaching the gospel. The devil had thought to restrict God's servant and frustrate his call to preach to that generation. Instead, God used Bunyan to speak to his own contemporaries **and** to millions in subsequent generations! In this, we see how God works all things together for good on behalf of His elect, creating expansion out of restriction.

4. Expansion through Renunciation

The true disciples of Christ must exercise self-discipline. We must take up our cross, renounce the world, deny ourselves, and follow Him. Every successful missionary has done this. We must not only forsake our idols, but all those things which are lawful, but not expedient, must be put away or kept under control.

When God called Moses, he had to cast down his rod, the emblem of his livelihood and the symbol of his independence. When Moses took it up again at God's command, it became **'the rod of God in his hand'**. With it he covered Egypt with plagues, subdued the proud Pharaoh, opened the Red Sea, and brought a river of living water from a rock.

Many years ago I heard a prophecy about Scotland. The Lord called upon the sons of the North, and He promised to visit Scotland. That day has now dawned. God is now visiting the North of Scotland in a remarkable way. **But where are the sons of the North?**

The spirit of sacrifice and broken-ness must reign before expansion can fully take place. Those who will lay their lives on the altar for God today, those who will renounce the prospect of worldly advancement, will find themselves involved in God's tremendous programme of expansion in the hour of divine visitation.

5. Expansion through Mortification.

Sadhu Sundar Singh, that great Indian Christian mystic, was travelling with a companion over the frozen heights of the Himalayas. As night drew on they came across a traveller fallen by the mountain path. Sadhu's companion refused to wait: 'I must press on to the next village,' he insisted. But the Sadhu remained with the wounded man, seeking to keep him warm through the bitter night. The heat from the mystic's body kept the man from freezing to death. Likewise did his frail body-heat sustain the Sadhu. When morning light broke, they set off together, struggling over the mountain-pass to the village. As they neared the village they found the frozen corpse of the mystic's companion. In seeking to save his own life, he had lost it. But the Sadhu, in seeking to give his life for another, had, in fact, saved it!

This is precisely what Jesus meant when He said; 'For whosoever will save his life shall lose it; but whosoever shall lose his life for My sake and the gospel's, the same shall save it' (Mark 8 : 35).

The corn of wheat abides alone until it submits to death. Then it lives again, increases, and multiplies. The death of self at the cross; mortification also through the Spirit; and resurrection in newness of life – these constitute God's formula for spiritual expansion.

153

56. GOD IN A BOX!

I came across the following story in the Summer edition of the Slavic Gospel Association Newsletter, *Break Through*. This extract is reproduced by kind permission of the S.G.A.

"When the woman entered the shop, she walked with a bit of a limp, but her stride was firm. The patrons and the shopkeeper could tell that she was not from their parts – her clothes were even more primitive than what most people in this village wore, and the cloth bag she carried was tattered and looked like something between a suitcase and a grocery bag.

"'I would like to speak to someone who knows everything that this shop carries,' the woman said to the shopkeeper.

"'What do you want?' he asked, a tenor of suspicion gracing his speech.

"She looked straight into the shopkeeper's eyes with an intensity that was disarming. 'You have probably already realised that I am not from this part of the country. I have been sent as a representative from my village far to the north-east of here. I have travelled over 1,000 kilometres. Now please help me, sir. I am looking for a church in a box.'

"The shopkeeper met the woman's simple face with an expression that was completely blank.

"'What did you say?' he asked.

"'A church in a box,' she answered, and then added, 'a box made of wood, I suppose.'

"'This way,' the shopkeeper said, and motioned her toward a counter. He reached down to a corner shelf and pulled out a decoratively carved wooden church. 'Our nicest one,' he said as he held it up for her to see. But to his dismay, the woman shook her head.

"'No,' she said. 'That's not it. I want a real church, one with heart and soul and power. In our village we have heard that there is such a church, and that it is in a box. I have come all this way to see if you have what we need. It's a church, but it's in a box.'

"The shopkeeper wasn't sure what he had here – had she lost her mind? 'These are all the churches we have,' he said, showing her a few souvenir-type onion-dome churches made of wood, glass, ceramic, even metal.

"'This church,' said the woman, 'can be turned on and off with a button. It can tell us what God thinks and says, and there are beautiful

154

voices, people singing.

'Have you anything like that?'

'Ah' said the shopkeeper, 'electricity!' He paused and wondered, could she be talking about a radio?

"He directed the visitor to the electronics department and she looked at their selection of shortwave radios. They didn't have much to choose from, yet the woman was amazed.

'Yes, I think this is what we want!' she said with a sense of triumph in her voice. 'This is what we need in our village. This is what I have come for!'

'And with that statement, the woman made her purchase and walked out of the shop with her 'Church in a box' and began her long journey back to her village."

As incredible as this story sounds, a Slavic Gospel Association missionary heard about it while visiting Christians in the Soviet Union. They told our missionary that they were in the remote Siberian village to which this woman took that shortwave radio. Now, because of her journey to find the church in the box, and because of God's work in the hearts of people, there is a thriving church in that distant village."

Is your God 'in a box?' Do you ever tune in to hear His inner voice? Do you increase the volume of your witness, so that others can hear the good news of the gospel?

Or is your God in the silent coffin of your own indifference? Nobody knows about His love by means of your testimony. Nobody hears from you that Jesus is alive. You 'jam' the 'radio-waves' of potential contacts for Christ with all other kinds of trivial conversation.

Clear the air. Turn up the volume. Let the whole world know that Jesus is a wonderful Saviour!

57. MAKING A SOCIAL IMPACT

Is the church making any impact on society? Does your life really make any difference to the cultural structure of your generation? Do you exert any influence at all upon the people in your locality, or upon the nation and its pattern of life-styles? Are the people of God really the salt of the earth and the light of the world that Jesus described?

The deteriorating quality of life in the nation could cause Christians to feel that they are not making much impact at all. The situation should drive the church to her knees in prayer. God has an answer to the obdurate attitude of the ungodly. He alone can heal the sickness of a dying society. But the Lord is looking for the willing co-operation of His people with His great purpose of national revival and restoration. 'A revolutionized church is the key to renewal in the nation.'

In his book, '*Great Revivals*', Colin Whittaker points out that '. . . In the 18th Century things were even worse than today – a large proportion of the population suffered from habitual alcoholism. Then revival led by men such as Whitefield and the Wesleys changed the lives of tens upon tens of thousands of people. This awakening directly prepared the way for the abolition of slavery and the creation of missionary and Bible societies, Sunday Schools, dispensaries for the sick, also benevolent societies for support of widows, orphans and the poor – the precursors of our present-day children's homes and our state health and social security services.'

When God moves in such a mighty way, His Spirit makes a lasting impact on society and history!

Whittaker continues: 'In the 19th Century another revival made a spiritual impact on Ireland . . . Judges throughout Ulster in 1860 often found themselves with no cases to try. At that time crime in Coleraine was reported to be almost non-existent and in Co.Antrim it was noted that there were no prisoners in police custody and no crimes were reported.'

Surely God can solve the complex problems that baffle politicians?

A more up-to-date cause for encouragement and hope comes from the good news of the *Teen Challenge Rehabilitation Centre for Men* at Gorslas near Penygroes, Dyfed. This inter-denominational arm of the church is making a social impact in the nation.

156

To make a mark upon the materialistic presuppositions of an unbelieving world seems a daunting task. But all the intellectual darkness in the world cannot quench one glowing light. Truth is stronger than error. Light is more powerful than darkness.

It is not only the humanistic philosophies and religious indifference of modern man that require the light of the gospel. In less sophisticated parts of the world, thousands of people have still not heard of Jesus and His love for them. Who is going to make an impact on them?

In their challenging and enlightening little volume, *Nine Worlds to Win*, Floyd McLung and Kalafi Moala reveal some startling statistics:

'In North America, the Zuni and the Hopi peoples of the Southwest remain amongst the most unreached tribal peoples on earth. Mexico has over 400 unreached tribal groups, and in the Amazon Basin there are dozens of groups who have had no contact with the outside world at all. In the Chittagong Hill Tracts of Bangladesh, the Chakmas, the Mogs and the Tripuraies remain some of the most unreached and restricted-access tribal peoples in the world. There are also many unreached tribal groups in Irian Jaya, Indonesia, Burma, Thailand, and in other areas of Asia.'

Now you know about them – what are you going to do for them?

Nine Worlds to Win contains encouraging news of Christian expansion in other nations. Information from the Third World throws into sharp relief the failure of the Western World to compete with the sacrificial efforts of the underprivileged countries in terms of missionary outreach. For example:

'At the present growth-rate there will be 100,000 missionaries sent out from Third World countries alone by the year 2,000. The number of North American Protestant missionaries has increased by 80% in the last decade, growing from 37,056 to 67,242. This surge of missions activity has resulted in unprecedented growth in the church . . . About 14,000 people are converted to Christ daily. There are 1,500,000 worship centres and congregations scattered around the globe and 1,600 new local churches are started every day. One group in Brazil is starting *8 new churches every hour!*'

There's no answer to that.

58. THE PERSECUTED CHURCH

The church of Jesus Christ is no stranger to persecution. The centuries have run red with rivers of martyrs' blood. Smoke from the fires of persecution has blackened the record of justice and fair-mindedness throughout history. Imprisonment, deprivation, discrimination, torture, grief and death have stalked the footsteps of the kindest and noblest of people. Why? Because they were Christians, following the example of Jesus their Master.

Jesus made no secret of the treatment His disciples could expect. 'If they have persecuted me,' He said, 'they will also persecute you.' Unbelieving and hostile men hounded Jesus to the cross. And many of His followers have received bitter persecution from sections of their communities in the same blind spirit of prejudice.

'In this world you will have trouble,' predicted Jesus. 'But take heart! I have overcome the world.' It was with that buoyant spirit of hope and victorious confidence that His followers faced cruel persecutions and won a martyr's crown! For the first three centuries of the Christian era political persecution was relentless. Rome regarded the church as a threat to government, simply because Christians recognised the kingship of Jesus and consequently could not pay homage or give total allegiance to an Emperor claiming deity for himself. Thousands of Christians became a spectacle in the arena. They met death with courage, whether thrown to the lions, burned in oil, crucified or killed with the sword. The blood of the martyrs became the seed of the church. The devil has never been able to prevent the harvest growing from that precious seed of devotion to Christ.

Despite all opposition, the church of Christ has grown and expanded geographically and historically. Jesus has kept His promise: 'I will build my church and the gates of hell shall not prevail against it'.

Yet, today persecution still persists. In many countries oppressive political regimes and prejudiced religious factions assiduously persecute Christians. More martyrs have died for Christ in the twentieth century than in all the previous centuries of church history put together. Still the church continues to grow and prosper numerically and spiritually. Satan cannot destroy it. It is God's universal instrument of aggression against the powers of darkness. It is His vehicle of spiritual government and it expresses His glory in every generation. It speaks His word to the nations with prophetic power and apostolic authority. It is the corporate international incarnation of the risen Christ, the habitation of God through the Spirit. It takes His love to the lost, His healing to the sick, and His truth to those yearning for reality. The church of God expresses His grace and demonstrates His power, proving to this planet that the Lord Jesus Christ is alive!

What methods are employed to persecute Christians today? Here is an extract from a pamphlet prepared some years ago by Dr. D. Rogers:-

'Vasili Shipilov is 65. He has been in prisons and psychiatric hospitals in the Soviet Union for 47 years. In the 1920's the farm belonging to Vasili's family was confiscated. The family was deported to Siberia as forced labour on a collective farm which was encircled by barbed wire. The crops failed. The family was starving. His father could not feed the family and was shot dead while trying to get out in search of food. His mother soon died of starvation.

'Some monks nearby cared for Vasili and taught him to read and write. He joined the clandestine seminary but was arrested when the secret police discovered it. In prison he was ordained by fellow prisoners who were orthodox priests. For his pastoral care of the other prisoners, and for performing baptisms, he was given a 25-year extension to his sentence but was amnestied in 1949 in the celebrations of the Soviet victory. He used his brief freedom to care for the starving population of a large area in central Siberia. At great risk to himself, he often tried to supply the needs of the 20,000 prisoners in a local labour camp by collecting berries in the forests. No other food was available. For a year he preached and cared for the sick and dying but was arrested in 1950 as an anti-Soviet.

'Labelled "schizophrenic" at Moscow's Serbsky Institute for Forensic Psychiatry, he was sentenced to indefinite confinement in institutions for the criminally insane. He spent many years in Prison Psychiatric Hospitals, first at Kazan, and later at Sychovka near Smolensk. There the officer in charge told him:- "If you don't give up your faith you will stay here – unless they kill you." Doctors told him:- "No-one knows about you. No-one will ever find you. Anything can happen to you."

'In 1977 he was transferred to the closed wing of an ordinary psychiatric hospital near Krasnoyarsk in Siberia. He has suffered from dangerously large doses of insulin even though he is not diabetic. He has sustained a severe skull fracture and has developed epilepsy. He is repeatedly beaten for crossing himself and fasting. He is in a section for incurables but is apparently still expected to fulfil a work-norm or be punished. He was officially declared discharged in 1979 but he is still there. No place could be found for him in a Soviet old people's home. The state refused to let Vasili live with a Soviet host who offered to open his home to him.

"A fellow prisoner, who has now emigrated, remembers Vasili well. *"He is a small man, always very sad. Twice a day he would pray fervently for those responsible for the suffering."*

Remember Vasili, and pray for the persecuted church world-wide.

PART V

PRAYER

Items 59 – 65

59. THE DOORWAY INTO THE NEW DIMENSION

You enter God's new dimension for your life when you are born again. At that dynamic moment you become a new creation in Christ, and the old sins, concepts and ideas are removed from your record by the power of the blood of Jesus. In one miraculous sweep you are transferred from the kingdom of darkness into the kingdom of God's dear Son. Instantly you become a child of God with all the rights, privileges and responsibilities of a citizen of Heaven. The regenerating Spirit of God starts to take control of your life, producing new aspirations and aims for living. Regeneration is the doorway into the new dimension.

God's new gift of eternal life to you must be sustained and maintained in the way that He has provided so that you will grow more like Jesus, and your Christian life will develop.

Feed your new life on the word of God. Faith will be generated in your heart and manifested in your deeds. The Spirit of God will lead you into avenues of truth and revelation. He will give you vision and victory.

Like the early patriarch and prophet Enoch, you will be able to walk with God, cultivating a life of fellowship with Him in prayer. As your relationship with God develops, you will become more and more sensitive to His voice, and more and more conscious of His constant presence. He will share His heart with you, and you will delight yourself in the Lord. The doorway of the new birth must inevitably lead to the pathway of prayer.

Personal prayer will cultivate your fellowship with God. praying with others will bring His blessing into your church and your community. Prayer produces both power and purity. It supplies both the desire and the dynamic energy for evangelism. Prayer is the hallmark of new-dimension living. The supernatural is a way of life to the praying Christian.

F.J. Huegel wrote: *'It has often been said that prayer is the greatest force in the universe. This is no exaggeration. It will bear constant repetition. In this atomic age when forces are being released that stagger the thought and imagination of man, it is well to remember that prayer transcends all other forces.'*

The forces of darkness are so subtly strong in our land that the tide of iniquity can only be stemmed by united prayer. Victory belongs to Christ and His church. But fervent united prayer is the way to achieve it. United intercession in the Spirit is a spiritual inspiration to the individual Christian soldier.

Our nation needs to be evangelized. Consider the timely words of T.A. Hegre: *'If the church would only awaken to her responsibility of intercession, we could well evangelize the world in a short time. It is not God's plan that the world be merely evangelized ultimately. It should be evangelized in every generation. There should be a constant gospel witness in every corner of the world so that no sinner need close his eyes in death without hearing the gospel, the good news of salvation through Christ.'*

Prayer is the energising air you breathe in the life of the new dimension!

60. THE PRELUDE TO REVIVAL

In his study entitled *The Role of Prayer in Spiritual Awakening*, the great Church historian of revivals, Dr J. Edwin Orr, outlines the appalling state of the churches in America following the American Revolution, and explains how this situation was reversed by intense, prolonged, united prayer.

He quoted the words of Dr A.T. Pierson: *'There has never been a spiritual awakening in any country or locality that did not begin in united prayer.'*

This kind of praying is the prelude to revival. Dr. Orr reminds us of the roots of some of the great movements of prayer which issued in revival. A Scottish Presbyterian Minister, John Erskine of Edinburgh, being burdened with the desperate need for concerted prayer by the churches, wrote a pamphlet entitled: *Pleading with the people of Scotland and elsewhere to unite in prayer for the revival of religion.*

Erskine sent a copy of his treatise to the great theologian Jonathan Edwards in New England, USA.

Edwards was deeply moved and took up the theme in a book to which he gave the impressive title: *A humble attempt to promote explicit agreement and visible union of all God's people in extraordinary prayer for the revival of religion and the advancement of Christ's kingdom.*

Following this, there was a revival of prayer in the USA. The prayer movement had begun in Great Britain through William Carey, Andrew Fuller, John Sutcliffe and others. It was called the Union of Prayer, and in 1792 the results of this intensive praying were seen when the second Great Awakening began and swept Great Britain.

Jonathan Edwards' exhaustive and rather quaint title for his book contains three vital principles which must be included in the prelude to any revival. These three factors are: **Explicit Agreement; Visible Union of Christians**; and **Extraordinary Prayer Times.**

When God's people sink their denominational differences in a common concern for the salvation of the lost; when they reach explicit agreement to make this burden their top priority; and when this agreement is visibly expressed to the world and to the powers of darkness in terms of sacrificial times of extraordinary, sustained, united prayer – then the stirring music of the prelude to revival will begin to resound throughout the nations.

Satan knows the power of a praying nation. That is why the devil will try in every way to divide Christian from Christian, and to pre-occupy believers with secondary matters, in order to divert the churches from the vital business of united prayer.

'No one is a firmer believer in the power of prayer than the devil' wrote Guy H. King – **'not that he practises it – but he suffers from it!'**

United intercessory prayer is the top priority for every church. Don't leave it too late. In his volume, *The Master Secrets of Prayer*, Cameron V. Thompson includes this sobering and poignant passage:

'One poor soul entered the school of prayer after his arrival in hell. He asked for relief from his agony; it was refused. He asked that a beggar warn his brothers; he was turned down. He was praying to Abraham, a man; he could not locate God. He dared not ask to get out; he plainly knew that he was beyond all hope. Prayerless on earth, unanswered in hell, he suffers on as the man who tried to learn to pray too late.'

Revival will follow genuine, united prayer. Intense prayer. Fervent prayer. Holy-Ghost prayer.

Don't leave it too late.

61. ARE YOU RECEIVING ME?

God is a speaking God. He is continually transmitting truth. He speaks in the majesty of creation: 'The heavens declare the glory of God.' He speaks through the Bible – God's revelation to mankind. He is constantly pleading with sinners in the loving tones of the gospel. He declares His word through apostles, prophets and preachers world-wide. Most comprehensively of all, God has spoken through the life, death, resurrection and ascended ministry of His exalted Son. It is as if the whole universe has united its resources to transmit the divine message to men. But who is listening to God?

If the ruler of a great nation were to broadcast an urgent message to the people, and yet receive little or no response to the declaration, it could be assumed that the nation had rejected the statement of the sovereign. Anarchy would loom on the horizon.

By their indifference to the words of God, men and women are indicating that they think they can do without His advice and instruction. International chaos and social disorder are the consequences. Personal confusion and individual frustration are the results.

Even within the circle of God's own people in the church, there so often seems to be an unwillingness (or perhaps an inability) to hear clearly what God is saying to us today. This problem is, of course, nothing new. In His correspondence to the seven churches of Asia, dictated in the first century by the risen Lord to His servant John, this exhortation appears seven times: 'He who has an ear let him hear what the Spirit says to the churches'.

There is never anything wrong with the divine transmitter. It is always in good working order. For centuries God has unfailingly sent out His word to the whole of mankind. History has trembled at the thunder of His law from Sinai, sinners have wept in adoring wonder as they have caught the whisper of His love from Calvary; and the church has thrilled to the vocal expressions of His Lordship flowing from the throne of His exalted manhood and sovereign headship. Jesus Christ is Lord! He is still speaking by His Spirit today.

But do you have an ear to hear? In other words, is your spiritual radio tuned to Him? Are you receiving the message? It seems clear to me that if the whole church were receiving the whole message, there would be a whole lot of difference!

The transmission of divine revelation from the heart of God to the realm of mankind is a matter for God's sovereignty. But the reception of that truth is a matter of human responsibility. If our receivers are not in good working order, it is our responsibility to take action to get them repaired. How can this be done?

Hardness of heart can prevent the fruitful entry of His word. Jesus also spoke about materialism choking the growing seed of God's word. We can take action to deal with these matters. The real secret in being able to receive divine revelation consists in true preparation of heart. In this neglected spiritual procedure, prayer and fasting are vital factors.

Often people forget that prayer does not mean asking God for things all the time. In true prayer we do not do all the talking. Prayer means listening to God as well as talking to Him. It includes meditation as much as supplication.

Fasting indicates that we are abandoned to divine resources; that we can find no remedy in the energies of the flesh; that we have denied ourselves the measures of natural strength in order to trust completely in the grace and power of the all-sufficient God.

'I humbled my soul with fasting', cried the Psalmist.

Prayer and fasting will prepare the heart, and repair the spiritual radio-receiver. Then you will hear the still small voice of the Spirit. And no longer will God have to ask: 'Are you receiving Me?'

62. THIRST

Thirst is something we all understand. We have all been thirsty. In the physical sense, thirst is the sensation of dryness in the mouth indicating our need to drink. In the emotional realm, thirst is an insistent craving, a deep yearning for satisfaction.

The purest thirst is a thirst for God. An inward intense longing that only God can fulfil. David yearned for God with an unusual fervency: *'As the deer pants for streams of water, so my soul pants for you O God. My soul thirsts for God, for the living God.' (Psalm 42:1,2).* Wouldn't you like to long for God like that?

The major problem today is an absence of thirst for God. Even His own people do not seek for God with an intensity matching the ardent yearnings of the Psalmist. We are thirsty. But we are not thirsting for God.

Jesus is the great Thirst-Quencher. He can meet every need. Satisfy every longing. Fulfil the deepest and the most intense yearnings of the human heart. Your total personality can find complete wholeness in Jesus. He understands your emotional needs. He cares about your financial problems. He hurts when you are hurting. He feels the pain you suffer. He knows when you are sad and lonely. He shares your joy when you are happy. With an aching heart Jesus longs for you to be thirsty for Him.

On the last and greatest day of the Feast of Tabernacles, Jesus stood and cried out in a loud voice: 'If anyone is **thirsty** let him come to me and drink.' There are two points which are of great interest in this incident.

First, there is the deep intensity of Jesus conveyed by the use of strong Greek language. When Jesus called out to the people, He did so out of an intense suffering. The Greek suggests the idea of a **shriek**, an agonising cry.

Jesus had watched the ritual as the Jews re-enacted their ceremonies with the water, celebrating miraculous events in their history. But nobody knew that the Rock which gushed with water in the wilderness, stood now in their midst. *'For that Rock was Christ.'*

The priests had brought water from the Pool of Siloam, followed by a procession of festive Jews. But nobody recognised the true Fountain of Living Waters.

Jesus must have experienced the pain of frustration as he observed them involved so intricately with ritual, when they could have had reality! No wonder he cried out with such terrible intensity.

The second factor of interest is the day on which Jesus issued his great invitation to the thirsty: *'Let him come to me and drink.'* After the crowd had spent seven or eight days of festive eating and drinking, Jesus stood up and cried out with passion: 'If any one is still thirsty, let him come to me and drink.' In other words: 'If there is anyone who is dissatisfied with mere ritual and who longs for reality – let him come to me. If any one is conscious that an abundance of material festivities still leaves an aching hunger and thirst in his soul – then let him come to me – and drink.'

Before you can drink of the Spirit, you must come to Jesus. But when you do come to him, you will discover that he really is the great Thirst-Quencher.

63. POWER AND AUTHORITY

POWER IS THE ABILITY OR CAPACITY TO TAKE EFFECTIVE ACTION. AUTHORITY IS THE RIGHT TO EXERCISE POWER.

The gospels are full of demonstrations of power and authority by the Lord Jesus. He displayed authority over men, angels, demons, disease, death, darkness, sin, fear, distance, tradition, storms and Satan. He could walk upon the waves of the sea, command the wind to be still, turn water into wine, wither a tree in a matter of hours and feed thousands from the meagre resources of a lad's lunch.

The staggering fact is this: Jesus said: 'I tell you the truth, anyone who has faith in me will do what I have been doing. He will do even *greater* things than these, because I am going to the Father. And I will do whatever you ask in my name, so that the Son may bring glory to the Father.'

Anyone with faith in Jesus can do greater miracles than He did. Why? There are three reasons. First, *true faith in Jesus implies the recognition of His authority, and the reception of delegated authority from Him.* This question of delegated authority is made very clear in the dialogue between Jesus and the centurion who asked Him to heal his servant. When Jesus responded to the appeal by offering to visit the centurion's home, the soldier replied: 'Just say the word and my servant will be healed.' The centurion understood the principle of delegated authority. His authority over his soldiers was the result of his own submission to the throne. Men obeyed his commands because he spoke with delegated authority from the Emperor.

The centurion recognised this principle in the life of Jesus who expressed the delegated authority of an invisible throne over disease, and whose word carried authority through time and space. It was this quality of faith that astonished Jesus.

Christians should understand that Jesus has delegated to them authority to do miracles in His name. A dynamic faith exercising delegated authority is the first step toward doing great things.

The second reason for the promise of Jesus is: *'Because I am going to the Father.'* Jesus went to the Father through the avenues of crucifixion, resurrection and exaltation, and having reached the throne, He sent the Holy Spirit. But Jesus did not take these steps merely as an individual, but rather as the Cosmic Man, the Representative Man, the Federal Head of a new and elevated humanity, and He sent His Spirit to make His work effective in the lives of believers.

There is a third reason for the stupendous claim of Christ: *'And I will do whatever you ask in my name.'* Obviously Jesus made His promise in the context of a life of prayer. His miracle-workers will be those living in unbroken fellowship with Himself.

The matter is now crystal-clear. You can do tremendous exploits for God, provided that you are submissive to His throne and qualified to exercise His authority; also that you are, by faith, completely identified with the steps Jesus took to the throne; further, that you are filled with the Holy Ghost and living in His power; and finally that you are experiencing a life of prayer and fellowship with the Lord.

After His resurrection, Jesus came to His disciples and said: 'All *authority* in heaven and earth has been given to me. *Therefore*, go and make disciples of all nations.'

Delegated authority, issuing in a life of great things for God, is the only way to fulfil the command of Christ!

64. DANGER! MAN AT WORK

During His earthly life Jesus was a busy Man. After recording many wonderful events and miracles in the life of Jesus, the Apostle John wrote at the close of his gospel: *'Jesus did many other things as well. If every one of them were written down, I suppose that even the whole world would not have room for the books that would be written.'*

The most energetic and zealous business-man jetting his way across the world and using the most sophisticated electronic equipment, could not compare with the work-load of Jesus as He moved in the power of the Spirit to carry out the Father's will and purpose for mankind. Jesus was a busy Man.

Since His ascension He has been busier still! The sphere of His operational activities has extended beyond the borders of Israel to cover the whole universe. He guides the destiny of the church, controls the political and military strategies of the nations, overrules the machinations of ungodly men and hostile demons, and directs His Spirit throughout the world for the ingathering of the elect in salvation, and the blessing of His church in revival. All this dynamic activity spells *danger* for the kingdom of darkness!

Jesus is the one Mediator between God and men. He is our Advocate with the Father, our Defence against Satan, and our Intercessor at the right hand of God. He is the Inheritor of all the vast empire of God, the Ruler of kingdoms visible and invisible, the Saviour of mankind, and the Head of the church which is His body. At the cross He culminated a sinless life in a perfect sacrifice of atoning death, bringing complete satisfaction to the heart of His Father. In His nail-pierced hand, the crucified, risen, ascended, exalted and glorified Christ holds the sceptre of universal and eternal dominion, exercising His supremacy and superintendency over every realm of God's kingdom. Jesus is a busy Man!

Whilst there are some responsibilities which are exclusively His, the Lord Jesus nevertheless involves His church with many of His ascension-activities. He incorporates His people into various aspects of His elevated work. By the Spirit of God the redeemed are linked to the Head of the body. Thus, millions of men and women in every nation of the world share the risen quality of His life, and the exalted privileges of their enthroned Lord. This international involvement of mankind with the eternal purpose of God increases the threat of *danger* to the kingdom of darkness.

One of the most effective spheres of co-operation with the Lord is, of course, the activity of intercession. This is a work very close to God's heart. Jesus ever lives to make intercession for us. The Apostle Paul defines the Holy Ghost as the Spirit of Intercession.

It was my privilege to attend Scotland's Day of Prayer for the Nation, held in the Scottish Exhibition Centre at Glasgow. We left home at 8.00 am, returning fourteen hours later at 10.00 pm. What a thrill to join with one thousand Christians whose one desire was to see God glorified in revival power in Scotland! The unique blessing of God was on that gathering as denominational differences paled into insignificance in the light of the presence of the risen Lord by the power of His Spirit.

All aspects of national life were discussed through the phases of the day, and periods of fervent intercession followed. How inspiring it was to witness children praying under the evident anointing of the Holy Ghost, interceding for their generation and taking authority over the powers of darkness which were afflicting many of their school chums through the dark avenues of occult practices!

As we prayed on that notable day, there came a time when I felt in my spirit that the forces of darkness were shuddering under the impact of the united prayer of the church. Demons cowered in dismay as they were forced to relinquish their grip upon our nation.

Colin Urquhart taught us a chorus: *'There's going to be a revival in our land.'* I now know, without a shadow of a doubt, that those words are true.

Let's share God's great burden in the Christian activity of united intercession for revival. Let the devil discern the invisible sign which describes the spiritual function of united prayer:

'DANGER! Men at work.'

65. SPIRITUAL DYNAMITE

'Prayer and Fasting'
Matthew 6 : 5-18

The instructions of Jesus to His disciples concerning their prayer life are penetratingly clear in the words of the New International Version of the Bible: 'But **when you pray**, do not be like the hypocrites, for they love to pray standing in the synagogues and on the street corners to be seen by men. I tell you the truth, they have received their reward in full. **When you pray**, go into your room, close the door and pray to your Father, who is unseen. Then your Father, who sees what is done in secret, will reward you. And **when you pray**, do not keep on babbling like pagans, for they think they will be heard because of their many words. Do not be like them, for your Father knows what you need before you ask Him.'

'**When** you pray . . .' said Jesus; not '**If** you pray . . .'. Obviously, Jesus expected His disciples to follow His own example in the matter of prayer. '**When you pray** . . . **Pray sincerely** . . . do not be like the hypocrites . . .'. **Pray secretly** . . . 'go into your room, close the door, and pray . . .'. **Pray sensibly** . . . 'do not keep on babbling like pagans . . .'.

With equal expectation, Jesus went on to say: '**When you fast**, do not look sombre as the hypocrites do, for they disfigure their faces to show men they are fasting. I tell you the truth, they have received their reward in full. But **when you fast**, put oil on your head and wash your face, so that it will not be obvious to men that you are fasting, but only to your Father, who is unseen; and your Father, who sees what is done in secret, will reward you.'

It is evident that Jesus regarded fasting as something joyously uplifting, not at all the ordeal that most Christians think it to be.

Prayer with fasting is God's way for the church to receive His choicest blessings. It is the key to **revival**. It is spiritual **dynamite**.

In his book about fasting and prayer, entitled *Atomic Power with God*, Rev. Franklin Hall relates how the holy Spirit led him into his first revival meeting in July, 1932. He knew only three families in the Oklahoma oil town of Nowata. One of these families believed and practised fasting and prayer.

He continues: 'Together we prayed and fasted ahead of time for the meeting that we knew God was going to give us there. The foundation was properly laid for a revival, and a revival we certainly did have! There was no building big enough to take care of the crowd, so we secured three acres of ground and had an open-air meeting. People packed the place out from the first service on. We kept building seats and the crowd continued to increase every evening. People gathered from all over North-eastern Oklahoma and South-eastern Kansas for the meetings. Scores of people were healed of all types of afflictions. One lady who had been in a car-wreck with broken ribs was carried to the services on pillows; she was instantly healed. A deaf and dumb boy was instantly healed. A man who could not lift his arm and had been paralysed was also healed; many more received notable healings. Folk were under the power of His Spirit. Many were baptised in the Holy Spirit. Within three months from the time we started the meeting, **we built a church and got it paid for**, so the people could continue to have a place to worship in truth and in Spirit. **All of these results were traced directly to prayer and fasting.'**

God did those mighty things through **one family** who fasted and prayed.

What would He accomplish if the whole church were to unite in prayer and fasting for ten days?

PART VI

PRAISE AND WORSHIP

Items 66 – 70

66. THE SONG OF MOSES

The Apostle John, with Spirit-inspired insight into things to come, was granted a glimpse into the glory:

'And I saw as it were a sea of glass mingled with fire: and them that had gotten the victory over the beast, and over his image, and over his mark, and over the number of his name, stand on the sea of glass, having the harps of God. And they sing the song of Moses the servant of God, and the song of the Lamb, saying, "Great and marvellous are thy works, Lord God Almighty; just and true are thy ways, thou King of Nations. Who shall not fear thee, O Lord, and glorify thy name? For thou only art holy: for all nations shall come and worship before thee; for thy judgements are made manifest"' (Rev. 15 vs. 2-4).

Moses – that comprehensive genius – legislator, administrator, leader, prophet, and judge of Israel, was also an inspired poet and composer.

Psalm 90 was written by Moses. Two other songs of Moses are preserved in Exodus 15 and Deuteronomy 32. Their mighty themes and majestic words are in sharp contrast to the trivial and superficial lyrics of modern music.

These three songs of Moses constitute an inspiring anthem, the dominant theme of which is the revelation of the glory and sovereignty of the Eternal God. **'He hath triumphed gloriously!'** (Ex. 15 vs. 1).

The voice of Moses has been silent for over 3,400 years, but it is his Spirit-inspired song that is destined to be sung by the triumphant Tribulation martyrs standing by the fiery sea of glass in glory. The redemptive themes are embraced and incorporated into an exultant anthem entitled 'The Song of Moses, the servant of God, and the Song of the Lamb'. In heaven, priorities are corrected, and everything is seen in proper perspective. Moses slips into the minor key: 'Moses the **bond-servant** of God'; whilst the victorious martyr-choir exult in the dominant-major theme of Eternity: **'The Lamb'**! 'The Lamb is **all** the glory in Immanuel's Land'.

F. H. Rawley, the hymnist, has captured the scene in verse:
I will sing the wondrous story, Of the Christ Who died for me;
How He Left His home in glory, For the Cross on Calvary.
Yes, I'll sing the wondrous story, Of the Christ Who died for me;
Sing it with the saints in glory, **Gathered by the crystal sea.'**

This thought in Revelation 15 vs. 2 of the triumphant throng praising God beside the sea, is clearly parallel to the experience of the joyful children of Israel singing praises to the Lord following the destruction of the Egyptians at the Red Sea (Ex. 14 vs. 30-31 and Ex. 15 vs. 1-21).

Both companies are redeemed by blood and by power. To both companies the Lord grants a victorious experience. Both are seen praising the Lord exultantly in song. They all acknowledge the sovereignty of God, and give Him all the glory (Ex. 15; Rev. 15).

The redeemed of the Lord commence their song of praise on earth, and they climax it in heaven.

The redemptive work of God generates revelation which inspires the song of praise.

There is an **understanding**, a measure of appreciation, concerning the God of redemption, issuing in true praise.

Rev. W. F. Bryan, of Ohio, points out: 'To be acceptable to God, praise must spring from **an awareness of God** and be directed to Him.'

The children of Israel at the Red Sea, viewing the corpses of their enemies, had this awareness. Let us consider Israel's awareness in more detail:

1. **An awareness of God Who is glorious in triumph**. 'I will sing unto the Lord, for He hath **triumphed gloriously**: the horse and his rider hath he thrown into the sea.' (Ex. 15 vs. 1).

'Thus the Lord saved Israel that day out of the hands of the Egyptians; and **Israel saw** the Egyptians dead upon the sea shore. And Israel **saw** that great work which the Lord did upon the Egyptians' (Ex. 14 vs. 30-31).

Israel **saw** something. They had **VISION**.

They had vision, and hence an **understanding**, an awareness, of the absolute triumph of the Lord over all their enemies. Everything that had threatened them had been dealt with completely by the sovereign hand of the Almighty.

Do you have such an awareness? Our Lord is **glorious** in **triumph**. At Calvary he defeated all the powers of darkness. In His resurrection he defeated death. In His ascension he led a multitude of captives, expressing His Lordship through every spiritual region of time and eternity. In His exaltation to the Throne, His absolute supremacy was manifested. One day there will be a **universal** recognition and declaration concerning His glorious triumph: '**Every** knee should bow . . . every tongue should confess that Jesus Christ is Lord, to the glory of God the Father' (Phil. 2 vs. 10-11).

All things are under His nail-pierced feet and He is the head **over all things** to the church which is His body.

A spontaneous song of praise will rise from our hearts when we have this awareness of a Lord Who is glorious in triumph!

Moses and the children of Israel had also:

2. **An awareness of God Who is glorious in power.** 'Thy right hand, O Lord, is become **glorious in power**' (Ex. 15 vs. 6).

God is omnipotent. He is the Almighty Lord! The Apostle John heard the numberless throng thundering this tremendous truth through the arches of eternity: 'And I heard as it were the voice of a great multitude, and as the voice of many waters, and as the voice of mighty thunderings, saying, ALLELUIA: for the LORD GOD OMNIPOTENT reigneth' (Rev. 19 vs. 6).

God is **glorious in power.** His power is evident in the created universe; in the great galaxies of outer space, the fiery sun, the silver moon, the orbiting planets, the mighty sea, the fruitful earth, the tiny atom, the multitude of creatures – and in man – the crown of His creation.

But God's power is not like a firework that sparkles gaudily for a moment and then fizzles out into nothingness. He not only brought the universe into being by His creative word, but He still **sustains** it and **upholds** it by the word of His power.

He is the great **Provider.** 'Thou openest thine hand, and satisfiest the desire of every living thing' (Ps. 145 vs. 16). He is **glorious in His power** to satisfy every need and every desire in every realm of His creation. Surely such a God can meet **your** need?

The triumphs that Jesus won are not temporary victories. They are eternal!

Because the Lord is **glorious in triumph**, He has defeated every foe. But because He is **glorious in power**, He is able to exploit and employ His triumphs continually and to communicate, as gracious **gifts** to the **believer**, the victories of Christ!

'Now thanks be unto God, which **always causeth us to triumph** in Christ' (II Cor. 2 vs. 14).

'But thanks be to God, which **giveth us the victory through our Lord Jesus Christ**' (I Cor. 15 vs. 57).

God's people with Moses also experienced:

3. **An awareness of God Who is glorious in holiness.** 'Who is like unto thee . . . **glorious in holiness,** fearful in praises, doing wonders?' (Ex. 15 vs. 11) God is **unique.** There is none like Him. He is the wonder-working Lord – fearful in **praises.** He is **glorious in holiness.** Therefore His redemptive triumphs and mighty power have certain holy aims in view.

(i) His power has a **moral** purpose: 'Thou in thy mercy hast led forth the people which thou hast redeemed: thou hast guided them in thy strength unto **thy holy habitation**' (Ex. 15 vs. 13). Holiness is the goal.

(ii) God's power has also a **spiritual** purpose: 'All the inhabitants of Canaan shall melt away. Fear and dread shall fall upon them; . . . till thy people pass over, O Lord, . . . which thou hast purchased. Thou shalt bring them in and plant them in the mountain of **thine inheritance**' (Ex. 15 vs. 16-17).

God's spiritual purpose in bringing His people out of the bondage of the world is to cause them to strike dread into the hearts of every opposing force. This demands a life of faith and spirituality. God intends ultimately to bring His people in; and to establish them in the place of His inheritance on the high and holy hill of the Lord.

(iii) God's power has an **eternal** purpose. God is eternal in His own nature and person. Moses understood this: 'From everlasting to everlasting thou art God' (Ps. 90 vs. 2). God's plans were laid in the eternities past. He outworks His purpose in the realm of time, moving inexorably toward the consummation of His purpose in the eternities yet unborn.

'Thou shalt bring them in and plant them in the mountain of thine inheritance, **in the place O Lord which thou hast made for thee to dwell in – in the Sanctuary, O Lord**, which thy hands have established. The Lord shall reign for ever and ever' (Ex. 15 vs. 17-18).

The faith and insight of Moses leaped over the boundaries of time into the eternal ages. He saw more than the promised land of an earthly Canaan. He had a vision of the Sanctuary of God where the Lord sits as Priest and King upon a throne.

How wonderful to realise that the majestic theme of the 'Hallelujah Chorus' was not conceived originally by Handel, nor by the inspired seer on Patmos, nor even by the illustrious prophet Isaiah, who beheld the enthroned King 'high and lifted up' – but was sung on the shores of the Red Sea in BC 1491 by Moses and the children of Israel: **'The Lord shall reign for ever and ever'!** (Exodus 15 vs. 18.)

It has been said that the things that belong to God are indestructible. Like Himself, they are eternal. His Word is eternal; His name is eternal; His throne is eternal. The glorious song of the eternal Lordship of our Redeemer King is destined to be the anthem of eternity, for it has become 'the song of Moses, the servant of God, **and the Song of the Lamb**'!

67. NEW WINE

The last promise that Jesus made to his disciples just before His ascension was a promise of power:

'You will receive power when the Holy Spirit comes on you; and you will be my witnesses in Jerusalem, and in all Judea and Samaria, and to the ends of the earth. After He said this, He was taken up before their very eyes, and a cloud hid Him from their sight.'

Some of them recalled His earlier command: 'I am going to send you what my Father has promised; but stay in the city until you have been clothed with power from on high.' So one hundred and twenty of them met in Jerusalem and prayed together for nine days. On the tenth day – the Day of the Feast of Pentecost in A.D.33 – the Lord fulfilled His promise. At nine o'clock in the morning the Holy Spirit came from the throne of God and entered into the stream of human history in a new way to carry out His dispensational work of forming, energising and directing the church of Jesus Christ.

Such was the impact of the Holy Spirit upon the waiting disciples that they were instantly and completely transformed! Tongues of fire sat upon each head, and their liberated and emboldened lips began to praise God miraculously in new languages. This phenomenon baffled the inhabitants of the city. Unable to explain or to understand what was happening to the followers of Jesus, the outsiders rationalised the event in terms of their own experience. Hearing the Galileans utter ecstatic praise in foreign languages, the mocking crowd cried out: 'These men are full of new wine!'

New Wine! What scenes of uninhibited joy the phrase evokes! New wine always made people different from normal. In the mind of the Jew it was always associated with gladness. 'Wine to make glad the heart of man' was the Old Testament expression. Wine was the symbol of joy. New wine also came to represent an unprecedented factor that would require new structures to accommodate it. Jesus made that point when he said: 'No-one pours new wine into old wineskins. If he does, the new wine will burst the skins, the wine will run out and the wineskins will be ruined.'

New wineskins were flexible and would expand to accommodate the fermenting wine, which gave off gas. But old skins were hard and lacking in elasticity. They would not give with new pressures, and eventually they would burst. Consequently the wineskins would be ruined and the wine lost.

When the Holy Spirit pours His new wine of joy and power into the churches they must be ready to receive Him. Administrative structures must be flexible enough to move with God. Thought processes must be renewed. Cherished traditions must give way as the wine begins to bubble. Entrenched prejudices must be abandoned. Minds must find a new elasticity to allow new ideas to replace old concepts.

God is a God of expansion. It is the nature of His Spirit-wine to expand as it ferments. The tragedy is that immovable and inflexible ecclesiastical structures (if they do not change to accommodate God's move of renewal) can be broken and destroyed by the very power which they so desperately require.

Visitation is vital! The churches need a visitation of God's Holy Spirit. But the essential prerequisite to God's visitation is man's preparation.

God's people, when seeking His face in preparation, are in fact, providing His Spirit with the opportunity to renew thought, and to readjust programmes so that the resultant structures are flexible and spiritual enough to move on with God when His new wine of revival is outpoured.

God has uncorked a new bottle. He is waiting for a renewed people with whom He can make merry. These are the last days – and God has kept the best wine until now!

68. PRAISE

'The dead praise not the Lord' (Psalm 115 vs. 17)

The Bible is full of exhortations to praise God! The Psalmist is particularly prolific in his commands to praise the Lord.

In the first part of Psalm 115 the Psalmist contrasts the Living God with dead idols. He is not very complimentary to the idolators! '**They that make them are like unto them; so is everyone that trusteth in them**' (v 8).

By verse 17 he reaches the conclusion that: '**The dead praise not the Lord**'. In other words, people who don't praise the Lord are, in the Psalmist's view, no better than dead things in which they trust.

It is possible to have a mouth, and yet never to speak His praise; to go to God's house, yet sit dumb in His presence, never uttering a word of praise or thanksgiving to the Lord of glory. '**They have mouths, but they speak not**' (vs. 5).

How opposite to the activity of praise and worship that God desires!

In Psalm 150 David calls for praise in the sanctuary. He sings of the various methods by which God's people can praise Him without inhibition. He exhorts every **living** thing to praise God: 'Let every thing that hath breath praise the Lord'.

Praise and **life** go together. They are inseparable 'twins'!

No praise – no life.
No life – no praise.

The Lord is worthy to be praised. Why be reluctant to put Psalm 150 into practice? There is great victory in praising the Lord.

You may feel as dry as dust. That's just the time to recall the Psalmist's question: '**Shall the dust praise Thee?**' (Psalm 30 vs. 9).

'**For he knoweth our frame, he remembereth that we are dust**' (Psalm 103 vs. 14).

Dust alone cannot praise the Lord. But dust touched by His hand, and breathed upon by His Spirit, can throb with spiritual vitality, and declare the praises of the Lord.

In Psalm 88 vs. 10 the Psalmist asks another penetrating question: **'Shall the dead arise and praise thee?'**. David had no answer. But the prophet Ezekiel found the answer! When confronted with the daunting prospect of addressing the most unresponsive audience possible – a valley full of dry bones – he launched out in faith and obedience: **'So I prophesied as he commanded me, and the breath came into them and they lived, and stood upon their feet, an exceeding great army'**! (Ezek. 37 vs. 10.)

The word of the Lord and the breath of God transform dust and dry bones into a mighty throng that can praise and glorify His name!

'Praise God in His sanctuary' (Ps. 150 vs. 1). (Remember that command next time you go to God's house.)

'While I live I will praise the Lord: I will sing praises unto my God while I have any being' (Ps. 146 vs. 2).

Praise Him with Hallelujahs – for Jesus is Lord!

69. HARMONY

Harmony is pleasing to the ear. Discord jars; it offends our musical sensitivity. A great choir of a thousand voices singing in harmony with perfect timing is almost a miracle! Yet it has been achieved on countless occasions. A symphony orchestra, each player, under the control of the conductor, producing thrilling and majestic sound from the unity of corporate co-operation – this also is a phenomenon which we often take for granted. To achieve perfection, there has to be not only musical and instrumental harmony but a togetherness of mind and spirit – an internal harmony.

This sense of togetherness where each does his own part, being sensitive to the needs and place of others, is essential for success in any project. Think, for example, of the interdependence and mutual co-operation that exists in the team of scientists and astronauts carrying out a space-programme. Men would never have set foot on the moon if the ground-staff scientists had lost interest or failed to give constant back-up and support. Members of that memorable team were often separated from each other by hundreds of thousands of miles – yet they continued to work together in an internal harmony of spirit and mind. Brilliant success was the historic outcome of their sustained and united effort.

If choirs and orchestras and space-teams can work together in harmony, why is there often so much discord amongst Christians? Heaven is an environment of harmony. Can Christians feel convinced that they are fitted for such a destiny if they cannot live and work together with fellow-Christians here on earth?

Jesus understood the futility of discord. He said: 'If a house be divided against itself, that house cannot stand.' Jesus recognised the value of people being able to work together for success. That is one of the reasons He sent out His disciples in twos. In His initial programme of evangelism He didn't seem to make provision for 'loners'!

God pointed out to the Old Testament people that one man could chase a thousand but two could put ten thousand to flight! The fellowship of one man with another did not merely double his strength – it made him five times as strong! No wonder the enemy is always trying to cause schism and division. Harmony amongst believers means defeat for the devil. Unity is strength.

A certain farmer had seven sons whom he resolved to test in order to find out the one most suited to inherit and govern his estate. Calling his sons around him, the farmer laid before them a bundle of sticks, tightly bound together with cords. 'He amongst you,' cried the father, 'who breaks the sticks, shall inherit my property and be ruler of all.' Thinking it to be a test of energy and colossal strength, his sons began to flex their muscles in anticipation of the task.

The first-born stepped forward and bending his brawny back strained with might and main to break the bundle of sticks. After several minutes, bathed in perspiration, he had to abandon his attempt. He stood back, exhausted by his great effort. The next five sons tried in vain to achieve what they now thought to be impossible. The bundle remained intact.

There remained only the seventh son. Youngest of all and of slighter build than his big brothers, he had been following the proceedings with keen interest.

At last, to the great amusement of the rest of the family, the boy stepped forward for his turn. His brothers grinned. What could this mere lad achieve?

The boy took up the bundle, then, to the astonishment of all, he untied the string and snapped the sticks one by one. The farmer declared him to be the winner. The lad had the wisdom and insight to see that it was the tightly bound unity of the bundle that had defeated his brothers. His mind had penetrated into the very nature of things and, with a simple yet brilliant ingenuity, he had broken the bundle by dividing it. Unity is strength. Sing life's song in close harmony with your brothers and sisters: 'Bind us together in love'.

70. A NEW SONG

'O sing unto the Lord a new song' (Ps. 96:1)

The world of today is split into two. Half of mankind groans in starvation and slavery, whilst the rest are bent on self-destruction in a materialistic society that forgets God.

And all the time there hangs over the peoples of this planet the black cloud of nuclear war, threatening to destroy millions in deaths of unprecedented terror. The outlook is far from bright today. There doesn't seem much to sing about – not a lot of inspiration for 'new songs'.

But God has His society within society. He has a people whom He has redeemed. He builds His church in every generation – and the people of the nuclear age are no exception.

God's Spirit inspires a million songs every day. The redeemed multitude on earth, and in heaven, sing His praises continually. The Comforter is constantly composing songs of praise – and a host of God's children are making melody in their hearts to the Lord. Lyrics of love to Jesus rise incessantly from earth to heaven. 'From the rising of the sun unto the going down of the same the Lord's name is to be praised' (Psalm 113 vs. 3).

The phrase 'a new song' is mentioned in the Bible at least eight times: – and six of these references are in the book of Psalms! God gave to the Psalmist a fresh appreciation of the many qualities of the new song:-

1. **A Song of Joy. Rejoice** in the Lord, O ye righteous; for praise is comely for the upright . . . Sing unto Him a **new song** . . .' (Psalm 33 vs. 1 and 3).

David also came to realise that it was:

2. **A Song of Deliverance**. 'He brought me up also **out of an horrible pit**, out of the miry clay, and set my feet upon a rock, and established my goings. And He hath put a **new song** in my mouth, even praise unto our God . . .' (Psalm 40 vs. 2-3).

3. Furthermore, the Psalmist was aware that there was something to sing about, because **God's saving power was at work throughout the whole earth**: 'O sing unto the Lord a **new song**: sing unto the Lord, **all the earth** . . . Declare His glory among **the heathen**, His wonders among **all people**.' (Psalm 96 vs. 1 and 3).

4. The total victory of the Sovereign Jehovah, constitutes another theme in the Psalmist's song: 'O sing unto the Lord a **new song**; for He hath done marvellous things: His right hand, and His holy arm, hath gotten Him the **victory.**' (Psalm 98 vs. 1).

Every Christian should grasp the concept of the complete Conquest of Christ over all the forces of darkness. The Lord is on the throne! Our God reigns! This is as true today as ever it has been.

5. A Song of Praise. David understood the importance of **praise.** He knew that a praising people would experience the blessing of God and become a happy and victorious people. Therefore, King David **determined** to lead by example: **'I will sing a new song** unto thee, O God: upon a psaltery and an instrument of ten strings will I sing **praises** unto thee.' (Psalm 144 vs. 9).

This determination to praise the Lord in song and with instruments of music arose out of David's understanding of the saving and delivering power of God in his own **personal** experience: 'It is He that giveth **salvation** (victory) unto kings. Who **delivereth David** His servant from the hurtful sword.' (Psalm 144 vs. 10).

We have as much to praise God for as David had. Let us be as determined and as eager as he was to do so.

6. A song of congregational worship. In Psalm 144 David expressed his own personal determination to praise God. But in Psalm 149 vs. 1 he develops the theme of individual praise into the mighty anthem of **congregational** worship. His thoughts flow forward from the voice of an isolated new song, to the chorale of **united praise**: 'Praise ye the Lord. Sing unto the Lord a new **song** and His praise in the **congregation of saints.'**

There is also a reference to '**a new song**' in the prophecy of Isaiah, who unveils the revelation that it is:-

7. A song of Faith! 'Behold, the former things are come to pass, and new things do I declare: **before** they spring forth I tell you of them. Sing unto the Lord a **new song** . . .' (Is. 42 vs. 9-10).

Faith in God's word will inspire a new song! The Apostle Paul sang this song above the howling of the wind and the screaming of the storm at sea! Standing majestically on the deck of the doomed vessel, he lifted his voice above the sound of the crashing waves – '**I believe God!**'

Stalwart hearts down the centuries have caught the echo of the Apostle's song, and have joined him in sublime declarations of faith, quelling the roaring of the flames at the martyr's stake; silencing the iron clang of the dungeon doors of persecution; bringing praise to God despite a lifetime of pain, sorrow, sickness, poverty, misunderstanding and suffering of all kinds.

God has made many wonderful prophetic promises to us.

Let us '**believe God**' and '**before** they spring forth,' let us sing unto the Lord a **new song of faith.**

The hymnist Mary Peters has well expressed the thought in her verse:-

> 'We expect a bright tomorrow;
> All will be well;
> Faith can sing through days of sorrow,
> All, all is well:
> On our Father's love relying,
> Jesus every need supplying,
> Or in living or in dying,
> All must be well.'

8. **An eternal song.** A new song, inspired by the Holy Spirit and based on the acts of God as expressed in His word, will last through time and eternity. That is why the Bible gives us a glimpse into glory, enabling us to view the majestic scene around the throne of God and the Lamb. This new song has a glorious, **eternal** theme: 'And they sung a new song saying, THOU ART WORTHY to take the book, and to open the seals thereof: for thou wast slain, and hast **redeemed** us to God **by thy blood** out of every nation.' (Rev. 5:9).

God's redeemed people can sing that **new song** throughout each year, and on through the unborn eternities!

PART VII

EVANGELISM

Items 71 – 76

71. THE SHORTEST SERMON!

This generation emphasises evangelism and church growth, – subjects which obviously involve the church in vocal witnessing. Clear, Bible-based preaching is also implied. Pastor I. Howells has said: 'It is not the method that matters. What we want are results!' People sometimes excuse themselves from preaching, and even from witnessing vocally, by saying, as Moses said thousands of years ago, 'I am not eloquent'; or 'I'm not a good speaker'; or 'I can't get a message together'.

I have been amazed to discover that the most effective sermon recorded in the Bible is the shortest one! Homiletically it was hopeless. It had no literary value, contained no emotional appeal or stirring language, and it carried no exciting challenge. Furthermore, it offered not a glimmer of hope should its hapless hearers repent and turn to the Lord. Not only that, but the preacher himself was an unpleasant personality without a shred of charisma. And he had no love at all for the foreign recipients of his eight terrifying words of doom!

Despite all this, over one hundred and twenty thousand souls from every strata of city society repented in sackcloth and ashes, with prayer and fasting. The reluctant preacher was the bigoted prophet Jonah, and his short sermon to the city of Nineveh was: *'Yet forty days and Nineveh shall be overthrown'*! Just eight ordinary words – but they brought conviction to the whole city population. From the king in the palace to the beggar on the pavement, everybody repented and turned to the living God! Not an eloquent message – but what tremendous results!

This message had, however, come from God. The preacher did not proclaim his own thoughts. He delivered the word of the Lord – in eight words! (Preachers and prophets please note!). It must also be recognised that Jonah, after turning this way and that, was now in the right place and was doing what God had told him to do. No doubt he could have preached a more eloquent sermon and delivered a more acceptable prophecy in Tarshish, to which place he had tried to flee. Disobedient Jonah, instead of going to warn Nineveh as God had instructed, had set out on a sea-voyage to Tarshish. But God, with dramatic sovereignty, eventually brought His messenger to the place of submissive obedience where he could be effective in his ministry.

So don't say: 'I'm not an eloquent speaker'. You can speak eight words can't you? But get your eight words from God! That will involve you in fervent prayer, and in seeking the face of the Lord. Be obedient to His will. Be in the right place at the right time. Don't do your own thing. Do what the Lord wants you to do. Then speak up for Jesus, and let God surprise you with the tremendous results! It's amazing what He can do with an eight-words sermon!

72. SOUL WINNING

The alternative to winning is losing. If people are not won for the Lord, they will be eternally lost. There seems to be no middle ground. It is as frighteningly stark as that.

The gospel is God's good news for a lost world. God loves you. Jesus Christ has power to transform your life. He laid upon the slender shoulders of His earliest followers the task of preaching this good news to every human being. Quite a tall order, in view of the phenomenal difficulties that confronted them.

The Lord has never removed that mantle of responsibility from His church. In this sophisticated, technological world, we are charged to tell the good news to every tribe and nation.

In one way we have an advantage over the early church. Because of modern communication methods, we can reach thousands every day by radio and television; by audio and video cassette. But are the masses being touched? Are we reaching the people? Do we make an impact? Are our churches reflecting the success of the gospel by a steady inflow of converted people?

The early disciples had none of our technology. Yet the church grew and multiplied at a tremendous rate. Whole communities turned to the Lord, and society grudgingly acknowledged: 'These men have turned the world upside down'!

Impression without expression leads to depression. Their lives were filled with the power of God, and their minds with His word.

They were actively and effectively vocal in giving expression to their inward faith. They did not fear the awful terrors of the arena, the persecution of the state, or the scorn of their neighbours. They knew that Jesus Christ, who had died an agonizing death on the cross, had risen from the grave, and the Holy Spirit gave them the constant assurance of Christ's presence with them. Therefore they spontaneously told everybody about God's good news for mankind.

Harnack, the church historian, has reminded us that: 'All the early conquests of Christianity were carried out by informal missionaries.' 'Everybody who received the gospel gave the gospel.'

Ordinary people achieved extraordinary progress because they were

197

given over to the power of the Holy Spirit. They had a vision to win the world for Jesus – and they were dedicated to the task.

The Communists had a vision of world domination, and they dedicated themselves to this objective. The Moslems, with fanatical zeal, bend all their energies toward making Islam the world-faith. Both of these philosophies can still influence the minds of the people.

Let those Christians who can use radio and television for the gospel employ their talents in that way; and let us pray for them. But I want to point out the possibility of success by using the simplest of all soul-winning methods – personal contact.

If in 1977 your church had ten members, and if those ten won one soul each in one year and brought those folk to the church, then by 1978 your church would have doubled its congregation. Witnessing at the same rate (each person winning just one per year), what would your congregation have been in 1987? The answer is 10,240. And by 1997 (even allowing for deaths), your numbers should be well over ten million!

What went wrong?

Nearly three thousand years ago, Solomon recognised the importance of soul-winning, and he wrote in one of his immortal proverbs: 'He that wins souls is wise.'

73. SHARING YOUR FAITH

What does it mean to 'share your faith'? Basically, it involves letting others know your convictions concerning Christ as Lord and Saviour and as the only hope for the world.

Christians who are enjoying fellowship with the Lord and who are filled with His Holy Spirit are often bubbling over with enthusiasm to share the good news about God's love and salvation through faith in the risen Jesus.

Sharing your faith involves a lot more than that, of course. You can share your faith doctrinally as well as evangelistically. There are no limits to the depths of truth in God's word. But Jesus is coming soon – and millions of people, even in our own land, have not yet responded to the gospel. The crucial need of the hour demands a simple, effective sharing of the good news with everybody, so that the lost can have the chance to be saved.

Satan will do his utmost to prevent this redemptive operation from taking place. Every kind of excuse and objection will be whispered into your mind. For example, it is often said that *'religion is a private and personal matter.'* Or: *'I keep my beliefs to myself.'*

It is true that Christianity is a personal experience with God for each individual. But that secret life of fellowship with God must always issue in an outward witness to the world. There must always be a yearning over the lost, and a longing for them to come to Christ. There is no more fitting example than the life of Jesus. No one spent more time in prayer and fellowship with the Father than Jesus did. And yet His whole ministry was an outreach to the lost, the broken, the despairing, the sick and the helpless.

Everything that Jesus received from God he shared with the disciples. *'I have called you friends, for everything that I learned from my Father I have made known to you.' (John 15 vs. 15).*

Jesus prayed for his friends. But he also prayed for those who would come to faith through their testimony: *'I pray also for those who will believe in me through their message.' (John 17 vs. 20).*

Thousands believed the gospel when they heard the preaching of the Apostles. But millions more have come to Christ by hearing or reading the Apostles' written testimony in the inspired New Testament. The prayer of Jesus is thus still being abundantly fulfilled.

It is clear that Biblical Christianity implies personal faith becoming productive in outreach to others. The New Testament knows nothing of a clandestine Christ. We cannot keep Him to ourselves, personally, ecclesiastically, nationally or doctrinally. Jesus must be shared with others. He cannot be hidden.

Every real Christian can share Christ with others. You don't have to wait until you're more experienced. No matter how young you are, you can share your faith with those in need.

One of the most beautiful of Old Testament stories tells of a little captive girl who shared her faith in a heathen household. She lived in the great house of Naaman, Captain of the Syrian army, and she was the maid of Naaman's wife. One day the marauding hosts of Syria had invaded this little Israelite girl's home and had taken her captive into a strange land, where she was forced to work as a slave.

She could have been bitter and angry and resentful. Who would have blamed her if her little heart had been filled with hatred for her alien masters?

Captain Naaman was an incurable leper. Instead of hoping that he would die from the disease, the little maid longed for him to be cured! So she told Naaman's wife about Elisha, the miracle-working prophet of Israel. As a result of her testimony, the great Captain Naaman was eventually healed, and the God of Israel was glorified in the eyes of the heathen.

It all happened because a little girl saw a deep need, had compassion in her heart, and, in child-like simplicity, shared her faith with others.

If a little slave-girl, living before Calvary and prior to Pentecost, could so boldly stand up for her Lord – what's stopping you?

74. THE LOST GENERATION

So terrible was the carnage in the Great War of 1914-1918, that the number of promising young men who died as soldiers in the conflict became known as the Lost Generation.

What a tragic waste! A whole generation lost! Lost hopes, lost potential, lost love, and lost fulfilment. Thousands of young lives snuffed out on the muddy battlefields. The ambitions of a whole generation draining away with their life's blood into the desolate trenches of No Man's Land.

But there is an even greater tragedy than that. It is the horror of a generation who, not threatened by war, nevertheless waste their lives in mindless destruction and violence, commit slow suicide by drug addiction, or fall down and worship the gods of alcohol and nicotine. By pursuing this course of madness, they become dead while they live. They constitute another lost generation. Unaware of God, they are lost to His purpose. Insensitive to spiritual realities, they are lost in the morass of materialistic pressures and values. The Bible is a closed book to them. The church is an archaic institution in their estimation. Christ is a blasphemous curse upon their lips. The dimension of the Spirit is, to their blind minds, nothing but a mystical delusion. They are lost.

From the divine perspective, all people who are not in a saving relationship with the living God are, in fact, lost. You don't have to be an alcoholic to be lost. You don't have to be an addict, a junkie, a football hooligan, or a criminal to be lost. You can be perfectly respectable and yet be lost. You can be the most sweetly reasonable person in the world – and be lost. You can even be religious – and you can still be lost.

Sir Arthur Conan Doyle wrote a book called *The Lost World*. In it he described the discovery of a prehistoric world forgotten by time and progress – a hidden, secret world inhabited by terrible monsters in primeval conditions. Unexplored and undiscovered by successive civilisations, Doyle's 'lost world' had remained unseen and unimagined for thousands of years. Men had strutted over the stage of time for centuries. But in planting their tiny foot-prints upon the shifting sands of history, they had remained totally unaware of the existence of a world populated by dreadful monsters.

Most people today do not feel that they live in a 'lost world'. In an affluent society they just don't imagine themselves as being among the lost. They seem totally unaware of that hidden world where, just beneath the surface of respectability, lurk the terrifying monsters of a sinful, fallen and God-rejecting nature far more destructive than any prehistoric beast.

Jesus came to live amongst the Jews – the most religious people upon the face of the earth. Yet He said He had come to seek and to save the lost! Under the veneer of religious ritual there existed a whole world of monsters – hatred, envy, anger, avarice and spite. Religious people were lost in this 'lost world' of ungodliness and sin.

When Adam disobeyed God, he became conscious of his sin. One of the awful consequences that followed was a state of 'lostness'. He tried to hide from God. *'Adam, where are you'?* All the pathos of God's heart was wrung into that cry. Man had fallen, and mankind was lost.

This is why Jesus came. And that is why Christians who have been sought and found by the Good Shepherd must spend their lives in seeking to reach, with the gospel, every lost soul in this Lost World.

75. TRIUMPH OR SUCCESS?

The modern world has little time for the unsuccessful. If you are not clever, prosperous, popular and successful – than you will be left behind in the rat-race to reach the top of the social ladder.

Jesus, however, viewed people from quite a different perspective. He spoke of the meek inheriting the earth. He described himself as *'gentle and humble in heart'*, urging his followers to find rest for their souls by learning from him. Meekness, gentleness and humility – not really much of a recipe for success in this rough-and-tumble world.

But Jesus was never interested in popular worldly success. His aim was to change human hearts and teach people to live in triumph whatever their circumstances. From the divine view-point, there is a vast difference between a triumphant life and a successful life.

There is a very grave danger today of being conditioned by the clamour of the world for visible immediate results which can be quantified in terms of evident success. Jesus always resisted that kind of pressure. The cross was not a success viewed from the contemporary perspective of the world in the time of Jesus. It looked like a failure for Jesus and his followers. It appeared to be the end of his mission and the desolation of all their high hopes.

'Come down from the cross' sneered his enemies.

But Jesus knew what the will of God was for him. He had come into the world for this very purpose of dying on the cross for the sins of mankind. Neither worldly sneers nor Satanic strategies could make him swerve from his Father's will.

Jesus waited for God's time. The Saviour believed in something better than coming down from the cross. He believed in coming up from the grave. That was God's will for him.

Coming down from the cross would have been regarded as a sensational success in materialistic terms. A carnal target would have been hit. A worldly aim achieved. Something immediate and tangible would have been produced for fevered worldlings to admire and gape at. But coming up from the grave in God's time was a supreme triumph – the results of which have been incalculable.

The tycoon trampling on others to reach the top of the financial tree is an example of worldly success. According to the values of materialistic society, the rich and the powerful are successes in life. But Jesus went into the temple one day and stood by the treasury. There he observed the ostentatious offerings cast into the treasury-box by the wealthy.

Jesus also noticed the humble gifts of a poor widow who cast into the treasury two tiny coins. It was all she had. And she gave it all to God. Jesus remained unimpressed by the other gifts, but he commented on the widow's offering. To the world it must have seemed that her gift was negligible – hardly worth her while walking to the temple just to put in two of the tiniest coins.

But Jesus illuminates God's assessment of giving. The rich, Jesus explained, always give an offering out of their vast abundance. However much they put in, they still have plenty left. No real sacrifice is ever involved. But the poor widow gave everything she had. It becomes clear that God measures our giving not by how much we contribute, but by how much we have got left. God looks for the sacrificial heart motivated by sheer love for Him.

Some Christians are wealthy and prosperous. Others are poor. They have inadequate incomes and they find it a struggle to cope with the economic pressures of life. Yet many are faithful to the Lord in their giving, and in their tithing. They may not be successful in materialistic terms. But they are certainly triumphant, because they serve God sacrificially. And this is precisely what pleases Him.

The same principle applies to churches. Some are rich (Laodicea was like that). But other companies of God's people struggle against tremendous odds, and still find it difficult to pay their way. Recession, unemployment, redundancy – all take their toll in some areas of economic depression. Such churches cannot be described as 'successful' in monetary values. But if they remain faithful to the principles of God's word, they are triumphant in Christ.

Some servants of God seem to have had phenomenal success in every aspect of their ministry. Others have found life a struggle. I read about one man who worked for twenty years amongst the Moslems, but only brought three or four of them to Christ. Yet he felt that he was doing the work that God had assigned to him. It is allegiance to the will of God, not 'success', that measures a man's ministry. Such a life is a life of triumph in Christ.

All that I have said must not be construed as an excuse for complacency. All Christians long for the true spiritual success that we believe God desires us to have. We yearn for revival. We pray for churches to become full of people praising and serving God. But there nevertheless remains a complex mystery about the will of God for certain people. And that mystery can never be fully understood or explained in terms of immediate evidence.

True triumphant Christian living is the outworking of an unshakable faith.

76. THE TRUMPET OF JUBILEE

'Consecrate the fiftieth year and proclaim liberty throughout the land to
all its inhabitants. It shall be a Jubilee for you . . .'

(Leviticus 25 v 10. N.I.V.)

The first Jubilee was instituted by God for His people Israel about 3,500
years ago. The word '**Jubilee**' comes from a Hebrew word '**Yobel**' –
which means 'a ram's horn **trumpet**'.

On the Day of Atonement Israel's High Priest took the blood of certain
slain sacrificial animals, passed within the veil that separated the Holy
Place in the Tabernacle from the Holy of Holies, and sprinkled that blood
upon the mercy-seat where God's presence shone in glory.

God accepted the substitutionary blood of the sacrifice, and covered
His people's sins. Thus was atonement made annually on 10th October
for the nation of Israel.

The High Priest then laid his hands on the head of a live goat,
transferring to it the sins of the people. This animal – the scape-goat –
was then led away by a chosen man, who released the goat far away in
the wilderness (illustrating prophetically that Christ would one day bear
away the sins of His people).

Each year, on the Day of Atonement, the people mourned for their sins
in repentance.

But God instructed that once every fifty years something special should
take place following the Atonement. He commanded the **Trumpet of Jubilee**
to be sounded throughout the land, announcing the exciting news of the
Year of Jubilee! (It is not difficult to see how the Hebrew word **Yobel**,
ram's horn **trumpet**, became synonymous with the concept of **Jubilee**).

Some of the special features of Israel's Jubilee Year contained
arrangements for all debtors to be absolved, all slaves and prisoners to be
set free, and all inheritances to be restored to the original owners!

The national mood of Israel at Jubilee time was obviously one of great
joy, peace, and liberty.

But it was **rejoicing after repentance**. The blood had been shed.
Atonement had been made. The people's sins had been covered and carried
away. It was not a facade of festivity. The root of their problem had been

dealt with, and their joy was built on the basis of righteousness – a right relationship with God.

The true joy of Jubilee celebrations must always be set within a context of repentance and righteousness. After the cries of repentance, the glad notes of rejoicing can be heard. The Jubilee Trumpet still sounds out its joyful message!

The trumpet of Jubilee has three major notes – and they are all in perfect harmony – making the music of God's good news.

First, there is the welcome note of **Forgiveness**. (All debtors absolved!) Jesus told a parable of a man who owed his king a vast sum of money. The servant had no way of clearing his debt, so he threw himself upon the mercy of the monarch and begged for time in which to pay the money back. The kind-hearted king was moved with compassion '**and forgave him the debt.**' (Matt. 18 vs. 27).

We all owe God a debt we could never pay. But Jesus paid our debt on the cross of Calvary. When we repent and cry for mercy, we hear the glad note ringing out: 'Your sins are forgiven. Go in peace!'

The second note is that of **Freedom**. (All slaves and prisoners set free). Our sins not only drive us into debt, they also bring us into bondage. It is Jesus who sets the prisoners free. By His death and resurrection He has power to liberate from every bondage, to snap every fetter, and to deliver from every dungeon of sin and Satan.

'This is the year of Jubilee, – when all the captives are set free! Come ye halt, ye blind, ye lame, leap and shout for joy again!

This is the year of Jubilee!'

Third, there is the dominant note of **Family Restorations.** (All inheritances restored).

The family is God's unit for building the structure of society. Satan has the family under attack in these days.

All around us are broken homes; broken hearts; families in feud; and a society rapidly disintegrating into despair, lawlessness, and anarchy.

The gospel trumpet of God's grace has a clear message of hope for our society. It is this: **Jesus can mend broken hearts and restore shattered family relationships.**

True repentance includes elements of reconciliation, restitution, and a returning to responsibilities. Only in this way can genuine **restoration** be achieved in families and in churches.

PART VIII

JESUS IS COMING AGAIN

Items 77-81

77. READY FOR THE RAPTURE

What is the Rapture? And how can we be ready for it? The word 'rapture' comes from a Medieval Latin word *raptura* meaning ecstasy – and this is its most common usage today. But the archaic connotation of the word *rapture* is 'the transporting of a person from one place to another, especially to Heaven'. The word's primary roots may well be in the Latin *rapere*, 'to seize', or 'to catch away'.

Jesus promised that He would come back again one day, and the early church lived in constant expectation of His immediate return. Some Christians were confused about the order of events, and the Apostle Paul found it necessary to write two letters to the church at Thessalonica clarifying this important matter. In this first letter, the Apostle wrote about the event which we now call the *Rapture* – the catching up of the living Christians to the Lord in the clouds. This is what Paul wrote:

'According to the Lord's own word, we tell you that we who are still alive, who are left to the coming of the Lord, will certainly not precede those who have fallen asleep. For the Lord Himself will come down from heaven, with a loud command, with the voice of the archangel and the trumpet call of God, and the dead in Christ will rise first. After that, we who are still alive and are left will be caught up with them in the clouds to meet the Lord in the air. And so we will be with the Lord forever. Therefore encourage each other with these words.'

That is the Biblical prediction of the Rapture. And the Apostle considered it to be a topic of encouraging conversation and faith. It should still be so today. The thought of Jesus coming to catch us away from this vale of tears to Himself in glory should excite and stimulate us with joy and anticipation.

The Rapture is the next great event to happen to the Church internationally. With the removal of Christians from the earth, unbridled evil will cover the planet. A time of great tribulation will ensue when the Anti-Christ will rise to power, demanding universal allegiance and putting to death all those who will not receive his mark upon them. Terrible persecution will be the fate of the Jews, and Jerusalem will become the bone of contention in the teeth of the dogs of war. The scene will be set for the battle of Armageddon. The cause of the Jews will seem to be lost

211

as their holy city becomes surrounded by the alien forces of Anti-Christ threatening total destruction.

At the last moment, when all seems lost, Jesus will appear in glory with the armies of heaven. He will destroy the hosts of Anti-Christ, and His people will at last acknowledge Him as their true Messiah. He will initiate the inauguration of His kingdom on earth for one thousand golden years of peace and prosperity. King Jesus shall rule this planet Earth.

When is all this to happen? Nobody knows the exact date. But from the Scriptural signs which are being fulfilled all around us, we can assert with confidence that the Rapture will take place very soon. And the subsequent events will follow very quickly thereafter.

How can we get ready for the Rapture? First, by accepting Jesus as Saviour and Lord. Second by living in loving fellowship with Him daily. And third, by being prayerfully vigilant in watching for His coming, not forgetting our responsibility to tell others about the return of the Lord.

Apply these principles and you will be ready for the Rapture.

78. PROPHECY COMES ALIVE!

Prophecy is history announced in advance. It is a glimpse of the future, viewed from the divine perspective. It involves the omniscience, omnipotence and omnipresence of the Eternal God. Omniscience, because prophecy reveals perfect knowledge about circumstances, details and events that could be centuries away in the future. Omnipotence, because the Almighty has the amazing ability not only accurately to predict the distant future, but also powerfully to control the minds and movements of men and of nations, thereby ensuring the perfect fulfilment of His prophetic word. And omnipresence, because there is no sector of the universe outwith His intense interest, or excluded from His wise providence. Neither is there any place beyond the scope of His absolute sovereignty. Prophecy is not a trivial thing. It is a mighty miracle expressing to all humanity the wonder and majesty of the living God. It is an articulate revelation of the secrets hidden in the heart of the Eternal.

'Prophecy comes alive!' This phrase does not imply that prophecy has ever been dead. It is merely a figure of speech to emphasise the perfect, detailed fulfilment of God's predictive word.

There is nothing dead about prophecy. It is as full of life as God Himself. His word pulsates with the vibrant energies of His own life. It is creative, predictive, redemptive and administrative. It cascades in cataracts of clear revelation from the throne of God, to irrigate the barren deserts of humanistic speculation and philosophy.

Many of the words of Jesus were prophetic revelations. A perusal of Matthew 24 will reveal to every unbiased mind that the predictions of Jesus concerning His return are being fulfilled in our day. Prophecy is coming alive. The forecasts of Christ can be seen daily on our television screens and in our newspapers . . . He spoke of wars and rumours of wars; of pestilence and of famine; of fear and distress; of revolution and rebellion; of earthquakes and of excessive violence socially; of persecution and of prison; of the rise of the cults – false prophets and false Christs; of international unrest and of planetary disturbances.

Jesus also spoke of the gospel being preached in all the world – something that was not technically possible until today. The whole world was not accessible in previous centuries. But, by using aeroplanes, missionaries have been able to reach hitherto inaccessible tribes. Nations which are politically closed to Christianity can receive the good news of God's love by radio, television and satellite. Revolutionary changes in Europe have opened up to God's word and to His evangelists, many nations which were formerly gripped in the uncomprehending iron fist of Communism. The warmth of God's grace is melting the iron in Europe.

The re-establishment of the nation of Israel was another of Christ's prophetic forecasts. In the long context of history, this event has taken place relatively recently, reinforcing our understanding that we are living in the last days immediately preceding the return of the Lord.

Referring to the sprouting of the fig tree a symbol representing the re-birth of Israel, Jesus said: *'Now learn this lesson from the fig tree; as soon as its twigs get tender and its leaves come out, you know that summer is near. Even so, when you see all these things, you know that it is near, right at the door.'*

Time has not weakened the impact of the prophecies of Jesus. Neither has the passing of many centuries diminished the power and eternal relevance of His words. Nothing can prevent their complete fulfilment.

Have you learned the *'lesson of the fig tree'*? Prophecy is still coming alive in our generation. Look up! Our redemption is getting nearer, and our generation could well be involved in the rapture of the church when Jesus returns.

79. THE MEANING OF LIFE

As soon as we are born we begin to die. That is a sobering thought. Paradoxically, death is the only experience of which we can be certain in our lifetime. Apart from the rapture, we can be sure of dying. Mankind is constantly aware of approaching death.

Serious-minded people must, however, think not only about the inevitable conclusion of their personal lives, but also about the purpose and consummation of history. In fact, there is a whole branch of theology devoted to the study of these very matters. It is called eschatology and it is concerned with the ultimate or last things, such as death, judgment, heaven and hell, and God's future programme.

Is there a pattern in human history? Is there a programme being out-worked in the individual and corporate experience of mankind? Is there any real meaning to life?

Marxist philosophy seeks to explain life in terms of dialectical materialism, regarding matter as the basic subject of change, and viewing all change as the product of a constant conflict between opposites. This theory, when applied to the interpretation of history, is known as historical materialism, a concept perceiving the social order as basically economic, punctuated by a series of class conflicts eventually evolving into a classless society.

But as the philosopher Hegel said: 'History teaches us that history teaches us nothing.' Social conflicts have never produced a classless society. Even in the Communist and Marxist states which arose out of a context of revolutionary class conflicts, there was a wide gulf between the elite ruling class and the proletariat. The Marxist interpretation of history just doesn't fit the facts. Despite this, millions have been brain-washed into accepting Marxist philosophy, and many still seek to apply it in our educational and national life.

Above all the futile attempts to interpret the meaning of life and history, God's voice can be heard speaking direction and purpose. His eschatological programme for mankind is outlined in the Bible. Viewed from the Biblical perspective, history is analysed into phases concerning the person and work of the Lord Jesus Christ. There were the centuries of prophetic preparation for His coming into the world. There were the brief

215

but vital years of His incarnation. (His involvement then with mankind made such an impact, that ever since people have found true spiritual fulfilment through a relationship with Jesus.) Then came the church-age initiated by the coming of the Holy Spirit at Pentecost.

This church-dispensation is fast coming to a close. The rapture is imminent. But subsequently this war-torn earth, following the tribulation, will experience a golden-age of peace when Jesus will rule the planet in righteousness for a thousand years!

The Bible teaches us that Christ alone makes sense of history, giving purpose and meaning to all life.

80. THE KING OF PLANET EARTH

The rightful Ruler of Planet Earth is King Jesus. He created the Universe and He sustains and upholds it by the word of His power. He selected Planet Earth for His incarnate visitation, entering the stream of human history and experience through the womb of the Virgin. He demonstrated a life of sinlessly perfect Manhood and completely fulfilled the will of the Father in every detail of righteousness and obedience. He defeated Satan, the Arch-Usurper, died on the cross for the sins of mankind, and rose triumphantly out of the grave of death to ascend in glorious splendour to the throne of victory at the right hand of the Majesty on high.

If anyone has the right to rule Earth, it is Jesus the King of kings.

During His earthly ministry, Jesus promised that he would return to this planet. First of all He will come to the air to snatch away His Bride, the Church of Christ. This event is called the Rapture and all the signs of the times indicate that this momentous occasion could take place very soon.

Following the Rapture, this planet will pass through a seven years period of unprecedented disaster known as the Great Tribulation. Mankind will witness the rise of an international dictator – the Anti-Christ who will openly oppose God and persecute His people. The principal purpose of the Anti-Christ will be to destroy the nation of Israel in order to possess their land. When his godless troops will have surrounded Jerusalem, leaving Israel no escape, suddenly Jesus will appear out of heaven leading the celestial armies into the battle of Armageddon. The forces of Anti-Christ will be destroyed and Israel will acknowledge King Jesus as their Messiah and Deliverer.

The Lord Jesus will inaugurate His Millennial Kingdom on earth. This will be a thousand years of peace and plenty upon our Planet.

The reign of King Jesus will be visible. At the present time the Lord reigns in the hearts of His people, in the unseen realm. The effects of His Lordship are seen to a certain extent in the world, but His sovereign overruling power is largely unrecognised by mankind. But in the Millennial Kingdom things will be different. The majesty, power and authority of King Jesus will be clearly visible to the whole world.

His kingdom will be political. This does not imply that His realm will

217

be racked by the schismatic system of party politics.

But it means rather that Christ's kingdom will display 'a definite and organised policy, or structure of government', this being one of the root meanings of the concept of the word 'political.'

His reign will be beneficial. Nobody ever had a more definite policy for the good government of this planet than Jesus. His reign will pour unprecedented blessings upon the human race. It will be in sharp contradistinction to the rule of Anti-Christ, whose brief reign of terror during the Tribulation will wreak more damage on Mankind than has ever been suffered throughout the history of the human race.

The Millennial reign of Jesus will be visible, political and beneficial. It will also be regal. Jesus is the most majestic Person in the Universe. He is King of kings and Lord of lords. The whole thousand years reign will be stamped with the regal dignity of His Kingly Personality. Under His loving rule men will hold their heads high and walk without fear, without poverty and without shame, throughout the earth.

Because of Jesus, the hopes and dreams of all mankind will be realistically fulfilled for one thousand years of peace on earth.

81. THE KING IS COMING!

There are not many kings left on planet Earth. History has seen them disappearing one by one as the social tidal-wave of democracy has swept forward inexorably across the sands of Time.

Two of the most powerful nations on earth today are Russia and the United States of America. Neither of them has a king. Socialism and republics are the order of the day.

Ancient Rome challenged the doctrine of a divine Emperor, and their government fluctuated between dictatorship and republicanism. It is a conflict that has been reflected internationally for centuries, and will persist ultimately until the kingdom of the King of kings fills the whole earth.

The prophet Daniel predicted these facts six centuries before Christ was born in Bethlehem! In his interpretation of the dream of the despot Nebuchadnezzar, Daniel explained the course of world history, predicting the rise and fall of powerful yet deteriorating world-empires:- Babylon, Medo-Persia, Greece and Rome. These dynasties were depicted by an image of a man whose head was of gold, but whose feet and toes were part iron and part clay. The chest and arms of the image were silver, whilst the belly and thighs were of bronze, and the legs iron.

This clearly demonstrates the pernicious devaluation of each successive world-empire: gold, silver, bronze, iron and finally an incompatible mixture of iron and clay. Some scholars interpret the iron as dictatorship, and the clay as democracy. They also view the ten toes of the image as ten nations – some of which are dictatorships or monarchies and others democracies. Then there are some Biblical expositors who go as far as relating the ten toes of the image to ten countries in the European Economic Community, which, they claim, will one day be united within the territory of the ancient Roman Empire under the rule of the demonic-human despot, the Antichrist.

Nebuchadnezzar gazed at this image until he saw a great stone fall upon its feet, destroying the whole image and grinding it to dust which the wind blew away into ultimate obscurity. The stone itself grew into a huge mountain which filled the whole earth.

Daniel explained that this represented the kingdom of God upon earth – a kingdom that would subdue and crush all world-empires of opposition. All kingdoms must have a king – and God's kingdom is no exception.

219

He declares: *'I have installed my King on Zion, my holy hill.'* (Psalm 2.6). His name is King Jesus – once rejected by His own people the Jews, but vindicated by His Father God in terms of the resurrection, and destined to be not only the King of all the earth, but the Ruler of the whole Universe.

Two thousand six hundred years ago God showed His servant Daniel a clear picture of His coming kingdom. It is very near now. Soon will come the rapture of the church when the sound of the trumpet will wake the dead in Christ. Then will break upon this planet the awesome plagues of the great Tribulation, and the Antichrist's brief but bloody tyranny of terror. The nations will gather on the plains of Megiddo for the battle of Armageddon, and God's people Israel will be threatened on all sides by hostile powers eager to destroy them.

Out of this morass of hopeless despair will ring the cry: *'The King is coming'!* The heavens will open and the nail-pierced Messiah, King Jesus, will save His people, destroy their enemies and initiate the kingdom of God politically, visibly and universally for one thousand golden years of peace on earth.

This is not a delusion. The King *is* coming!

PART IX

THE POWER OF THE HOLY SPIRIT

Items 82 – 85

82. THE HOLY SPIRIT IN THE MINISTRY OF JESUS

'And Jesus being full of the Holy Ghost returned from Jordan, and was led by the Spirit into the wilderness, being forty days tempted of the devil. And in those days he did eat nothing: . . . And Jesus returned in the power of the Spirit into Galilee: and there went out a fame of him through all the region round about. And He taught in their synagogues, being glorified of all'.   (Luke 4 vs. 1,2,14 and 15).

The work of the Holy Spirit was predominant in the life and ministry of Jesus. For He lived His unique sinless life and exercised miraculous abilities, not merely in the strength of deity, but in the power of a Spirit-anointed manhood. The implication is that if we can be as yielded to the will of God and to the pressures of the Holy Ghost as Jesus was, then we too can live above sin and exercise the authority of a Holy Ghost ministry.

In the passage from Luke's gospel quoted above, there are three significant phases of the work of the Holy Spirit in Jesus.

1. First, the Plenitude of the Spirit

'*And Jesus being* **full** *of the Holy Ghost . . .' (v 1)*. Jesus was not full of His own ideas (though no one had more right to be so than He). He was **full** of the Holy Ghost.

John reminds us: '*For He whom God hath sent speaketh the words of God: for God giveth not the Spirit by measure unto Him' (John 3 : 34)*.

There was no limitation in the capacity of Jesus to receive. Therefore there was no restriction by God in the measure of His giving the Holy Spirit. We are limited by our small capacity for God. And God is Himself limited in us for the same reason. To be 'emptied of self and filled with God' is no light matter. But it seems to be an extremely rare experience.

To be effective for God we must be **full** of the Holy Ghost. On the day of Pentecost all the people in the upper room were filled with the Holy Ghost. Peter preached a short sermon and three thousand souls were saved! Why? Because he was full of the Holy Ghost.

Later on, Peter and John were confronted by a man who had been lame from birth. This man was instantly healed in the name of Jesus Christ of Nazareth! Why? Because Peter and John were full of the Holy Ghost. They were arrested, and instructed to explain their behaviour. They knew no fear in the presence of the authorities and rulers. The Bible says: *'they saw the boldness of Peter and John'. (Acts 4 : 13).* What was the secret of their courage? The answer is in verse 8: *'Then Peter* **filled with the Holy Ghost** *said unto them . . .'*

The first deacons of the early church were men full of the Holy Ghost (Acts 6 vs. 5).

Outstanding amongst them was Stephen, who, being full of the Holy Ghost, did great wonders and miracles! Arrested and arraigned before the Sanhedrin, he confounded his critics with his wisdom and his knowledge of the scriptures. The inward life of the Holy Spirit manifested itself upon his countenance, for his face was like 'the face of an angel' (Acts 6 : 15).

Full of the Holy Ghost, Stephen's vision penetrated into the spiritual realms and he beheld Jesus at the right hand of God! (Acts 7 : 55-56).

He died a triumphant martyr, forgiving his murderers, as Jesus had forgiven those who had nailed him to the cross. How could young Stephen do all this?

By being **full** of the Holy Ghost. There is no other explanation.

It is clear that the **plenitude of the Spirit** is for all who will make room for Him in their hearts.

2. Secondly, the Pathway of the Spirit

'Jesus **was led by the Spirit** *into the wilderness' (Luke 4 vs. 1).*

For every Spirit-filled life there is a Spirit-led pathway, which stretches right along the line of the Father's will.

Those who find and keep on this pathway of the Spirit are marked by maturity. *'For as many as are led by the Spirit of God, they are the sons of God' (Rom. 8 : 14).*

What a strange place for the Spirit of God to lead Jesus into: '**the wilderness**'! And what a mysterious experience for the sinless Son of Man to be led to endure: To be '**tempted** of the devil'! The devil! How awful to be led into a confrontation with the prince of darkness! We spend most of our time trying to avoid Satan. But Jesus was **led by the Spirit** to meet the devil in the wilderness.

In fact, the language of Mark's gospel is even stronger: *'And immediately the Spirit driveth Him into the Wilderness'. (Mark 1 vs. 12).*

Not since the creation of mankind had there ever been a man to resist Satan successfully and to overcome him. But the Father could trust Jesus. So the Spirit drove Jesus along the pathway of divine purpose right into the severest conflict with Satan in the wilderness. Adam had failed to overcome the devil in the garden paradise; but Jesus, although faint and weak from hunger, conquered Satan in the wilderness.

We ought not to be completely surprised when the Spirit leads us (or even drives us) into a wilderness experience. All wildernesses are not the same.

For the murmuring, unbelieving Israelites, 40 years in the wilderness became a frustrating experience. But for the obedient Jesus 40 days of prayer and fasting in the wilderness constituted a fulfilling experience – because He was on the pathway of the Spirit. And that pathway for Jesus was always in the centre of the Father's will.

Philip the Evangelist must have thought it strange when the Angel of the Lord came to him during a tremendously successful revival-campaign in the city of Samaria and told him to go down into the desert of Gaza! Out of the revival and into the wilderness! Away from the crowds with their many needs, and into the solitude of the desert! But Philip did not hesitate. He knew he was not indispensable; and he also knew that it was always best to obey the Lord's will. So he went into the wilderness and there he met the Chancellor of the Exchequer from the Court of Candace, Queen of the Ethiopians, whose chariot was traversing the desert of Gaza – just at that precise moment!

Philip was able to lead this palace official to Christ. Then he baptised him in water, and the new convert went on his way rejoicing! Thus it came about that the gospel touched the continent of Africa many years before Paul took it into Europe! And all because a man was prepared to be obedient, and went into the wilderness with God.

The aged Simeon was another of God's servants who knew what it was to tread the pathway of the Spirit. The Bible says: *'And he came* **by the Spirit** *into the temple'. (Luke 2 vs. 27).* What a lovely way in which to come into God's house!

Keep your eyes on Jesus, and your feet **on the pathway** of the Spirit. It will always lead you closer to God – and it is never a dead-end.

3. Finally, the Power of the Spirit

'And Jesus returned in **the power of the Spirit** *into Galilee . . .' (Luke 4 vs. 14).*

At the close of his gospel, John wrote: *'And there are also many other things which Jesus did, the which if they should be written every one, I* suppose that even the world itself could not contain the books that should be written' (John 21 : 25).

How was it possible for one Man to do so much? He did it in the power of the Spirit. His parables and His miracles were all in the power of the Spirit. He achieved more than anybody else because of the power of the Holy Ghost upon His life.

Notice that Luke explains that when Jesus returned in the power of the Spirit to Galilee, after His victory over Satan in the wilderness, *'He taught in their synagogues' (Luke 4 vs. 15).*

So it is interesting to observe that, according to Luke, **the first thing** Jesus did in the power of the Spirit was to apply Himself to **teaching**.

All who preach or teach God's word need the power of the Holy Spirit upon their ministry. It is necessary because of the forces that are in opposition to God's living truth.

Jesus taught in the Jewish synagogues. Think of the opposing powers that He faced there:- the traditionalism, legalism, unbelief, envy and pride of the Jewish religious rulers; and the fear and superstition of the people. He did not begin to teach until the **power** of the Spirit was upon Him. That is why His teaching was effective – and still is today.

We need the power of the Holy Spirit in order to accomplish anything at all for Jesus. It is His promise to us and His provision for us.

'You shall receive power after that the Holy Ghost is come upon you: and you shall be witnesses unto me' (Acts 1 vs. 8).

83. PROPHECY TODAY

IS IT GOD'S VOICE?

God is a speaking God. His vocal ability is highlighted by the Psalmist in sharp contrast to the idols of the heathen: 'They have mouths but cannot speak.'

It was by the power of His word that God created the universe. 'He commanded and it stood fast.' God spoke, and a million galaxies sprang into existence! This complex universe with its myriad life-forms is continuously sustained and upheld by the word of His power.

God made mankind in His own image. Man has creative and communicative potential. He is so constituted that he constantly requires to hear the voice of God. Jesus said: 'Man cannot live on bread alone, but needs every word that God speaks.'

God revealed His will through the prophets to His people Israel. Moses was a prophet, and to him God gave much detailed revelation to be communicated to His people. Moses stood in a special relationship to God. The Lord revealed His word to other prophets by dreams and visions, but with His servant Moses, God spoke face to face.

The history of Israel confirms that God continued to communicate prophetically through the centuries. Much of the Bible is, in fact, prophecy. Many predictive prophecies have already been fulfilled. Others will come to fruition in the future. There is no reason to doubt the veracity of God's word. The eternal, omniscient God to Whom the past, the present and the future appear as an ever-consistent 'NOW', will over-rule in sovereignty to bring His word to pass in every detail.

Prophets and the gift of prophecy are still required in the church. From His exalted position at the Father's right hand, our risen ascended Lord Jesus continues to give to His church channels of governmental revelation described as prophets. These men are expressions of His headship, and exercise a ministry that is foundational, doctrinal, and supernatural in the church. Prophets work best with apostles. This twin-ministry is vital for the spiritual prosperity of the church.

The Holy Spirit also gives gifts to the church. One of His gifts is the gift of prophecy, which he may choose to give to any believer. It is quite clear that God has a sincere desire to maintain communication with His church through prophets, and through believers exercising the gift of prophecy.

There are many voices clamouring for our attention on every hand. Various sects and cults claim that God has given them a revelation, and that He has chosen to speak through them.

How can we recognise genuine prophecy? Can we be sure it is God's voice?

There are certain principles to be applied in order to test the reality of prophetic utterance.

If prophecy does not come to pass, God has not spoken. But even if it does come to pass, that is not the only criteria for assessment. The essence of the prophecy should unveil the character of God, with a view to stimulating the people to be loyal to Him and His word. It has a moral as well as a mystical content.

If prophecy does not keep in line with Scripture, then it is not genuine. God will never contradict the revelation of His own word, the Bible. 'All Scripture is God-breathed.' Mature prophecy does not merely repeat what is already written, although God does often remind us of His written word and of His promises and predictions. Genuine prophecy must be in accord with the Bible, but it is more than a mere repetition of Biblical texts. True prophecy brings revelation, and if reference is made to scripture it will be in order to focus the word of God upon a specific situation and thus bring unprecedented enlightenment, or perhaps to bring prophetic wisdom which will solve a difficult problem.

Genuine prophecy in the church never generates fear, gloom, distress or uncertainty. Jesus is the good Shepherd and His sheep know His voice and they follow Him. His prophetic word brings comfort, strength and encouragement.

The word of the Lord is life-creating. It inspires the people with enthusiasm. Prophetic utterances that minister a sense of deadness are not likely to be the word of Him Who is the Resurrection and the Life!

When God speaks He generates life and faith.

'He who has an ear, let him hear what the Spirit says to the churches.'

228

84. THE ANOINTED CHURCH

Jesus was very aware of the anointing of the Spirit upon Him. Following his temptation in the wilderness, he went to Nazareth where he had been brought up. On the Sabbath day, in accordance with his custom, Jesus went into the synagogue and stood up to read from the scroll of the prophet Isaiah:-

'The Spirit of the Lord is on me because he has anointed me to preach good news to the poor. He has sent me to proclaim freedom for the prisoners and recovery of sight for the blind, to release the oppressed, to proclaim the year of the Lord's favour.'

He rolled up the scroll, returned it to the attendant and sat down. Everyone in the synagogue fixed their eyes upon him. Then he said: 'Today this scripture is fulfilled in your hearing.'

That was no idle boast. His matchless life, healing power, dynamic miracles and incomparable teaching all combined to demonstrate the reality of the Spirit's anointing upon him.

Years later, Peter recalled the practical and effectual ministry of Jesus, attributing His success to the Spirit's anointing. Addressing the household of Cornelius, the apostle Peter declared: 'God anointed Jesus of Nazareth with the Holy Spirit and power . . . he went around doing good and healing all who were under the power of the devil, because God was with him.'

Peter's statement makes four things very clear.

First, Jesus exercised his healing ministry and performed his mighty miracles in the power of the Holy Spirit. His invincibility arose from moving in the power of a Spirit-anointed sinless manhood – not necessarily by exerting the prerogatives of deity. 'God anointed *Jesus of Nazareth*' – that was the title denoting his humanity.

Second, his practical help to people and his social outreaches were accomplished in the power of the Spirit. *'He went around doing good.'* God cares about broken humanity. He loves people. Those who are truly anointed by God's Spirit will be burdened for the needs of others and will be moved compassionately to do something practical about it.

Third, the Spirit's anointing found an expression in a ministry of healing for all who were *'under the power of the devil'*. Satan's influence may often be manifested in the bodies of men and women, but the devil's

229

strongest chains hold the spirits and minds of his victims in bondage. It follows that there must be an inward, spiritual and psychological healing arising out of the Spirit's anointing, and not merely a healing applicable only to the outward, physical and visible areas of the human personality.

Fourth, the deep assurance of God's abiding presence with his Servant is authenticated by the Spirit of the Lord. *'God was with him.'* Furthermore, God's seal of approval on everything that Jesus did in the power of the Spirit's anointing constituted the evidence outwardly that God was with him inwardly.

Thus the anointing of the Spirit supplied the subjective factor of assurance, and at the same time manifested the objective reality of the divine approval. These are qualities which the Lord Jesus wants every believer to experience. The dynamic, successful life of Jesus is mediated to Christians by the power of the Holy Spirit. It must be expressed and implemented by faith.

The church is the body of Christ. God wants His church to exercise an effectual ministry to the current generation, just as Jesus did to his generation. This can only be achieved as the church becomes aware of God's anointing. It is the anointing of the Holy Spirit that makes the essential difference between theory and practice; between theological appreciation and personal possession; between orthodox exposition and dynamic demonstration of miraculous power.

The three Old Testament offices which required an anointing were the prophet, the priest and the king. Jesus is the Christ, the Anointed One. He is the archetypal Prophet, the Great High Priest, the King of kings. He wants to manifest Himself through his church in these ministerial capacities.

An anointed church will have a prophetic function, pointing the predictive finger toward the coming of the Lord, and proclaiming the truth of His word. Such a church will also exercise a priestly ministry of bridge-building, bringing mankind to God in prayer, and bringing God to mankind by means of the gospel. A church moving in the Spirit's anointing will also know kingdom authority, marching against the forces of evil with kingly dignity and regal power.

In his gospel, Mark relates that after the crucifixion, the women acquired spices so that they could go and anoint the dead body of Jesus. Their intentions were not quite in line with God's plan. Jesus was not in the grave. He had risen! God had not destined His Son to be embalmed – but to be enthroned! Jesus had hated iniquity and loved righteousness. Therefore God had anointed him with the oil of joy and gladness above his fellows.

What His church needs today is not the embalming fluid of a sterile traditionalism, but the energising dynamic of the Holy Spirit's anointing, which will thrust His people forward in faith toward the coming of the Lord!

85. 'MAJESTY'

The Biblical use of the word 'majesty' includes the ideas of greatness, dignity, splendour and magnificence.

Our God reigns! His reign is not the brief bid for power made by the usurper. It is not the outward show of worldly and decaying empires. Nor is it the iron rule of a totalitarian system led by a dictatorial megalomaniac.

Our God reigns in sublime majesty! In unimaginable magnificence! In supreme splendour, awesome dignity, and universal power! His throne is unshakeable; His purpose inflexible; His character immutable. His rule represents an ethical, as well as a governmental majesty. The magnificence of His reign is illuminated by the radiance of His sacrificial Calvary-love! The Lamb is in the midst of the throne. His nail-pierced hand wields the sceptre of righteousness, universally and eternally.

To behold Him in His majesty, authority and glory, is the greatest privilege of the godly.

To behold divine majesty is to experience dynamic change! Basically, it is not a mystical, but rather a practical experience, evoking from the enraptured beholder worship, reverence and repentance.

The prophet Ezekiel saw Him: '. . . as I was among the captives . . . the heavens were opened and I saw visions of God.' (Ezk. 1.1).

This transforming experience released the prophet's spirit from captivity into liberty, enabling him to receive tremendous revelation from God in the realm of prophetic insight.

Speaking of the power of the Creator in the universe, Elihu reminded Job: 'Out of the north He comes in golden splendour; God comes in awesome majesty' (Job 37.22, N.I.V.). But it took a personal revelation of God's majesty to transform Job's outlook and philosophy.

After his traumatic experience, Job could say: 'My ears had heard of you, but now my eyes have seen you. Therefore I despise myself and repent in dust and ashes. (Job 42.5-6, N.I.V.). The original Hebrew literally implies: 'I disappear. I retract all I have said. I repudiate the position I have taken up'. A vision of true majesty wrought that miracle in Job!

Isn't that precisely the vital need of the church today? Entrenched opinions, cherished traditions, and tenaciously-held prejudices must be repudiated, so that the church can continually undergo dynamic phases of progressive change, advancing in the will of God from glory to glory! Only a revelation of divine majesty can accomplish that miracle of developing transformation.

Our God reigns! May the full impact of this vision of enthroned majesty, effect God's perfect purpose in your transformed life.

PART X

THE SUPERNATURAL

Items 86-90

86. CHRISTMAS AND THE SUPERNATURAL

Christmas has become so commercialised that we are in danger of forgetting the supernatural element.

This generation takes the Christ out of Christmas and substitutes the sign of the unknown quantity, calling it Xmas. Modern man will have the seasonable holiday – but he will not have Christ as Saviour and Lord.

The Christ of God, however, can never ultimately be evaded. He is at the heart of Christmas. He is God's greatest gift to mankind, and because of Him countless lives that were in hopeless despair have been supernaturally changed.

Jesus puts the joy into Christmas. He produces the peace for which people yearn. His love satisfies the longings of a restless race.

The first Christmas was full of the supernatural. To begin with, there was **supernatural guidance**: 'Behold, there came wise men from the east to Jerusalem, saying, Where is He that is born King of the Jews? For **we have seen His star** in the east, and are come to worship Him. When they had heard the king, they departed; and, lo, **the star**, which they saw in the east, **went before them**, till it came and stood over where the young child was.' (Matt. 2, vs. 2 and 9).

The God of a million galaxies controlled the progress of a few wise men on earth by the movement of a heavenly body light-years away! Travellers and starlight are both 'natural' qualities. But when men are led to the King by the rays of His star – then the supernatural element becomes evident to all. **Supernatural guidance** – that is the first thing to note.

The second element is this: **Supernatural utterance**. 'Herod demanded where Christ should be born. And they said unto him, in Bethlehem of Judea: for thus it is written by **the prophet**' (Matt. 2, vs. 4-5).

Over seven centuries before King Herod made his enquiry, the prophet Micah had predicted the precise geographical location of the birth-place of the Messiah! (See Micah 5, vs. 2).

That exact **supernatural utterance** had lost none of its effectiveness, and it struck home to the evil heart of Herod, filling him with fear and apprehension.

Thirdly, there was a **supernatural appearance**: 'The **angel of the Lord appeared** to Joseph in a dream.' (Matt, 2, vs. 13). Angelic messengers fill the Christmas story. An angel had appeared to Zacharias, the father of John the Baptist. The same angel, Gabriel, had been sent to Mary with the astounding news that she was to be the mother of the Messiah. (Luke 1, vs. 11, 12, 26-38). The angel of the Lord had appeared to the shepherds on the first Christmas night, and then the whole sky had become full of the angelic hosts praising God! (Luke 2, vs. 9-14).

Now yet again, a **supernatural appearance** of an angel to Joseph warned him of Herod's evil intention to destroy the Christ-child, and instructed the family to flee into Egypt.

These **supernatural** elements stimulate our confidence in the ability of the Sovereign God to outwork His purpose to perfection.

The fourth factor to observe is **supernatural intelligence**: The wise men, 'being warned of God **in a dream** that they should not return to Herod, they departed into their own country another way.' (Matt. 2, vs. 12).

God is not limited in His methods of moving men. Whether it is a shining angel or a flaming orb in the heavens, millions of light-years away, beckoning the Eastern sages to the worship of the infant King of the Jews – or whether it is the communication of revelation in the depths of their subconscious minds by means of a fleeting **dream**, the lesson is crystal-clear – **God** is in supreme control. The careful student can not fail to observe this **supernatural intelligence.**

Finally, note what must be the most miraculous element of all – **the supernatural difference**: 'And when they were come into the house they saw **the young child** with Mary his mother, and fell down, and worshipped **him**.' (Matt. 2, vs. 11).

This was a young child with a difference. He was quite unique. Mary was his mother, but Joseph was not his father. The angel had told her months before: 'The Holy Ghost shall come upon thee, and the power of the Highest shall overshadow thee: therefore also that holy thing which shall be born of thee shall be called the son of **God**.' (Luke 1, vs. 35).

That is why the wise men fell down and worshipped the child. They did not worship his mother. It was to **the King** that the star had led them.

A child with a supernatural difference! Deity and humanity combined in one unique sinless personality. God upon the virgin's lap!

In the nineteenth century R.S. Hawker wrote a poem to try and express the mystery of the hypostatic union that took place in the womb of the

238

Virgin:

'The zone where two glad worlds for ever meet
Beneath that bosom ran;
Deep in the womb the conquering Paraclete
Smote Godhead on to man.'

What a sublime mystery it all is! Yet it is an historic fact. God has done it. He stepped out of eternity into the stream of human history. Yet the supernatural incarnation was but the stepping-stone to the cross! Bethlehem was the prelude to Calvary. Bearing the wounds of crucifixion in His sinless man-hood, Jesus has ascended to the throne of God.

As the living Lord, he can make each Christmas truly supernatural!

87. FREE FROM THE CURSE!

God's word commands us to 'bless, and curse not' (Rom. 12 : 14). Our heavenly Father desires His children to be like Himself. It is the nature of God to bless and to bestow benefits, even upon the unthankful and the undeserving.

It is the nature of Satan to curse, i.e. to invoke evil or injury upon mankind. Satan has his followers – his henchmen held in bondage by demon powers and occult forces, spawning the devil's influence in this generation.

Missionaries have reported the awful power of ju-ju curses, resulting in fear and sometimes in death for the victims.

Such practices are no longer confined to the jungle. Satanic forces have made terrible inroads into the sophisticated society of our day. The ungodly have no real power to resist the devil. But the children of the Lord can overcome him by the blood of the Lamb and by the word of their testimony.

There is power in the blood of Jesus. There is victory in the name of Jesus. We are more than conquerors through Him that loves us. The world neither knows nor understands that Satan and his forces are defeated foes, that Christ has gloriously triumphed, and that every believer can be completely victorious in Christ!

During his visit to Plymouth, Evangelist Hans Koornstra told of a young lady called Mary whose mother had placed a curse upon her. Her doom was to be cursed with blindness, and to be reduced to the gutter of the European city where she lived! How dreadful for a mother to hate her daughter so much! But such is the nature of Satan and of those that serve him. Such is the power of hatred.

Both of these terrifying maledictions came true! When the Evangelist found Mary she was blind and living in degradation. The devil appeared to have overcome and to have brought another precious soul into bondage. But Jesus had other plans!

Mary came to the Gospel Campaign, where she gave her life to Christ and was cleansed in His precious blood. When the Evangelist placed his hand upon her head she fell to the floor under the power of God – and the awful curse was broken!

Later on, the Evangelist saw her again in a café. Her face, once lined with guilt and fear, was now radiant with joy and peace. 'I now feel clean for the first time in my life!' she said. There is power in the blood of Jesus. Mary, however, was still blind.

She was brought to another meeting. The Evangelist prayed for her in the name of Jesus – and she was wonderfully healed. Her eyes were opened, and she received her sight! There is power in the name of Jesus. As a result of this miracle, her mother and father and many of her relatives were gloriously saved. What a wonderful Saviour!

'Believing, we rejoice, **to see the curse remove,**
We bless the Lamb, with cheerful voice
And sing His bleeding love.'

88. THE EXORCISTS

Christ's command to evangelise the world included the commission to cast out demons (Mark 16 vs. 15-18).

Critics have challenged the authenticity of this portion from Mark's gospel, but it is evident from the New Testament that Jesus opposed the kingdom of darkness by casting out many demons, and that the early church followed fearlessly in His footsteps.

The current intensification of interest in the occult, and the increase of Satanic activity, should awaken the church to the necessity of resisting the powers of darkness in the name of Jesus!

'Let courage rise with danger,
And strength to strength oppose'.

Every true believer is delegated with the authority of Jesus to cast out demons in His name. Women as well as men have this authority: 'These signs shall follow them that believe'.

We need, however, the mighty power of the Holy Spirit for this militant task. Without His gracious anointing we could fall into failure, as did the seven sons of Sceva!

Concerning His own death at Calvary, Jesus said: '**Now** is the judgment of this world: **now** shall the prince of this world be cast out. And I if I be lifted up from the earth will draw all men unto me' (John 12 vs. 31-32). The powers of darkness were defeated at the Cross!

Because the Man of Golgotha has conquered the 'master of gloom', every believer who, empowered by the Spirit, stands in that Calvary Victory, can oppose the kingdom of darkness, and in the name of Jesus – cast out demons!

It takes more than the muttering of mystic medieval mottoes to deal with the minions of hell! Demons are not impressed by elaborate rituals or ceremonies of exorcism. Souls in bondage are not brought into liberty by those methods.

The vital prerequisite for dealing with the 'powers from below' is – '**power from on high**'! The name of Jesus must be proclaimed by Spirit-filled believers.

The dynamic anointing of the Holy Ghost on Christians full of faith and exercised in prayer and fasting will prove more than a match for the upsurge of spiritism and satanism in the current occult revival.

The disciples of Jesus were given power and authority to cast out demons:-

'He called His twelve disciples to Him and gave them authority to drive out evil spirits and to heal every disease and sickness.' (Matthew 10 v 1)

That same demon-defeating dynamic is the vital need of Christ's followers today.

89. 'THE SUPERNATURAL' – GOD OR SATAN?

There was a time when the Western world denied the reality of a supernatural realm. Science dictated: 'If it can't be seen, weighed and analyzed, then it isn't real.' That excessively materialistic view is now being challenged. There is a reaction against a culture where materialism reigns supreme, but which fails to recognise the spiritual dimension, and leaves the human spirit empty, longing for inward reality.

The great psychiatrist Carl G. Jung said: 'The central neurosis of our age is emptiness.' How right he was! People are empty, void of spiritual satisfaction, because they have filled their lives with materialistic prosperity but have not catered for their deep spiritual needs. The real spiritual dimension has been ignored.

So it has really been for pragmatic reasons rather than because of theological convictions that there has been a swing toward the spiritual world of the supernatural. That trend has, however, brought with it some terrible dangers.

There *is* a supernatural dimension; but the energies being exercised in that realm are both good and evil. The miraculous power of God works for good, but the counterfeit workers of darkness produce evil and confusion. The real danger consists in an inability to discern which energies are being manifested in the supernatural context.

People hunger for reality. But the power of Satan is as real, though not as beneficial, as the power of God. So multitudes are led astray and ensnared by the powers of darkness, in the mistaken belief that they are involved with God's power.

Over the last thirty years there has been a charismatic revival; an outpouring of the Spirit of God accompanied by the manifestation of supernatural spiritual gifts with signs and wonders. Challenging this move of God, there has been a Satanic revival, an upsurging of occult powers producing renewed public interest in the supernatural. School children have dabbled with ouija boards, practised levitation, taken a keen interest in witchcraft, sorcery and spiritism. All age groups have been ensnared by the drug scene; some have blown their minds with excessive doses of hallucinatory drugs. Others have had their lives destroyed by heroin addiction, hooked, and eventually assassinated by the needle of death.

Some, driven mad by demons and drugs, have committed suicide in order to escape from the intolerable horror of the addict's unreal world. Tragically, they have exchanged a temporal hell for an eternal one.

The Bible teaches that there is a link between addiction to drugs which affect the mind, and the activity of demons. 'For by thy sorceries were all nations deceived.' (Rev.18.23). The Greek word for sorceries is *pharmakeia*, which basically signified the use of medicine, drugs, spells, then poisoning, then sorcery. W.E. Vine reminds us: 'In sorcery the use of drugs, whether simple or potent, was generally accompanied by incantations and appeals to occult powers . . .' The same word *pharmakeia* is used by the Apostle in Galatians 5 verse 20, where the Authorised Version translates it as 'witchcraft'. In the Revised Version, however, and in the New American Standard Translation the word used is *sorcery* rather than witchcraft. There is, therefore, clear Scriptural light on the correlation between drugs and demons.

Many of the activities masquerading today as genuine supernatural experiences from God are the counterfeits of the enemy produced by drugs and demons. The human mind is also capable of psychologically inducing certain experiences which the uninitiated may mistake for true God-given spiritual supernatural phenomena.

The effective answer to all this confusion is for every Christian to be continually filled with the Holy Spirit and controlled by the revelation of God's written word.

90. THIS WONDERFUL WORLD

This is our Father's world. He provides for it. He loves it. The best known text in the Bible reminds us of this fact: *'For God so loved the world that He gave His one and only Son, that whoever believes in Him shall not perish but have eternal life.' (John 3.16).*

When God created planet Earth with its myriad varieties of teeming life, He pronounced His handiwork perfect. After each day's creatorial work: *'God saw that it was good.'* Summing it all up, the Bible says: *'God saw all that He had made, and it was very good.'*

A superficial glance at these apparently simple statements uttered by the Creator can give no real idea of the wonder, the majesty, and the complex mystery of sublime intelligence displayed by God in His universe.

There is an unbridgeable gulf between our meagre understanding of the phrase *'. . . it was very good'*, and God's understanding of it. John Downer's book, *Supersense,* and the BBC programmes displaying it, have surely highlighted the wonders and mysteries of creation, and have given us fascinating insights into the supreme skill and intelligence of the great Creator Who has endowed some of His humblest creatures with some of nature's greatest senses and powers. We are, of course, indebted to modern science and technology for a renewed understanding of the marvels of creation. But God knew all about it thousands of years ago, and that is why He could say: *'. . . it was very good.'*

If John Downer has given us a fresh insight into the creative energies of God demonstrated in nature, then Dr. Lyall Watson's works must surely require us to re-examine, and perhaps to re-define, the boundary between the natural and the supernatural.

There is so much wonder in the astonishing skills of the Creator displayed in nature, and there are so many mysteries not yet fully understood or explained, that it would be wise to keep these matters in mind when formulating views on the manifestation of the 'supernatural'.

Without a doubt, there is a spirit-world. There are demons oppressing mankind. There is a devil, the implacable enemy of God and of His church. There are angels serving God's children. There are principalities and powers – wicked spirits in high places whose power can be overthrown by prayer and fasting. And there are some people on earth who give

246

themselves over to evil spirits by becoming involved with the occult powers of darkness. There is a supernatural realm, in which both good and evil forces are locked in an invisible struggle for supremacy.

All these things are taught in the Bible. But this Biblical concept of the supernatural must be held in equilibrium with an equally Biblical insight into the mysteries of the natural realm.

Man is the crown of God's creation. Though inhibited by the fall and by the curse on the earth, I do not think that rare examples of his unexplained mysterious powers ought necessarily to be attributed to demonic forces, or even to the supernatural realm.

In my view, the current philosophy, and even the theology of the supernatural and the occult, requires regulation until a more balanced Biblical position is achieved.

This is our Father's world. He has not abdicated in favour of Satan. Neither has He handed over the administration to demons. God is absolutely sovereign.

The steel of the theological sword that carves out the pathway of man's responsibility in the world must not be forged in the inconsistent flames of human experience, but rather in the unchanging fires of God's word.

When the Apostle Peter opposed the idea of Jesus going to the cross, the Master said: *'Get behind me Satan! You are a stumbling block to me; you do not have in mind the things of God, but the things of men.'*

In addressing Peter as Satan, Jesus did not imply that Peter was demon-possessed or even oppressed. Neither did He say: 'You have outlined the strategy of hell, and the doctrine of demons.' No. The Lord contrasted the things of God with the things of *men*. In other words, he equated an unsubdued human will (Peter's mind unyielded to God's will and word) – with the aims of Satan.

Paul reinforced this view in his list of the acts of the sinful nature. The Apostle included *witchcraft* in this catalogue of evil things. But he did not attribute any of these activities to demonic agencies. Rather he contrasted them with a life full of the Holy Spirit. Even if there were no active demons, people devoid of the Spirit of God would still perpetrate evil practices and serve the enemy's purpose.

These concepts lead us to a logical and practical conclusion. The answer to many problems is not necessarily to be found by blaming the devil and seeking release from demonic bondage, but rather by submitting to the cross and being continually filled with the Spirit. Then there would be 'days of heaven upon earth' in this wonderful world.

PART XI

GOD'S BOOK

Items 91-94

91. THE BIBLE – GOD'S MIRACLE BOOK!

Science can do wonderful things. But it can't give peace to a troubled mind. It can't instantly transform a person's life. And it can't produce faith in an empty human heart. Science is powerless to satisfy the deepest yearnings of mankind. It is unable to solve the problems of restless souls longing for reality. But the Bible can do all these things. It is God's word pointing mankind to the living Lord Jesus – the Ultimate Answer to human need.

A Californian Lawyer, Dana Pankey, and his wife Ruth were involved in the Moscow Book Fair, collecting the names and addresses of people queuing for a New Testament. Dana relates the following incident, illustrating the power of the Bible:-

'A young lady who is with the Ministry of Culture from one of the most progressive governments of the Soviet bloc came over to our booth at the Moscow International Book Fair. She asked for some books in English. She wanted to learn about God and said she would be willing to exchange books from her booth to pay for our books. I walked with her from our booth to another building to see her display.

As we walked, I asked her if she knew of God. 'How can I?' she answered. 'Since I was a young child in school, they always told us there was no God. But my grandmother told me there is a God, that God is real. She told me that when I had problems, I ought to pray.'

'No matter what you've heard in your country,' I said to her, 'God is real, and He reveals Himself through His Son, Jesus Christ.'

When we got to the book display from her country, she asked me back into her office. We discussed how God could actually live within an individual, and we discussed Bible verses that explain the plan of salvation.

This young woman holds a doctor of philosophy degree. She speaks seven different languages. As she sat across the desk from me, she said, 'I was always taught by our government that the church is for old people and people who are not educated – people who are simple-minded and don't have good education.' I explained to her that I am a lawyer. I have a doctor of philosophy degree in education myself. She was overwhelmed as we talked about the simplicity of the reality of God and the simplicity of salvation through His Son, Jesus Christ.

After we went through the Bible verses about how Christ died for our sins, I could see the Spirit of God working in her life. So I took her through the entire plan of salvation. I told her that I believe in God, that I believe Jesus was the Son of God, that He died on the cross for my sins, that He hears my prayer now and will forgive my sins. Finally I asked, 'Do you want to know God? Do you want to have Jesus Christ living in your life?'

'Oh, I do,' she answered.

'Let's pray right here.'

'Can I pray in my language?'

'Yes, certainly,' I said, and she began saying the Lord's prayer. Then I said, 'Now I want to pray with you, and I want you to pray with me, and we are going to tell God exactly what we have been talking about, and exactly what you said you want to do, and that is to receive Jesus Christ and for Him to come into your life and dwell within you.' We bowed our heads and started to pray.

'But we can't pray here,' she protested. 'We can pray here. We can talk to God just like we talk to each other,' I replied. 'You pray with me right now, and you will be telling God what you have told me you want to do.'

After we finished praying, she suddenly rose to her feet. Her face lit up, her eyes were glassy. She walked to the opposite side of her office, turned around and said, 'I'm overwhelmed. I don't understand what's happened to me, but something has happened to me.' After we walked from her book display back to our display, I introduced her to some of the other workers. She said to them, 'The most wonderful thing that Dana has told me is that I can talk to God just like we talk to each other, in simple language.' As I introduced her to others, she gave testimony that Christ was her's now. 'I'm overwhelmed. Something has happened to me here,' she kept saying as she put her hand on her chest.

I praise the Lord for this marvellous testimony from this woman, who holds a very important place in the government of her country. She also asked me, 'How can I explain this to my husband and children – I have a 10-year-old child – how can I help my children understand what has happened to me and tell them about God and about Jesus Christ?' I had one of the colourfully illustrated children's New Testaments produced by the Slavic Gospel Association. I wrote a message on the inside cover and gave this book to her as a gift. She thanked me saying, 'Oh, that will be helpful for me to teach them, and this will also be helpful for me to understand more about the Bible and about God.'

How wonderful to see God at work right there in the middle of the Moscow Book Fair!'

Neither science nor philosophy could give that young lady in Moscow the reality for which she yearned. But Jesus could! And she was introduced to Him by believing God's plan of salvation outlined in the Bible!

Science does not contradict the Bible. Neither does the Bible fail to confirm science. But science has its limitations. God has none. It is His word that will count in the ultimate analysis.

[Acknowledgement to the Slavic Gospel Association.]

92. NO SUBSTITUTE

Satan can copy and counterfeit many good things in order to deceive people. But he has his limitations. Some tasks are beyond him.

The devil can dilute and distort doctrine. He can twist truth to suit his own perverse purpose, and wrench written words out of their correct context. But it is not within his power to imitate adequately or accurately the creative essence and the transforming energy of the word of God. Neither can he nullify or deaden the dynamic of scripture.

It is this unique quality of God's word for which humanity hungers. While millions despise and neglect the Bible, millions of others thirst desperately for its life-giving words. There is no substitute for the Bible.

Word in Action reported an incident of the miraculous power of the Bible to transform people. The story was first published by *Aid to the Persecuted* and highlights the wonder of the word of God.

A Soviet medical professor was sent from a military academy to an army unit in the Far East to determine the level of expertise among top military doctors. During one of his question-sessions he learned about a young recruit, a Baptist, whom the army could not 're-educate'. 'We have tried every scientific and psychological method,' complained an officer, 'but none of them has worked.'

The professor examined the Christian, and was amazed by his joyful countenance and his general stability. During the interrogation, an officer colleague of the professor finally asked: 'Tell me, where do you get all this from?'

'From the Bible,' replied the young man.

Eventually the officer asked the Baptist if he would get a Bible for him. The professor overheard the request, and later he went privately to the young man and also asked for a Bible.

'I will write to my father, and he will send you his.'

The professor obtained the young man's home address, and some days later he also wrote to the father requesting a Bible. After several months the professor had still not received his Bible.

'Comrade,' he wrote, 'I am really disappointed. Both your son and I have written to you, yet here I am still waiting for a Bible without so much as a single word for an answer.'

Upon receiving this second letter, the father, a lay-preacher, fell on his knees to ask God's forgiveness. The man had assumed the professor's first letter to be a trap. He searched all day for a Bible to send the professor. But without success. Finally he decided to send his own preacher's Bible, well-worn and marked with his notes. He asked for it to be returned to him in six weeks, as it was his only Bible for preaching.

The delighted professor devoured the Bible hungrily, and during his reading he became a Christian. Shortly afterwards, his wife, an engineer, also came to know the Lord. But then they had to send the Bible back.

The professor had two sons studying medicine in different cities. He was anxious to tell them about Jesus. But he no longer had a Bible. So he advised them both to secure Bibles for themselves, in order to discover the meaning and purpose of their lives.

The sons searched everywhere for a Bible – but they could not secure one. Eventually the student in Moscow recalled a book by Tolstoy entitled *The Resurrection* which he could obtain from the Lenin library. He knew that Tolstoy quoted the Bible in his works. The young man found 25 such books containing quotations from scripture. Taking them all home, he sat down and copied out all the Biblical quotations he could find.

Although he had only a small part of God's word, it was powerful enough to lead him to Christ, and later he was able to lead his brother to the Lord.

Because of his conversion, the professor was forced into early retirement. But this gave him more time to work for God, and both his sons are also serving the Lord.

What other book in the world contains such life-changing energy? There is no substitute for the Bible.

[Acknowledgement to the Bible Society.]

93. MIRACLES!

Miracles are no problem to God. He has all power in heaven and earth and is well able to do miraculous things. The Bible abundantly demonstrates this fact. Exclude the miraculous element from the Bible, and there is very little left. As far as God is concerned, miracles are the order of the day.

This does not mean, however, that God is involved in stunts, gimmicks or showmanship. The miracles of Jesus were oracles – each one designed to teach some particular aspect of truth or to unveil a specific quality of His personality. The gospel of John is particularly rich in examples of the teaching claims of Jesus being undergirded and backed up by miraculous happenings. When He said 'I am the bread of life', He substantiated the statement by feeding 5,000 men with five loaves and two fishes. The assertion 'I am the light of the world' was backed up by the miraculous healing of the man who had been born blind. And when Jesus said 'I am the resurrection and the life', He proved it by bringing out of the grave Lazarus, a man who had been dead for four days!

From Genesis to Revelation, God's written word is packed with miracles. In fact, the Bible is itself a miracle, unsurpassed in the literary history of mankind. It is a miracle of perfect harmony and precise prophecy. Some Biblical predictions are still being fulfilled in these days, adding more evidence to the mountain of proof that the Bible is divinely inspired. The signs of the times outlined by Jesus as events which would take place prior to his personal return can be clearly seen all around us. Check for yourself. Read Matthew 24 and Luke 21 in the light of current events and you will see the miraculous precision with which the Lord indicated the state that the world would be in at the time of His return.

Creation, with all its variety and majesty, is a miracle. It is surely miraculous that God could produce, out of nothing, this marvellously intricate universe with its myriad forms of life. And it is no less miraculous daily to sustain the whole cosmos by the word of His power! Galaxies of incredible energy and magnitude are ordered by His word in the unimaginable vastness of outer space. Planets, quasars, pulsars, comets, stars, suns, moons and meteorites are all under His supreme control. He daily opens His hand and satisfies the desire of every living thing. His

Spirit renews the face of the earth. The cycle of the seasons is energised consistently by His power, so that spring-time and harvest never fail. A little child can confidently play on the edge of the mighty ocean because God has set the boundaries of the tides, and has commanded the seas: 'Thus far, and no further!' This is our Father's world – and it is full of miracles.

The crucial questions uppermost in the minds of many folk are these: 'Does God take an interest in my circumstances?' and 'Will He do a miracle for me?' Yes, God is interested in you, He will do miracles for you. But you must have faith. On several occasions in the gospels Jesus made this principle of operation clear. Descending into the valley from the mount of Transfiguration, Jesus was confronted by a boy possessed by a violent evil spirit. The boy's distraught father cried: 'If you can do anything, have compassion on us and help us.'

But Jesus replied: 'If you can believe, all things are possible to him that believes.'

It is evident that Jesus was teaching a principle. What was it? Simply this: *When you live in the dimension of faith, you move in the realm of miracles, where all things are possible!*

94. THE LAST LAUGH

God has a grim sense of humour when it comes to petty men pitting their pathetic powers against Him. They set themselves against His Son in defiance of His immutable word. But 'He that sitteth in the heavens shall laugh: the Lord shall have them in derision.'

The Psalmist wrote those words over 3,000 years ago, but the ungodly have not paid much attention to his warning. God, however, remains inflexible in His attitude of apparent amusement as sinful rebels futilely hurl into His face their threats to abolish His word from the earth.

The French infidel, Voltaire, a writer of great talent, abused his skills by writing against the Christian faith. He blasphemed Christ and boasted: 'In twenty years Christianity will be no more. My single hand shall destroy the edifice it took twelve apostles to rear.'

Not long after his death in 1778, the premises in which he printed his blasphemous literature became the depot of the Geneva Bible Society. (I can almost hear the divine chuckle echoing down the corridors of Time!).

How did the boaster die? His end was terrible! The nurse attending Voltaire said: 'For all the wealth in Europe I would not see another infidel die.' His physician, Trochim, who was with Voltaire at his death, reported that he cried out most desperately: 'I am abandoned by God and man: I will give you half of what I am worth if you will give me six months' life. Then I shall go to hell and you will go with me. O Christ! O Jesus Christ! I am lost! I am lost! O that I had never been born!'

What a dreadful doom! The infidel had mocked God and His word, but at the hour of death, facing the inevitability of divine judgement, Voltaire could find nothing to laugh about. It was too late when he finally realised his lost condition. At the end he knew in his heart of hearts that the Bible was true after all – but he was too late to repent; too fixed in his unbelief to change his ways.

Terrible as that infidel's death-bed scene is, there is nevertheless something even subtly worse, that is the case of the blind leaders of the blind – men who enter the pulpit to undermine the Christian faith and deny Biblical truth. On such treachery the late Dr. Joseph Parker was scathing in his judgement: 'The man in the pulpit who insults the Bible on which he lives, and wriggles out of the profession by which he climbed to

258

the pulpit he dishonours, I charge with worse crimes than those which blackened Barabbas or damned Iscariot.'

Despite satanic strategy, the supreme authority of God's word stands secure. Let foolish men mock the Bible – God will have the last laugh.